The news media have become the central arena for political conflicts today. It is, therefore, not surprising that the role of the news media in political conflicts has received a good deal of public attention in recent years. *Media and political conflict* provides readers with an understanding of the ways in which news media do and do not become active participants in these conflicts. The author's "political contest" model provides a new approach to this important issue. The best way to understand the role of the news media in politics, he argues, is to view the competition over the news media as part of a larger and more significant contest for political control.

The book is divided into two parts. While the first is devoted to developing the theoretical model, the second employs this approach to analyze the role of the news media in three conflicts: the Gulf war, the Palestinian *intifada*, and the attempt by the Israeli right wing to derail the Israeli–Palestinian peace accord.

Media and political conflict

Media and political conflict

News from the Middle East

Gadi Wolfsfeld

The Hebrew University of Jerusalem

CAMBRIDGE
UNIVERSITY PRESS

Published by the Press Syndicate of the University of Cambridge
The Pitt Building, Trumpington Street, Cambridge CB2 1RP
40 West 20th Street, New York, NY 10011–4211, USA
10 Stamford Road, Oakleigh, Melbourne 3166, Australia

First published 1997

Printed in Great Britain at the University Press, Cambridge

A catalogue record for this book is available from the British Library

Library of Congress cataloguing in publication data

Wolfsfeld, Gadi.
Media and political conflict: news from the Middle East / Gadi Wolfsfeld.
    p.   cm.
ISBN 0 521 58045 5. – ISBN 0 521 58967 3 (pbk.)
1. Mass media – Political aspects.   2. Press and politics.
I. Title
P95.8.W65   1997
302.23 – dc20   96-8611   CIP

ISBN 0 521 58045 5 hardback
ISBN 0 521 58967 3 paperback

CE

To Annette and Bernie for their love, their support, and their wonderful sense of family

Contents

Figures

Tables

Acknowledgments

It is never easy to decide how far back to search when one decides to thank all of those who have helped along the way. I would say my first debt of gratitude goes to my earliest mentor, Ithiel de Sola Pool. Ithiel was the first person to introduce me to the field of political communication. His fierce dedication to the world of ideas and evidence was an inspiration to hundreds of graduate students. It was he, more than anyone, who pointed me in the direction of the most enjoyable voyage imaginable: forever trying to understand the role of the media in politics.

I was fortunate enough to find a second mentor later in life. Bill Gamson's influence on this project should be apparent to all those who know and admire his work. Bill has read many versions of the manuscript and spent countless hours helping me to sort out the ideas presented herein. He has been a wonderful friend and advisor and a constant source of encouragement and guidance for many years.

I also want to thank Marvin Kalb, director of the Joan Shorenstein Barone Center on the Press, Politics, and Public Policy at Harvard. An important part of this manuscript was written while I was a fellow at the Center. Marvin, his dedicated staff, and the other fellows and guests provided a marvelous atmosphere for intellectual discussion and debate.

Several other colleagues were generous enough to read earlier versions of this manuscript and to provide reactions that proved critical in the final revisions. I want to thank (in alphabetical order) Marion Just, Elihu Katz, David Paletz, and David Riccie for investing so much time and effort to help me. I also want to thank the two anonymous reviewers who provided valuable criticisms.

While many students were helpful over the years, there are three I would especially like to thank. My research assistants, Einat Lochover and Motti Neiger, carried out most of the interviews and a good deal of the content analysis reported in the case study on the peace process. They each possess one of the most important attributes for scholars: the ability to ask questions. This proved to be important not only in the field, but also when they returned to the office, where a healthy dose of skepticism can prove invaluable. Samara Oberlander-Agam was my first editor. I found her blue pen to be a magic wand capable of turning difficult, wordy writing into a text that could be read and understood.

My editor at Cambridge University Press, John Haslam, has been extremely supportive and helpful from the very first. The relationship between authors and publishers is full of anxiety and uncertainty; a good editor like John can make all the difference in the world.

Finally, I want to thank my family, Lauren, Noa, and Dana. Lauren has always asked the perfect questions when I got stuck, and has always been willing to listen to "just one more" version of the answer. Only someone as special as Lauren would be willing to hear me agonize about the same book for over three years and not throw me out of the house. Noa and Dana provide us with the joy and love that makes everything else possible.

Introduction

Imagine, if you would, a not-so-mythical world in which conflicts are fought within a magnificent arena. The arena was built with the latest technology and allows millions to hear stories about the battles that take place throughout the day without even coming to the event. The crowd who actually views the battles is surprisingly small. It is composed of professional storytellers (sometimes called journalists) who are responsible for turning even the most monotonous of contests into exciting drama. Sometimes managers send spies to scout the land looking for new talent, but for the most part gladiators come from miles around hoping to fight in a major event, or at least a side show. For those who are lucky enough to be chosen the benefits seem almost too good to be true: fame, fortune, and the chance to appear again. While winning the battle is always preferable to losing, everyone knows that it is better to have appeared and lost than never to have appeared at all.

The rules of entry have been handed down for generations. The soldiers of the emperor, of course, need no special permission to enter. They enter through the Royal Gate, they have an elaborate dressing room, and the management treats them with the respect they deserve. The soldiers of the noble class enter through a similar door and while their entry is not as routine as that of the rulers, they appear within the arena regularly. Finally, there is a very small door, known as Deviants' Gate, which is located in the back section of the arena, the darkest part of the stadium. The gate contains a small peephole and a particularly nasty gatekeeper whose major responsibility is to pick out the freaks and loonies who add spice to the show. Those who come through this gate usually come from the poorer classes of society and while many realize the enormous risks they face in the arena they also know that it represents their only chance for fame. To gain entry they must prove to the gatekeeper that their act will be more entertaining than their competitors'. In their desperate attempt to catch the gatekeeper's eye they dress themselves in ornate costumes and carry out bizarre, even frightening, feats. They are expected to remain in costume and character throughout the performance, a requirement that makes the road to honor even more difficult.

Occasionally, however, a challenger comes along who inspires the crowd with his or her bravery or cunning. Then the arena lights up with excitement as word begins to spread that a David has been found who is worthy to fight Goliath. The enthusiasm of the journalist crowd at such moments is a joy to see as they cheer for the victory of justice over evil. They dance, they prance, they pat each other on the back, tell ancient tales about a land called Watergate, and only reluctantly return to business as usual.

The news media have become the central arena for political conflicts. It is not surprising then that the role of the news media in political conflicts is an issue that has received a good deal of public attention in recent years. Policy-makers, journalists, and social scientists all point to the important role of the press in events such as the war in Bosnia, the conflict in Somalia, the Gulf war, the Palestinian *intifada*, the events at Tiananmen Square, and the massive protests throughout Eastern Europe and Russia in the dying days of the Communist regimes. Yet, when compared with other issues studied, this topic has been severely neglected by researchers.

The competition over the news media is a major element in modern political conflicts. The Pro-Choice and Pro-Life movements in America, the Serbians and the Muslims in Bosnia, Amnesty International, Russia, Chechnya, and the American government all compete for media attention as a means to achieve political influence. Each antagonist attempts to promote its own frames of the conflict to the news media in an attempt to mobilize political support for its cause. If we can understand the rules of combat and the factors that lead to success and failure in the arena, we will be one step closer to understanding the role the news media play in such conflicts.

The focus in this book will be on the role of the news media in *unequal political conflicts*. These include all public confrontations between a government and at least one other antagonist in which the state (or one state) has a significantly superior amount of coercive resources at its disposal. As detailed below, the news media are most likely to have an impact on just these types of conflicts and this is the reason for this choice. Nevertheless, many conflicts fall under this category: protests, terrorist acts, riots, rebellions, revolutions, and all-out wars between powerful countries and weaker ones.

The term "antagonist" refers to any group, institution, or state involved in an ongoing conflict with another group, institution, or state over a political issue. I shall refer to the more powerful antagonists as the "authorities" and to the weaker ones as "challengers". I adopt the term "challenger" from Tilly (1978) who makes a distinction between two types of "contenders": those who have low-cost access to resources controlled by the government (members) and those who do not (challengers). The present discussion does not therefore deal directly with the competition between political parties which takes place during and between elections. While many ideas developed here can be applied to that realm, the number of studies about the media and elections far exceeds those that look at the more intensive conflicts.

The book is designed not as a research report, but as a theoretical work that uses several case studies to illustrate the model. It is intended to put forth an approach, a way of looking at the role of the news media in political conflicts. It is also hoped that the ideas presented here can serve as a useful contribution to efforts being made to build a comprehensive model of political communication.

The theoretical model presented here is called the *political contest model*. The thrust of this model is that the best way to understand the role of the news media in politics is to view the competition over the news media as part of a larger and more significant contest among political antagonists for political control. I want to put the politics back into political communication. Many of those who have studied this issue have made the same mistake as novice protest leaders. They have been so blinded by the radiance of the news media that they have lost sight of the more powerful political forces that lay beyond them.

The model rests on five major arguments. First, that *the political process is more likely to have an influence on the news media than the news media are on the political process*. The political process has a major impact on the press because political power can usually be translated into power over the news media, because the political culture of a society has a major influence on how the news media cover conflicts, because the news media are much more likely to react to political events than to initiate them, because political realities often determine how antagonists use the news media to achieve political goals, and because political decisions have a major influence on who owns the media and how they operate.

This does not mean that news media do not also influence the political process. They help set the political agenda, they can accelerate and magnify political success and failure, they can serve as independent advocates for victims of oppression, they can mobilize third parties into a conflict, and they are central agents in the construction of social frames about politics. The press serves as a powerful catalyst for political processes and it is therefore essential to understand better how this catalyst operates. This cycle of influence, however, usually begins within the world of politics.

The second argument is that *the authorities' level of control over the political environment is one of the key variables that determine the role of the news media in political conflicts.* Political conflicts are characterized by moves and counter-moves as each antagonist tries to initiate and control political events, to dominate political discourse about the conflict, and to mobilize as many supporters as possible to their side. Those who have success in these areas also enjoy a good deal of success in the news media.

The news media's role in these conflicts is directly affected by the outcomes of such struggles. When authorities succeed in dominating the political environment, the news media find it difficult to play an independent role. When, on the other hand, the authorities lack or lose control it provides the news media with a much greater array of sources and perspectives from which to choose. This offers important opportunities for challengers to promote their own frames to the press.

The third major argument is that *the role of the news media in political conflicts varies over time and circumstance.* This contention emphasizes the need to develop a dynamic approach to the study of this issue. Those who attempt to find a single unified role for the news media in political conflicts are wasting their time. When covering political violence and terrorism in wars such as Vietnam and the Israeli war in Lebanon, the press were accused of being virtual saboteurs who undermined military effort through biased anti-government reporting. Social movements, on the other hand, often accuse the press of being an instrument of government propaganda. Similar accusations were leveled at the press during the Gulf war and to a certain extent in the Falklands, Grenada, and Panama.

The role of the news media in conflicts varies along with such factors as the political context of the conflict, the resources, skills, and political power of the players involved, the relationship between the press and each antagonist, the state of public opinion, the ability of the journalists to gain access to the conflict events, and last but certainly not least what is happening in the field. All of this is beyond variations in the antagonists' control over the political environment mentioned above. Thus, not only does the role of the news media vary across conflicts, it can also change within the course of a single conflict.

The fourth argument is that *those who hope to understand variations in the role of the news media must look at the competition among antagonists along two dimensions: one structural and the other cultural.* The best way to learn about the rules of combat is to watch the battle. Antagonists compete over the news media along two major dimensions. They compete over *access* to the news media and they compete over *media frames*. The model will use two dimensions of analysis, each of which contributes an important perspective on these struggles. The *structural dimension* looks at the extent of mutual dependence between the antagonists and each news medium to explain the power of each side in the transaction. This offers important insights about which political actors are most likely to gain access to the arena. The *cultural dimension* of analysis focuses on how norms, beliefs, and routines all have an influence on the construction of media frames of conflict. This second dimension serves to remind us that political contests are also struggles over meaning in which success within the news media can lead to higher levels of political support.

The fifth and final argument is that *while authorities have tremendous advantages over challengers in the quantity and quality of media coverage they receive, many challengers can overcome these obstacles and use the news media as a tool for political influence.* The literature on this topic presents mostly one side of this picture. It is a story of gloom and doom in which powerful governments can exploit the dependence of the news media to drown out alternative frames and agendas. Authorities have routine access to the news media and the staff, skills, and resources to take full advantage of that access.

There is, however, another part of the story that is just as important to tell. Challengers can and do compete with the authorities in the news media. Some of these opportunities emerge from the political blunders of the powerful while others can be attributed to outside events. The news media keep a large stock of anti-authority frames for those antagonists who have the resources and skills to use them. Researchers should focus their attention on the exceptions as well as the rules.

When taken as a whole, these five arguments suggest a process that is neither linear nor constant. The competition between authorities and challengers over the news media is as fascinating and unpredictable as politics itself. In some ways the central arena resembles the modern sports facility that can be converted into several structures, each designed for a different type of event. Sometimes the arena is used for lavish spectacles in which officials show off their most colorful costumes and weapons. At other times it is a place for fierce contests in which challengers and authorities square off in brutal combat. And at yet other times it becomes a theater-in-the-round putting on tragic morality plays about the plight of the oppressed and the need for social change. The goal of this study is to understand better the political, social, and situational factors that dictate how and when the arena is transformed.

Methods and approaches

There are two major methodological approaches in the social sciences: quantitative and qualitative (Glassner and Morena, 1989; Wimmer and Dominick, 1991). The quantitative approach is based on the natural sciences model of hypothesis-testing through statistical analysis and is best used in studies that look at the relationship between individual level variables. The qualitative approach is especially appropriate for research such as this that attempts to explain social interaction between two or more systems. Qualitative methodologies employ inductive logic by learning as much as possible about a particular social reality and then attempting to build a more general theory based on those findings (Denzin and Lincoln, 1994).

The ideas presented in this work are based on about ten years of research looking at the interaction between political antagonists and the news media. I started studying the interactions between protesters and the news media (Wolfsfeld, 1984a, 1984b) and then moved on to the issues of insurrections and war (Wolfsfeld, 1993a, 1993b, 1991). In the second part of this book I present three of these studies to demonstrate the varying role of the news media in political conflicts: the Gulf war, the Palestinian *intifada*, and the attempt by the Israeli right wing to derail the Israeli–Palestinian peace accords. Details of the methodology of these three cases can be found in the appendix at the end of this work. The model, however, derives from a much broader set of research.

The process of reasoning was very much an inductive one in which I kept trying to understand how the role of the news media varied over time and circumstance. My goal was to try to develop an understanding of the basic rules. Previous works on this subject have been limited to looking at the role of the news media in either a particular conflict (such as the Gulf war) or a particular *type* of conflict (such as terrorism). This fragmented approach to the topic inhibits our ability to develop a more comprehensive understanding of how the role of the news media varies.

There were two central research questions that guided these studies:
1. Which factors best explain how political antagonists and the news media influence one another?
2. When is the news media most likely to play an independent role in political conflicts? The formulation of the first question assumes a two-way flow of influence in which it is just as important to study the impact of antagonists on the news media as it is to look at the influence of the media on political actors. The second research question forces us to look at the issue comparatively to understand better the varying role of the news media.

Thus, the goal of the work is to build theory. One will find very little normative analysis within this work. There is no attempt, for example, to make any value judgments about whether the news media should be given more or less independence in wartime. The assumption is that governments generally prefer a less independent news media during war and that most journalists would like to break away. The model is designed to explain which factors increase the likelihood of each of these scenarios coming true.

I used a similar methodology in all these studies. I interviewed activists, journalists, and officials about the quantity and quality of interactions among them. When possible, I also tried to be present to observe the interactions directly. I then attempted to look at how the media covered the conflict, combining systematic content analysis with a deeper, more qualitative type of reading. My field experience was also supplemented by the work of my students at the Hebrew University of Jerusalem who carried out many similar studies for seminar papers. I was also very conscious of the work of my colleagues in political communication who had carried out comparable studies in other countries, especially the United States.

A qualitative methodology does have its drawbacks. The model that has emerged can never be completely "tested": it can only be applied with greater and lesser success. One can demonstrate but not "prove" the validity of one's conclusions; the goal is to be convincing. Researchers must make a conscious decision to sacrifice precision in hopes of attaining at least some vision. The method is unabashedly subjective. Researchers find themselves constantly moving back and forth between two worlds: one composed of political actors and journalists who are constantly negotiating over news stories, the other of social science that tries to place these interactions within a broader context. Attempting to interpret systematically other people's interpretations is a risky way to make a living.

A significant part of this work deals with the social construction of political reality, about the construction of frames. I feel compelled, therefore, to say something directly about my own political frames rather than leaving the reader to infer them from my analyses. I was born in the United States and moved to Israel for ideological reasons about twenty years ago. My political affiliations run left of center and I generally support the Labor party. I did reserve duty in the Israeli army during the Lebanese war, the *intifada*, and the Gulf war. During the time of the *intifada*, I believed Israel should recognize the PLO and attempt to achieve a political compromise. My position on the Gulf war ran along the same lines as the vast majority of Israelis: I supported the Allied war effort against Iraq. I also support the peace process that began with the Oslo agreement between the Rabin government and the PLO.

Nevertheless, although it may suggest some character flaw, I find myself capable of empathizing with most of the antagonists I have studied over the years. I sympathize with Palestinian attempts to free themselves of Israeli occupation and yet I also understand those who believed that the violence must be put down by force. Despite my support of the peace process, I fully understand the right-wing protesters in Israel who believe that it will bring nothing but death and destruction. I also understand Saddam Hussein's aspirations to defy the West during the Gulf conflict, despite my support for the Allies in that confrontation. The key in qualitative methodology is to develop an empathy with each antagonist while avoiding over-identifying with any of them.

Finally, a note about the ethnocentrism of this study. The fact that so much of my research has been carried out in Israel has both advantages and disadvantages. On the one hand Israel is a place with a great deal of conflict that gets an enormous amount of attention in the news media and thus provides an especially intriguing site for this research. It can also be argued that the fact that so much previous work has been carried out in the United States makes it essential to look at other cultures for the purposes of comparison.

Critics will nevertheless be justified in being suspicious of any model whose author has spent so much time in such an unusual political milieu. There is a tendency in American political science to label any research conducted outside the United States as "comparative politics." While there is nothing inherently offensive about such a classification, I do believe that the ideas presented here are applicable to other countries. The theoretical discussion in the first part of the book purposely avoids using examples from the Middle East to underscore this point. In the end, however, readers must decide whether the arguments presented here also explain the role of the news media in their own countries.

Organization of the argument

The book is divided into three parts. Part 1 is devoted to developing the political contest model and Part 2 is dedicated to applying that model to the three case studies mentioned above. The final part of the book consists of a single concluding chapter.

The argument begins in Chapter 1 by looking at the competition among antagonists over access to the news media. The discussion focuses on when political power can and cannot be translated into power over the media. This is the structural level of analysis that looks at the relationship between antagonists and the news media by considering the relative need each side has for the services of the other. The analytical tools provided should allow researchers a method for monitoring this aspect of the conflict.

The second chapter looks at the contest over media frames that constitutes the cultural level of analysis. This is a competition over the meaning of the conflict as each antagonist attempts to promote its own interpretations to the news media. The factors that determine success and failure in this realm are more subtle and more difficult to discern, but just as important in determining the media's role. Here too one finds that one can only understand the role of the news media by looking to the political and cultural forces that help shape the story.

While the first two chapters are devoted to explaining how antagonists influence the news media, Chapter 3 examines the influence of the news media on the antagonists. A "continuum of influence" is put forth with three ideal points, each representing a different role for the news media in political conflicts. The discussion looks at some of the political outcomes that can be attributed to the press and provides some guidelines for evaluating the extent of media influence on a given conflict.

The second part of the book begins with a discussion of how the model can explain the role the news media can play in attempts by social movements to influence government policy. As noted, the case study chosen to illustrate the dynamics of this process was the protest in Israel against the Declaration of Principles signed between Israel and the PLO in the fall of 1993. This conflict offers many advantages for those interested in understanding how the role of the news media varies over time and political circumstance. Chapter 4 uses the political contest model to explain the competition over access to the news media during this period, while Chapter 5 looks at the struggle over the meaning of the peace process. The analyses focus on how differences among movements, news media, and political control all had significant influences on the ability of challengers to promote alternative frames to the news media.

Chapters 6, 7 and 8 are devoted to discussing the role of the news media in insurrections and wars. Here the importance of control over the political environment becomes even more important in deciding the role of the news media. The dynamics and consequences of this process are explained in Chapter 6 through a detailed comparison of the struggle over the political environment that characterized the *intifada* and the Gulf war. Chapters 7 and 8 are devoted to exploring the contest over media frames in those two confrontations. The analytical tools developed in the first part of the book are used to explain how both political and journalistic factors combined to produce very different outcomes.

The final part of the book is intended to bring the argument full circle. The news media played a very different role in each of these conflicts and hopefully the model helps explain why. Those who want to capture what is happening in the arena had better be equipped with a wide-angle lens and some high-speed film. While taking the photograph may become more difficult, the added effort should produce a more realistic picture.

Part 1

The rules of combat

1 The structural dimension: the struggle over access

The contest over the news media has become an important element in almost every political conflict. The purpose of this chapter is to outline the central rules of passage into this arena. It is critical to understand the struggle over access for there is much more at stake than mere publicity. It is a struggle over the national and international agenda. The very fact that policy-makers and citizens are encouraged to think about some challenges rather than others is, by itself, likely to affect the allocation of public resources and how people relate to the political world.

Nevertheless, one cannot, and should not, distinguish between the contest over the news media and the more general contest over political control. Political actors view the news media as one of many tools that can be used to achieve their goals. The political process has a life of its own and only by monitoring this process can one understand the victories and the defeats.

The structural dimension of analysis

The concept of structure as it is used in this study is best detailed in an article by Sewell (1992). Sewell defines structures as "sets of mutually sustaining schemas and resources that empower and constrain social action and that tend to be reproduced by that social action" (1992, p. 19). This type of analysis relates to the basic "rules of the game" as they are understood by the various players.

The relationship between political antagonists and the news media can be described as a "competitive symbiosis" (Wolfsfeld, 1991) in which each side of the relationship attempts to exploit the other while expending a minimum amount of cost. Each side has assets needed by the other to succeed in its respective role (Blumler and Gurevitch, 1986). Political activists and leaders rely on the press to get their message to a variety of publics and the press relies on the antagonists for information and events that can be turned into news. It is this exchange of information for publicity that explains an important part of the relationship between the two systems.

There is a formula that clarifies this part of the relationship between antagonists and the news media. The initial principles are based on exchange theory (Blau, 1964; Grossman and Rourke, 1976; Waldman, 1972) and/or power dependency theory (DeFleur and Ball-Rokeach, 1989; Ball-Rokeach and DeFleur, 1976; Emerson, 1972; Reese, 1991). The relative power of either side – a given news medium and a given antagonist – is determined by the value of its services divided by its need for those services offered by the other. Power is a question of relative dependence: who needs whom more at the time of the transaction. As noted, while some aspects of this relationship remain fairly constant, others change over time and circumstance.

Presidents of the United States, for example, have a tremendous amount of news value and journalists are willing to "pay" a lot to receive information from them. The ways in which the press accommodates Presidents come in many forms. The news media are much more likely to allow Presidents free air time to make speeches to the nation than other political actors, more likely to quote them directly in news reports, more likely to treat them with respect in interviews, and more likely to station journalists permanently with the explicit purpose of collecting information from the President.

Presidents, however, must also accommodate the press. They need the media to promote their image and their policies. This adaptation comes in many forms that range from the staging of media events to the creation of an informational infrastructure that facilitates the distribution of information to reporters. The amount of need will vary within different political contexts. Presidents' dependence on the news media often rises at election time, for example, because of their increased need to send information to the public. This increased dependency will be reflected in a more conscious attempt to carry out newsworthy behavior and to give public speeches with the appropriately placed sound bites.

The notions of value and dependence also determine which challengers gain access to the news media. Here then is a second struggle over access: the contest among challengers. Once again the choices made by the news media will depend on the relative value of the information being offered by the various actors while the willingness of each actor to adapt to the news media will depend on their need for publicity.

As Sewell points out, however, the reproduction of structure is "never automatic" (1992, p. 19) because of the effects of "agency." Social actors are free to accept, reject, interpret, and modify structural rules and these decisions vary among agents. This is certainly true in the relationships between antagonists and the news media. Ideology often serves as one of the most important factors that limits the exercise of power in this area. Social movements are often unwilling to humiliate themselves, sully their self-image, or carry out especially violent acts to obtain a higher level of publicity. When television cameras appear, political actors are perfectly free to ignore them despite any benefits that might be achieved by adapting one's behavior.

Similarly, the news media may refuse to carry out an interview with certain groups of terrorists even if such an interview would dramatically increase the size of their audience. Despite the way reporters are often portrayed in recent years, journalistic ethics do set important limits on the willingness of the news media to give in to demands by even the most powerful of authorities.

An analysis of the structural relationship, therefore, tells us what to *expect* but not necessarily what will happen. The key to understanding the nature of these relationships is to monitor the transactions between the antagonists and the news media (Wolfsfeld, 1991). The structural principles developed here serve as an analytical base line that explains an important part of the relationship between antagonists and the news media. There are, however, many important deviations from this base line because of changes in the actors involved and the particular circumstances that define a given political situation.

We need to look, then, at two issues. The first issue has to do with the inherent advantages which political power brings to those attempting to gain entrance to the news media. The second has to do with why the importance of such advantages varies over time and circumstance. The major reason, it will be argued, is that authorities often find it difficult to take control over the political environment and this sets important limits to the extent of political power. Scholars who only look at the advantages miss some of the most interesting parts of the game.

Translating political power into power over the news media

A major theme in the scientific literature on the news media concerns the advantages that the news media afford to those with political power. It is important to go beyond this truism and attempt to understand how and why political power can be translated into power over the news media. If one understands *why* the politically powerful usually have more access to the news media, one can also understand how that relationship can change. The way to understand this dynamic is to look

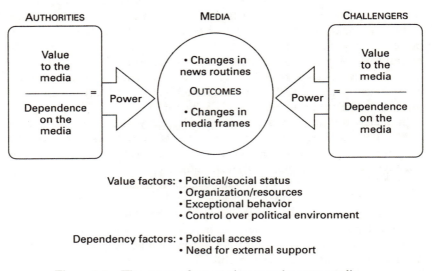

Value factors: • Political/social status
• Organization/resources
• Exceptional behavior
• Control over political environment

Dependency factors: • Political access
• Need for external support

Figure 1.1   The power of antagonists over the news media

at the *intervening variables* that serve as the bridge between political power and power over the news media.

The power of a given antagonist over a given news medium is based on the antagonist's level of perceived news value on the one hand and the antagonist's need for the news media on the other: the higher the value and the lower the need the greater the likelihood of an antagonist having an influence on the press. This influence will be manifested in terms of more access and an increased ability to have one's preferred frames adopted by the news media. An outline of these initial principles is shown in Figure 1.1.

There are four major factors that increase the inherent news value of antagonists: their level of political and social status, their level of organization and resources, their ability to carry out exceptional behavior, and their level of control over the political environment. I shall discuss the first three of these factors now and then turn to the issue of political control.

Political and social status

Political and social status can be defined as the formal and informal standing of an actor, group, organization, or country within a particular political and social system. When elites plan strategy, make decisions, or carry out policies, it is considered news. The news media consider elites inherently newsworthy and rely on them as their major sources of information (Bennett, 1983; Paletz and Entman, 1981; Molotch and Lester, 1974; Entman, 1989; Gans, 1979; Reese, Grant, and Danielian, 1994; Shoemaker and Reese, 1991). The ways in which status increases demand can be easily illustrated by simply considering "who chases whom." While high-ranking officials, politicians, and celebrities are constantly surrounded by journalists awaiting their every statement, those with lower status move about in relative anonymity and must make special efforts to obtain publicity.

Bennett (1990) has suggested that this reliance on political elites as sources has had an especially important effect on the setting of the political agenda. Bennett argues that: "Mass media news professionals, from the boardroom to the beat, tend to 'index' the range of voices and viewpoints in both news and editorials according to the range of views expressed in mainstream government debate about a given topic" (p. 106).

He goes on to show how closely the debate within the *New York Times* about the conflict in Nicaragua during the middle of the 1980s reflected the debate in the US Congress. When opposition in Congress to Reagan's policies rose, so did the number of opinion pieces against it; when Congress stopped dealing with the issue, so did the *New York Times*. Lacking institutional sources, the *New York Times* was either unwilling or unable to play an independent role in covering this issue. This system of indexing offers an extremely narrow definition of the political climate by being too dependent on the rise and fall of debate within official circles.

The advantages enjoyed by the political elites are institutionalized through the "beat system" (Bennett, 1983; Fishman, 1980; Gans, 1979; Molotch, Protess, and Gordon, 1987; Molotch and Lester, 1981; Tuchman, 1978). Journalists are assigned to a particular institution or subject area on an ongoing basis to allow for the routine collection of information from sources with higher levels of political and social status. This allows for both medium- and long-term planning by editors, correspondents, and political elites. Clearly such a system leads to tremendous inequalities in access for those who are not included in such beats, but it is hard to conceive of an alternative structure that could enable the press to continue to function in its present form.

While many previous scholars have noted the advantages that high-status political elites have over other news sources it is important to take this principle a few steps further. First, differences in political and social status tell us something important not only about variations in access *between* the authorities and challengers, but also *among* them. There are status rich and status poor among all political actors.

As an example, consider what would happen if two groups of differing political status – say the American group Common Cause (an interest group that works for "good government") and a new group called "Citizens for Honesty" – each sent press releases to different news media about certain politicians taking bribes. The press release of Common Cause would be treated seriously while the press release from the unknown group would either be ignored or followed up by contacting alternative sources with higher status. The higher status of Common Cause leads journalists to assume that the organization is more credible, and more likely to have an impact on the political process.[1] The same would be true of such international groups as Amnesty International and Greenpeace who can be considered elites among challengers.

In addition, although one normally thinks about the high status of authorities when compared to the low status of challengers, there are challengers who enjoy higher status than some politicians. A low-status politician might very well have more trouble making claims about the political system in the United States, for example, than Common Cause. In addition, if that same politician were attacked by Common Cause, he or she would find it extremely difficult to divert attention because his or her other activities are not considered newsworthy. The point to keep in mind is that in any political conflict one must examine the *relative* status of each of the competing antagonists.

The importance of political and social status to access should also be extended to the role of the news media in international conflicts. Here too, editors make certain assumptions about the status of various international actors and assign reporters accordingly. Just as every American news medium wants to have a journalist stationed at the White House or the Congress, so every foreign news agency that can afford it attempts to place a reporter in Washington, London, and Moscow. Here too, assumptions about political impact influence the access afforded to various political actors.

The dilemmas facing less powerful countries run along similar lines as those facing domestic challengers. Only natural disasters or very high levels of violence justify sending journalists to Third World countries, and this has a critical influence on both the quantity and quality of coverage of these countries (Hawk, 1992). Countries such as Rwanda

---

[1]   For more about the relationship between Common Cause and the press see Paletz and Entman (1981).

only make the news when there are vast numbers of dead. This means that international challengers will only have access to the international news media when they carry out exceptional actions.

The ongoing conflict between Argentina and the United Kingdom over the Falklands, for example, only came to the attention of the international press when the Argentine army took over the islands. Only then did the international press begin to deal with Argentinian claims of sovereignty. As with many such challenges, Argentina began the struggle over world opinion with two strikes against it. First, international audiences were much more familiar with British leaders who had been given extensive attention in the years preceding the Falklands conflict. Second, the use of force by Argentina was considered far more newsworthy than any Argentinian claims of injustice. Argentina found itself in the classic dilemma for challengers: damned to infamy if they act and damned to obscurity if they don't.

The relationship between international status and informational flow is an issue taken up by the United Nations. Resolutions have been passed that call for a "new world information order" (Dordick and Wang, 1993, Galtung and Vincent, 1992; Roach, 1990) in which poorer countries will get a larger part of the informational pie. It is doubtful, however, whether such resolutions can have much of an effect on norms and values of international journalism, especially within the Western press. Soderlund and Schmitt (1986) carried out a study of North and South American coverage of the civil war in El Salvador. They found that US and European sources were more likely to be used not only in US newspapers but even in South American and Canadian newspapers. It is odd that Western sources are given more credibility in South American newspapers about a Central American conflict, but this is the privilege of international status.

Organization and resources

Antagonists with a high level of organization and resources are in a better position to create news because the creation of major events is organizationally expensive (Alinsky, 1971, Bennett, 1983; Gans, 1979). The ability to produce a major demonstration, for example, demands organization, people, and money. In addition, actors with resources are more likely to be considered inherently newsworthy even before they act, due to assumptions about their potential for political impact. A mere threat of a strike by a large union is considered news, as are rumors that the government may send troops to quell political disturbances, or that a major international power is contemplating economic sanctions against a smaller country. It is useful to distinguish between hard and soft resources although both can increase the power of an antagonist over the news media. Hard resources are concrete assets such as the number of members in an organization, the amount of funds available for collective action, and the number of paid professionals working for the antagonist. Soft resources are intangible assets such as the degree of group solidarity, and the extent of knowledge and experience, especially regarding the news media.

Money can be used to buy knowledge and experience and the use of professional spokespeople has become an especially important factor in any public conflict (Manheim, 1991). As information is the major commodity being offered by the antagonist it must be carefully guarded, packaged, and distributed. A skilled professional in public relations is a trained soldier with knowledge of weapons, strategy, and terrain. Amateurs enter the arena at their own risk, and these disparities are often directly reflected on the battlefield. While many journalists are proud of their ability to get around such spokespeople, the truth is that such public relations systems provide an important subsidy for news organizations who would otherwise spend much more time and effort independently gathering information (Gandy, 1982; Fishman, 1980; Reese, 1991; Turk, 1986).

It is sometimes helpful to refer to status, organization and resources as *production assets*.[2] These are the assets that an antagonist can use in the production of newsworthy information and events. While an antagonist's level of assets can change, they tend to be more stable than other variables that will be discussed. These three factors offer important information about the inherent news value of a given antagonist. Intrinsic advantages, however, are not enough: one also has to act.

Exceptional behavior

The third major factor that increases the news value of an antagonist is the degree to which they carry out exceptional behavior. The word "exceptional" carries two different meanings that provide important insight about the construction of news. Behavior can be considered exceptional in the sense of being either unusually important or unusually deviant. This returns us to the notion of a Royal Gate for VIPs and a Deviants' Gate for challengers. There are indeed two gates for entering into the media arena. The front gate is reserved for those regarded as

---

[2]   This is a term used by Bill Gamson in his work on this topic.

exceptionally eminent while the rear is intended for the exceptionally weird.

Challengers are often forced to carry out exceptionally strange or violent acts as a substitute for their lack of status or resources. Dissidents may burn an American flag, dress up in weird costumes, or even carry out terrorist attacks to obtain access to the central arena. Leaders of smaller countries may choose to give an especially provocative speech or make threatening moves to gain an international platform for their demands. In the fall of 1994, for example, Iraq set off a mini-crisis with the West by moving troops toward the Kuwait border. CNN immediately sent Peter Arnett back to his old stomping grounds to produce stories about how painful UN sanctions were to the country. Until then, Iraq's pleas for attention had been ignored. Iraq moved the troops, and it got the coverage. Such actions serve as a crude but effective battering ram for breaking down the gates of the central arena.

Challengers must pay a heavy price for this type of entrance: they must remain in costume. Weaker antagonists only remain newsworthy if they remain deviant and this widens the gap between the haves and the have nots. The Yippies of the 1960s are remembered primarily for their outlandish costumes and war paint; the most memorable photographs of the Black Panthers have them holding guns; the PLO was long linked with the pictures of the masked terrorists taking hostages at the Munich Olympics; and the concept of the early women's groups as radical "trouble-makers" remains etched in the collective memory of many Americans. Having gained access to the media, such groups must then fight an uphill battle for legitimacy.

In addition, the notion of what is considered exceptional varies over time and culture. Acts considered exceptional when they are first carried out become less exceptional as they drag on. As pointed out by Hilgartner and Bosk (1988) issues and actions reach a certain saturation point and lose their dramatic value, and drama is an important element in the competition over public attention. The journalist approach to antagonists is pretty much summed up the obnoxious question: "What have you done for me lately?" The news is created on a daily basis and those who want to compete for media space must constantly prove their newsworthiness. Hackett (1985) makes a similar point in his study of Canadian peace movements. Movements, he argues, must often choose between "disappearing from the front pages, or of constantly escalating its tactics and rhetoric to stay above the media's rising boredom threshold" (p. 79).

Still, even Presidents can be boring. The newsworthiness of a given antagonist is related not only to whom they are but also what they do.

Status, organization, and resources are not enough. The first obligation of any journalist is to produce a "good story" and when challengers provide better stories than authorities, they get more – though not necessarily better – coverage.

Dependence on the news media

One cannot calculate the total level of power without also considering an antagonist's level of dependence on the news media. The greater the need for the services offered by the news media, the more vulnerable the antagonist is to being influenced by the news media, and the weaker its bargaining position compared with competing antagonists. Dependency leads to adaptation.

There are two major factors that lead to an increase in media dependence. The first is a *lack of alternative access to political influence*. A major reason for turning to the news media is to gain access to political decision-makers. The press, however, is a rather crude and even dangerous communication channel. Those who have more direct access to such decision-makers can work privately and have less need for media attention.

While the reasons for this are clear with respect to challengers they may be less obvious concerning the authorities. After all, the authorities *are* the decision-makers. Nevertheless, not all the authorities are in an equally advantaged position to have an effect on policy. Those who are further down on the political influence ladder are more dependent on the news media than those further up.

The second factor which influences dependence on the news media is the *need for external support*. This is the other major service the news media provide for political antagonists: access to third parties (Schattschneider, 1960). The need for public support varies among antagonists and over time. Social movements, for example, usually depend on the public because their goals are long term and broad based (Gitlin, 1980). Labor unions, on the other hand, can frequently avoid turning to the press. They clearly look for public support during a strike but at other, less intensive times union leaders will prefer working directly with authorities (be they private or public) and to stay out of the public eye.

The interests of political leaders also vary among issues and circumstance: public mobilization is essential for some policies and less important, or even detrimental, for others. As the need for public support rises and falls so does the willingness of antagonists to change their message, tactics, and behavior to meet the needs of the media.

Thus, dependence on the media is determined by the need for an antagonist to send its message "up" (to major decision makers) and "out" (to the public). As before, these concepts tell us something important not only about the gap between authorities and challengers but also about the difference among them. Members of the US Congress need the news media more than senators, who need the news media more than the President. Poor interest groups need the press more than rich ones and weak social movements need the press more than strong ones. These distinctions are important for they tell us a good deal about which antagonists are most likely to be influenced by the news media.

The same principles can also be applied to international conflicts. A weaker country or group conflicting with a larger, more powerful one will be more dependent for external support and this will have an impact on its relations with the international news media. While the Serbs would have preferred to keep the war with Bosnia as an "internal affair," the Bosnians' only hope for salvation was external intervention. The stories of Muslim casualties, especially in Sarejevo, were the only way for the Muslims to mobilize external support. Journalists in Sarejevo provided the lifeline for the citizens living in that city.

NATO only issued an ultimatum to the Serbs to end their blockade of Sarejevo in February of 1994 when stories of a particularly bloody attack in which sixty-eight civilians were killed were broadcast around the world. *Newsweek* (1994) reported that "the horror of the marketplace massacre shown on CNN pushed him [President Clinton] and his advisers into the Oval Office on Saturday afternoon to review once again what, if anything, America could do to stop the slaughter" (p. 9). One could argue that it was the event rather than the broadcast that was central but this is contradicted by the fact that the United States and NATO ignored similar incidents that were not reported both in other parts of the former Yugoslavia and the world.

The extent of dependence on the news media and the willingness to adapt is not simply a matter of objective criteria. As discussed more thoroughly in Chapter 3, antagonists make subjective decisions about the centrality of the news media in their general political strategy. While most groups must consider such factors as their need for public support, many have ideological reasons for avoiding the news media that override any structural needs. Even the most desperate of antagonists will set limits to the extent to which they are willing to humiliate themselves to achieve news coverage. Ideology sets important limits to any structural dependency on the press.

The principle of cumulative inequality

It is now obvious why so many observers have stressed the advantages which political power brings to those seeking media attention. It is possible to summarize this axiom by referring to the *principle of cumulative inequality*.[3] This principle states that those who most need the news media are the ones who find it the most difficult to obtain them; the rich get richer and the poor remain poor. The major reason for this Catch 22 is the already-stated correlation between political power and all of the factors that lead to a higher news value and a lower dependence on the news media. Political power leads to political and social status, organization and resources, the ability to carry out exceptional behavior in the positive sense of the word, more direct access to political decision-makers, and less need for external support to achieve political goals.

There is also a clear correlation among these factors that goes beyond their relationship with political power. Organization and resources bring status and status facilitates access to decision-makers. Easy access to the news media becomes simply another indicator of wealth and power. The politically powerless find themselves in the same trap as all members of the underclass: they lack the clout to gain resources and they lack the resources to gain clout.

Political power and power over the news media are not, however, perfectly correlated. The discussion turns to dealing with this important gap.

Control over the political environment

From here, the playing field begins to level. The authorities' degree of control over the political environment, I shall argue, is the key situational variable that determines whether the news media will play an independent role in a political conflict. It is one of the most important wild cards that ensures that conflicts between authorities and challengers over the news media remain genuine contests.

Many communication scholars treat the political world as a given, and concentrate almost exclusively on variations within the news media. The political world is seen as something more stable and solid, even static. Nothing could be further from the truth. The political world is in a constant state of flux, and as political scientists have learned over the years, painfully difficult to predict.

---

[3]   This term grew out of work conducted together with Bill Gamson.

The ability of the antagonist to control the political environment can be understood in terms of three variables:
1. the ability to initiate and control events;
2. the ability to regulate the flow of information; and
3. the ability to mobilize elite support.

Each of these factors increases the ability of an antagonist to dominate public discourse about a particular issue. While the news media constitute the central area of the public space devoted to politics, they are hardly the only place where politics occurs. Politics happens in the legislature, in the courts, in the streets, on the battlefield and in discourse among elites, journalists, and the public. Those who dominate these forums will have little trouble dominating media discourse.

Here, too, authorities enjoy important advantages over challengers. They can bring their status, organization, and resources to bear within all these forums. After all this is what political power is all about. But there are definite limits to their power. Their inability to maintain full control over the political environment provides considerable opportunities for challengers to make significant inroads into the political process and the news media.

The first factor that determines control over the political environment is the *antagonist's relative ability to initiate and control events*. Political conflicts are often characterized by the attempts of each side to take the initiative and put the other side on the defensive. The news media respond to *events* and the competition for public attention is an important part of any political conflict. When the situation is under control, so is the story. Governments are in a much better position to coordinate their press relations when they can anticipate the events that will be covered. When, on the other hand, the powerful are forced to *react* to events it suggests that others are setting and framing the media's agenda.

Consider, for example, how easy it was for the Reagan administration to control the informational environment during the invasion of Grenada in 1983 (Sharkey, 1991). The fact that the battle plans for Grenada were known in advance, and that there were few surprises along the way allowed for a carefully orchestrated public relations campaign by the administration. They faced a very different situation in October of that year when the Marines were forced to deal with Shiite guerrillas in Lebanon. The inability to control the events led to an inability to control the story. All of the public relations experts in the world could not correct the damage in the news media that followed the explosion of the car bomb that killed over 200 marines.

There is good reason to believe that this was also one of the problems facing the "public relations campaign" surrounding the Vietnam war.

Hammond (1991) writes about the difficulties General Westmoreland faced in attempting to woo the US correspondents in Vietnam:

The effort had its effect, but in the end failed to compensate for major flaws in the American strategy. For by choosing to leave the enemy's sanctuaries in Laos and Cambodia intact and by refusing to invade North Vietnam or to block off the enemy's ports, the United States left the practical initiative to the communists. The enemy chose when and where to fight. (p. 13)

Losing the initiative meant losing control over the war and with it control over war coverage. As Hammond notes, the nightly briefings for the Saigon correspondents soon became known as "The Five O'Clock Follies"; the rising number of American casualties could never be "explained" away.

The need to carry out and control events offers a perfect illustration of the overlap between the structural and cultural dimensions of analysis, between the struggle over access and the struggle over media frames. The ability to draw the media's attentions from one issue to another increases the ability to promote certain conflict frames. The best-known example of this phenomenon comes from the reported preference of US Presidents to travel abroad when they lose popularity at home. They take the initiative, the television cameras follow, and they find themselves playing on a more convenient field.

Bennett (1983) makes a similar point about the importance of control by making a distinction between "fully controlled news," "partially controlled news," and "uncontrolled news." Fully controlled news occurs when politicians can stage "pseudoevents" (Boorstin, 1961) in which the politician can completely stage an event especially for the media. Bennett offers the example of an incident in which then President Richard Nixon took a walk on a carefully cleaned section of beach after a disastrous oil spill in Santa Barbara Channel in 1969. The rest of the beach remained filled with oil but journalists reported the story as it had been planned.

Press conferences, argues Bennett, are good examples of partially controlled news. While the authorities have some control over who will be invited and the format of the session, enterprising journalists can ask some embarrassing questions that can lead to unexpected stories. Many conflict stories fall into this category because the confrontation itself is what makes the story newsworthy.

The most dangerous sort of news for government leaders is uncontrolled news. Bennett describes a typical scenario:

A typical pattern in loss of news control is for an actor first to generate images successfully, only to eventually run afoul of leaks, blunders, or uncontrollable events in the world. Few news stories are bigger than the ones written about fallen political idols and struggling politicians. The greater the loss of control, the bigger the story. Reporters can be unmerciful in covering politicians who fail to manipulate the news effectively. (p. 51)

I would put it differently. Those who control the situation have little problem controlling the news. The key variable for researchers to monitor is the extent that a politician or a government maintains control over political events. While conventional wisdom puts a great deal of emphasis on the importance of "spin control," political events and developments can often become much more important than the quality of public relations. Molotch and Lester (1974) were the first to discuss the distinction between routine event and accidents. Whereas "news promoters" have little problem getting the appropriate coverage for routine events, accidents provide important opportunities for challengers. The ability to "manipulate" the news depends primarily on the ability to plan and execute political actions with a minimum of resistance and surprises.

A second variable that decides the extent of dominance over the political environment is the ability of the more powerful antagonist to *regulate the flow of information* about the conflict. As stated, information is the key commodity being exchanged by antagonists and, therefore, the ability to take control over information is a key factor in determining the value of one's information; it is just as important to take control over the supply of information as the demand.

The first step in regulating the flow of information is to ensure that one has control over one's own organization. A lack of control in this area can lead to leaks that lower the bargaining position of the antagonist in relation to the news media. Why should the news media "pay" anything for information from the main office that it can get free down the hall? This is an especially dangerous problem for antagonists because the information that is available down the hall is not only cheaper, it is often more exciting than any official press releases.

In addition, governments, both democratic and non-democratic, often find compelling reasons to employ censorship during political conflicts and this increases the value of official sources of information by eliminating competition. Powerful antagonists also have other means of controlling the flow of information to the press such as denying access or accreditation to journalists (or specific journalists), expelling them, shutting down press agencies working for other antagonists, or even placing rival news sources or journalists under arrest.

The ability of the powerful to regulate the flow of information to the press is affected by the nature of the *logistic and geographic environment*.

Powerful governments prefer to operate under conditions in which they can isolate the areas of actual conflict and regulate the entry and exit of journalists. But the powerful are not always able to choose the sites of conflict and this can greatly affect their ability to control the informational environment. While the physical circumstances of certain locales facilitate government control, other locations are more porous and offer easier access for reporters, thereby increasing the level of journalistic independence.

An illustration of this point can be made by comparing the ability of the British to control the press during the Falklands/Malvinas campaign (Glasgow University Media Group, 1985; Morrison and Tumber, 1988) with the difficulties they face attempting to regulate information about their conflict with the IRA. The most favorable situation from the authority's point of view is to have the conflict scene in an area that is as isolated as possible. This puts journalists at a serious disadvantage not only because they have to invest a good deal of ingenuity and resources into gaining access, but their lack of knowledge of the area increases their dependence on official sources. The worst case scenario for authorities, on the other hand, is a fight that takes place close to home in an area such as a major city, such as London, which is impossible to seal off from the press. The British government's claims of having "everything under control" look ridiculous when journalists are free to take pictures of the bomb sites, interview victims, and conduct interviews with IRA operatives. The issue of Northern Ireland takes a central place within the national agenda.

The emphasis on the logistic and geographic environment suggests that a good deal of the debate over "freedom of the press" in such conflicts is misguided. There have been countless studies that emphasize the normative aspects of government "censorship" during wars and far too little about the situational circumstances that either enhance or diminish the ability of authorities to control the flow of information. In this study I take as a given that authorities would prefer to have a monopoly on the information available to journalists and that journalists would like to break that monopoly. The question, then, is not so much whether governments *should* restrict information in the midst of a conflict but whether they *can*.[4]

The third and final factor that decides the powerful's level of control over the informational environment is the ability to *mobilize elite support*. Whereas elites are the most common sources for journalists, those who mobilize them capture an important part of the public space on the

---

[4]   I am not suggesting that the normative perspective is not an important one. The point is rather that other perspectives on this issue have been neglected.

issue. When the various factions within a government are promoting different frames about a conflict, it is more difficult to control the informational environment because journalists can choose among a variety of sources. When, on the other hand, the official frame is the only frame available among elites, journalists will have little choice but to adopt that frame.

In this case, rather than offering an illustration of how this varies among conflicts, the example will show how the political environment can change over time. Hallin's (1986) work on the Vietnam war offers an excellent case study of how media coverage is affected by the amount of consensus among elites. In the early years of the war there was a high level of consensus within Washington about the goals of that campaign and the methods being used to achieve them. The Cold War frame that dominated media discourse in those years was never really replaced by competing frames, but as the consensus among the political elite began to break down, other less positive frames of the war also began to emerge. As Hallin points out, it was not that the press stopped relying on elite sources for guidance and information, but that the anti-war movement had made serious inroads among the elite.

A legitimate question concerns the role of public opinion in all of this. If, after all, the news media reflect opinion then perhaps the emphasis on elite support would be unwarranted. As discussed, however, the news media take their cues from the elite. In Bennett's (1989, 1990) research on the Nicaraguan Contras, polls showed a clear majority opposed to Reagan's policy throughout the conflict. Nevertheless, media coverage focused almost exclusively on the debate within the Congress and barely mentioned the distribution of opinion on the issue. Therefore, the amount of public support within the public will be important only as reflected by the elites.

The goal of challengers is to mobilize as many elites as they can: to generate *dissensus* among the powerful. Challengers attempt to make inroads among elites, who represent more legitimate sources for providing alternative frames. This distinction in the level of aspirations between authorities and challengers provides an important insight into the relative ability of the two sides to increase the media's level of dependency. Whereas the authorities can sometimes achieve almost total control over the political environment, challengers can only hope to break that monopoly, not achieve it. While the authorities can sometimes attain exclusive access to the news media, challengers always have to share the stage with others. This point should be kept in mind in later discussions about the independence of the news media. Media independence, for the most part, refers to independence from the authorities.

Summary

There are then two parts to this story. The first, which is better known, is that political power brings important advantages to those who want to achieve exposure in the news media. Political power brings status, organization and resources, the ability to carry out exceptionally important behavior, and a reduced level of dependency on the press.

The second, less familiar, part of the story is that, despite these obstacles, challengers can and do compete. Authorities are never in full control of the political environment and these gaps provide important gateways for challengers to enter. The ability of the challenger to compete successfully with more powerful antagonists will depend to a large extent on their ability both to create and to exploit these opportunities. Some measure of success in this area will come to those challengers who can initiate and control events considered newsworthy, who find innovative ways to circumvent the powerful's control over the flow of information, and who make serious inroads among political elites.

Political successes and failures will often *precede* and *determine* success within the news media. The success of challengers in political mobilization will be reflected in their level of access to the news media that in turn will usually lead to an even higher level of mobilization. Political control and control over the media are perpetually intertwined, for better, and for worse.

Having established the basic rules for entrance, it is time to move to the battle itself: the contest over meaning.

2   The cultural dimension: the struggle over meaning

The transactions between antagonists and the news media are more than a business deal. They are a set of cultural interactions in which antagonists promote their own frames of the conflict while the news media attempt to construct a story that can be understood by their audience. The most useful way for researchers to deal with this aspect of the relationship is to focus on the interpretive *frames* constructed by the news media about political conflicts (Bennett, 1990; Gamson, 1989; Gamson *et al.*, 1992; Gamson and Modigliani, 1989; Gamson and Wolfsfeld, 1993; Gitlin, 1980; Ryan, 1991; Wolfsfeld, 1993b; Wolfsfeld, 1991). Here, we shall adopt the definition of frames proposed by Gamson: "A central organizing idea for making sense of relevant events and suggesting what is at issue" (1989, p. 35).

Many political conflicts center on disputes over frames as each antagonist attempts to market its own package of ideas to the mass media and the public. It is important to examine the level of correspondence between the frames adopted by the media and those offered by each of the political antagonists in order to understand better this competition.

I will attempt to explain the competition over media frames in three stages. The first section will offer a model of how the press constructs media frames of political conflicts. The second will explain the ramifications of the model for the struggle over meaning between authorities and challengers. The third and final section will suggest three framing questions that can be used as analytical tools for applying these theoretical principles to actual conflicts.

The construction of media frames

The concept of media frames is best understood within the context of the social construction of reality approach to the news media (Adoni and Mane, 1984; Berger and Luckman, 1966; Gamson, 1992,

Gamson *et al.*, 1992). Davis (1990) offers a helpful summary of this approach:[1]

Social construction of reality theory is grounded on the premise that we live in a fundamentally ambiguous social world – a world in which persons, objects, and actions have no inherent or essential meaning. If meaning is not inherent, then it must be created – imposed on action, events, or things through human action. But action is necessarily situated in a specific place and time. The meaning imposed is limited by and relative to the context in which meaning is generated. Moreover, because action in situations is inevitably structured by groups that dominate those situations, those groups enjoy an inherent advantage in determining the meaning derived from action in situations.

The notion of context is important: it serves to remind us that the transactions between the news media and political antagonists never take place within a political vacuum. They take place within a larger social and political context that has an important influence on the construction of frames by antagonists, the news media, and audiences. As Gamson and Lasch (1983) point out, every political discourse exists within a certain "issue culture" in which groups and individuals use a "catalogue of available idea elements" and "make use of a variety of symbolic devices to express their ideas" (p. 397). The extent to which a particular frame will resonate within the professional and political culture of the news media will vary over time and place because the political and cultural base of the news media varies. Scholars must, therefore, avoid the temptation of attributing too much power to the news media in the construction of political frames. Although the news media can play an independent role in the creation of these issue cultures, they are much more likely to serve as cultural time capsules which offer a brief glimpse of the political symbols, myths, and stories that are popular at a particular time and place.

Cultural frames exist at a variety of levels and as a rule one would expect that deeper frames would be less contested and thus more resilient to change. This formulation is similar to the one that is often made in the literature on public opinion and attitude change where a distinction is made between basic beliefs (or values), attitudes, and opinions (Graber 1984, Rokeach, 1960). The depth of a given frame can be judged by considering its level of specificity and its age: while the deepest cultural frames about conflict may go back thousands of years, those with less depth may be as recent as yesterday's news. The power of the deepest frames comes from the fact that they are rarely examined and usually taken for granted.

---

[1]   Davis also makes a point of distinguishing between the cultural studies perspective and the social construction of reality model although others have not.

The news media's professional focus on events means that they usually employ the shallowest level of frames. The rhetoric of antagonists, on the other hand, is more symbolic; leaders attempt to communicate on a deeper level. This is one reason why so many antagonists find it difficult to promote their frames to the news media: the news media are interested in current affairs, not ideology. Links to deeper frames can be found, however, in editorial pages.

The frames at one level usually suggest a deeper frame and this is why the choice of media frames is so important. Consider, for example, the different levels of frames employed by the American public and the news media in the early stages of the Vietnam war. One could speak about the deepest level of framing by focusing on the notion of *peace through strength*, a longstanding principle that suggests that aggression must be met with force. The next level of framing might be the *Cold War* frame that can be considered an application of the first principle to the conflict between the Soviet Union and the West (Hallin, 1987). A more specific frame which deals with Vietnam could be labeled the *falling-domino* frame that suggests that the struggle in Southeast Asia is a struggle against the spread of communism in that part of the world. Finally, one could talk about the framing of a particular event or campaign such as the Gulf of Tonkin incident which was framed as an *unprovoked communist attack on American forces* (Hallin, 1986).[2] Media frames which focused on communist attacks and the threat to the rest of Southeast Asia evoked deeper, more powerful frames.

While media frames are generally based on frames that are available in the surrounding culture, they are also designed to serve the specific needs of journalists. Gitlin (1980) offers a cogent summary about the use of media frames:

Media frames, largely unspoken and unacknowledged, organize the world both for journalists who report it and, in some important degree, for us who rely on their reports. *Media frames are persistent patterns of cognition, interpretation, and presentation, of selection, emphasis, and exclusion, by which symbol-handlers routinely organize discourse, whether verbal or visual.* Frames enable journalists to process large amounts of information, to assign it to cognitive categories, and to package it for efficient relay to their audiences. (p. 7)

The news media construct frames for conflicts by attempting to fit the information they are receiving into a package that is professionally useful and culturally familiar (Gamson *et al.*, 1992; Gans, 1979; Gitlin, 1980; Tuchman, 1973; Wolfsfeld, 1993b). The process is best understood as

[2] I am grateful to Bill Gamson for pointing to the importance of these distinctions in talking about frames.

one in which journalists attempt to find a *narrative fit between incoming information and existing media frames.*

It is useful to think about the similarities between this process and the ways in which individuals process political information. Those working in the area of schema theory (Graber, 1984; Fiske, Kinder, and Larter, 1983; Lau, 1986; Sears, 1985; Zaller, 1992) emphasize that people attempt to deal with new information based on what they have already come to believe about the political world. Existing schemas serve as organizing tools that allow individuals to recognize, sort, compare, and store new information.

Similarly, the construction of news is best thought of as a process in which journalists use established concepts and practices for "routinizing the unexpected" (Tuchman, 1978). This is especially true in ongoing conflicts where a strong story line has already been established by the news media. The story line in the American press for the conflict between the Catholics in Northern Ireland and the British government, for example, was well established in the last decades. The most common frame was one of *terrorism*, a frame that focuses on the innocent victims of brutal violence. Stories typically centered on the number of people who are killed or injured by the IRA, the extent of damage, and how the British government responded to the threat. It would probably be difficult to find an alternative story line in either the American or British press that framed the conflict as a legitimate struggle by an oppressed people against British occupation.[3] The terrorist story line provides an important shortcut for journalists in their search for sources, images, and context (Taylor, 1986).

Once the news media have their attention drawn to a particular conflict they begin a directed search for information. They then attempt to use the information and images they have collected to create news stories. They do so by trying to find an existing media frame that fits their data. The process is an interactive one in which the initial impressions about the nature of the conflict engage standard routines for the collection of information and the construction of media frames. *The creation of news is neither information driven nor frame driven, but rather, a combination of the two.*

Political events and the construction of media frames

There is an important ramification of this approach that will shock many of those who work in social construction theory: *events matter!* Or at least

[3]   I am not arguing that either of these frames is "correct," merely that there are always alternative frames which could be used.

those events that can be covered by journalists matter. The more radical version of constructionist theory implies that because events have no inherent meaning, and such meaning is constructed through social processes, the events themselves are irrelevant to the process. Journalists, it is argued, spend most of their time looking for facts and images that fit existing frames; contradictory information is either ignored or rejected. Newspeople are accused of carrying out a drunken man's search: always looking for the proverbial key under a well-lit lamp post – rather than where it was lost – because the light is much better under the lamp.

The model used here suggests a different process. It is true that newspeople have a long list of preconceptions about political conflicts and that these expectations have an important influence on their search for information and on the final construction of news stories. Nevertheless, journalists react to what they see and hear in the field, they look for the best narrative fit (Gamson, 1989; Snow and Bendford, 1988). A peaceful demonstration in which a thousand people walk in a quiet procession will not be framed in the same way as a violent riot in which stores are burned and looted. A police action guarding demonstrators against attacks will not be given the same story line as one in which the police open fire and kill twenty protesters.

For better and for worse, journalists focus on events; the events serve as the initial stimulus for the entire story-building process. Here, too, one can learn an important lesson from studying social psychology. The important questions in this field deal with how different individuals and groups respond to *divergent stimuli* within changing environments. Editors and reporters all come with certain predispositions and expectations that clearly influence the way they process information, but their reactions are also affected by the nature of the information they confront.

Consider, for example, the coverage of the events at Tiananmen Square. The assumption among journalists was that the Chinese government would avoid a confrontation with the student protesters (Joan Shorenstein Barone Center, 1993) and many believed that this was the beginning of the end of communism in China. These expectations were no doubt based on interpretive frames developed through observing the fall of communism in Eastern Europe and the Soviet Union. The events, however, took a very different course and so did media frames of that story. The *brutal repression* frame was familiar to both journalists and their audience; it simply had to be taken out and dusted off before it was applied.

Suppose, however, that the Chinese authorities *had* chosen simply to ignore the protesters, and that after several months the demonstrations had simply petered out. Or assume that the government had met with the students and offered concessions that were sufficiently forthcoming to bring an end to the protests. The information and images coming out of China would have been very different and so would the accompanying media frames. The Chinese authorities would have been framed positively, similar to the frames that had been used in most of Eastern Europe. The *brutal repression* frame would not have even been considered. It was the actions by the Chinese authorities – which ran *counter* to journalist expectations – that dictated the final narrative.

All of this is not meant to suggest that the *brutal repression* frame was the "correct" one. There is no such thing as a correct frame; there are always alternative frames that can be applied to an event. The Chinese leaders, for example, attempted to promote a *law and order* frame to justify their actions. Events, however, establish a starting point for the construction of news stories and thereby narrow the range of possible frames. Neither the Chinese leaders nor the Western press would have chosen to use a *democracy is blooming* frame to describe the events at Tiananmen Square. Frames are used to organize events into a meaningful pattern and while some aspects of narrative fit are culturally specific, others are universal.

It is also important to note that some events are more ambiguous than others. One or two civilians being killed is easier to explain than a thousand. An armed attack on an army base lends itself to a wider range of interpretations than an attack on a children's school bus. A war with no clear victor is more ambiguous than one in which one side surrenders to the other. The more ambiguous the event, the wider the range of media frames that can be applied.

Professional and political influences on media frames

While events normally serve as the starting point for the construction of media frames the attempt to find a narrative fit is also influenced by professional and political considerations. These considerations help define the range of existing frames, the search for information and events, and how frames are applied to a particular conflict. The attempt to find a narrative fit should be seen not as a mechanical process, but rather a cultural one in which journalists place the events of the day within a meaningful context.

The professional culture of the news media refers to the system of values, norms, beliefs, and practices held in common by those working as journalists. Journalists have certain routine frames used for covering political conflicts based on their definition of what makes a good story.

Whereas most of the previous discussion emphasized the routine advantages enjoyed by the authorities, it is useful to provide such frames that offer advantages to government opponents.

The first frame could be labeled: *power corrupts*. There is a long tradition in the Western news media that sets a high value on stories that show how those in power are corrupt, cruel, or incompetent. This genre of "investigative reporting" has become especially important in journalist culture since the days of Watergate. Many challengers can and do exploit the existence of these frames to compete successfully with the authorities in political conflicts. Journalists often express an obligation to serve as a public "watchdog" over government.

Many scholars deride the notion of an "adversary" press and argue that any criticisms against the government tend to be weak and superficial. Bennett (1983) is one of the most articulate of these theorists who claims that media criticism of authorities tends to be "ritualistic." Negative stories about those in power, he argues, are extremely selective in terms of the sources who are allowed to criticize (elites), the targets of such attacks (individuals rather than institutions), and the general tone of criticism (reform rather than radical change). The ritual of adversary reporting "creates an image of no-holds-barred reporting while circumscribing actual news content in the process" (p. 83). Bennett even belittles the significance of the press's role in the Watergate scandal because the final frame for that affair was that "the system worked" (p. 84).

There is an opposing school of thought that emphasizes the negative, cynical aspects of journalist culture. Patterson's (1993) research on changing patterns of political election coverage is an excellent example of this genre. Patterson found that press coverage of elections changed dramatically between 1960 and 1992. There has been a consistent tendency to publish more bad news about candidates than good news. Whereas in 1960, 70 percent of the evaluative references to Kennedy and Nixon were positive, only 40 percent of the references to Clinton and Bush fell into this category (p. 20). It is no coincidence, Patterson argues, that the public's negative opinions about Presidential candidates rose at about the same rate as the negative coverage.

Whereas earlier candidates had the luxury of being treated with a certain reverence and having their positions quoted directly, modern election coverage emphasizes the game-oriented style of reporting which views every political statement as a manipulative attempt to trick the public (see Robinson and Sheehan, 1983).[4] The emphasis on "what's

---

[4] One unfortunate conclusion of this line of research is that greater independence for the press does not necessarily mean better coverage.

really going on 'behind the scenes'," on the "spin-masters" and "handlers," provides an extremely cynical picture of the political process.

> The press makes . . . lies appear to be the norm. Candidates are said to change their positions as they campaign in different regions or talk with different groups, make promises they plan to break, make commitments that cannot be honored even if they try. Cynical manipulation is the story that is told of candidates' efforts to woo the voters. (Patterson, 1993, p. 11)

Neither side in this debate has much admiration for the way the news media deals with politics. One can accept Bennett's basic premise about news routines without accepting his conclusions. It is true that the news stories focus on specific events rather than ongoing processes, on individuals rather than institutions, and that elites are usually the preferred source of information. But journalistic norms and routines do not all work to the benefit of authorities. The fact that journalists see themselves as public watchdogs has a very significant impact on the ways in which many news frames are constructed and ultimately on the way society views the political processes. Prizes, awards, promotions, and prestige often depend on the ability of journalists to produce "hard-hitting" stories that "uncover" some aspect of the social or political world that is especially shocking or disturbing. It would be hard to think of a Pulitzer prize awarded for either a fluff piece on a particular political leader, or a routine story about one member of the Senate attacking another.

Journalistic norms and routines can, then, pull in several different directions. Some, such as the use of elite sources, do work to the advantage of the authorities. Others, such as the popularity of "investigative reporting," work to the advantage of challengers. And some, such as the emphasis on "bad" news, can go either way. The goal of research in this field should be to understand better the circumstances that bring each set of routines into play.

A second media frame for political conflicts that emerges from the professional culture of journalists can be called the *innocent victims* frame. Victims (and potential victims) are a major ingredient of news, especially news about conflict. Victims provide human interest, good visuals, and drama as well as important moral lessons about the evils of violence. News about victims is not restricted to the coverage of political conflicts: they are also a central part of stories about crime, natural disasters, accidents, and social problems.

Those who can latch on to this frame are provided with an extremely powerful conveyor belt for bringing their messages to the public. *Images* of victims are an especially important factor in building such frames. Pictures of protesters being beaten, of bodies being thrown out of planes by terrorists, of children dying due to the cruelties of war resonate powerfully in the news media. The fact that Rodney King's beating was filmed made all the difference in the world. Not all forms of incoming information are equal. I shall have more to say about victim frames in the final section of this chapter.

A final note about the professional culture of journalists. While most of this discussion has emphasized the similarities among news media, there are also some important differences. The professional culture of television news, for example, revolves around good visuals and very short pieces, whereas newspapers have a different set of priorities. Similarly, popular or tabloid newspapers have a different set of professional beliefs and values than news organs designed for more elite audiences. These variations will have a significant impact on which stories will resonate within each culture, and how information will be processed in the construction of news. This dimension should also be considered when examining the struggle over meaning.

Political influences

The political culture of the news medium also influences the search for narrative fit. Political culture refers to the norms, values, beliefs, and practices that define the ways in which each news medium relates to the world of politics.[5] The level of these beliefs can be as general as the notion that democracy is a better form of government than a dictatorship, or as specific as the belief that the United States should intervene in a particular conflict such as Bosnia.

While journalists are quite eager to talk about professional norms, most object to the idea that political ideology has anything to do with the way they report the news. Nevertheless, every news medium exists within a particular cultural base that defines the range of frames that are available for the interpretation of political events. The character of this base is influenced by such factors as the geographic location of the medium, who owns and/or regulates the news organ, the political leanings of the editors and reporters, the nature of the audience, and the historical period when the conflict is being covered (Shoemaker and Reese, 1991).

The effects of political culture on the construction of media frames are

---

[5]   Gamson and Lasch (1983) refer to the cultural resonance of various frames, while in this work I will talk about political resonance. I consider political culture to be a subset of the more general culture.

perhaps most obvious when one examines how the news media from different countries cover foreign conflicts. Whatever their beliefs about the need for objectivity when it comes to internal disputes, journalists inevitably interpret the world from a national – or even a nationalistic – perspective. This is especially true when they cover conflicts involving their own country, but such national perspectives also shape the construction of frames about other foreign conflicts.

Paletz and Vinson (1992) carried out research on the ways in which newspapers from around the world covered the downing of KAL flight 007. Soviet pilots shot down this Korean plane after it violated Soviet airspace and flew over Soviet military areas. A bitter dispute broke out between the United States and the Soviet Union about whether the downing was a legitimate mistake or a premeditated attack. The researchers demonstrated how the frames of nineteen different newspapers could be explained in part by the political orientation of their home countries. Claims made by the antagonists were either emphasized or dismissed based on the degree of political alignment with one of the two sides. A similar piece of research was conducted by Entman (1991). His work showed the difference in media frames used to cover the KAL incident on the one hand and the downing of an Iranian airplane by the US navy on the other.

Political influence is not limited to the expression of support or opposition by the news media. In keeping with the more general process of framing, the political ideology of a news medium will also be reflected in ways in which the news package is constructed to make it more familiar to domestic audiences. American coverage of the protests in Tiananmen Square offers a very good example of this phenomenon. A report by the Joan Shorenstein Barone Center (1993) shows the ethnocentrism of US media coverage of this conflict. The American media generally adopted a Cold War frame that defined the student protesters as "pro-democracy" even though they were not. This frame made it easier to tell a very American story with familiar heros and villains, but it masked the reformist nature of student demands. The Chinese students were protesting for greater party responsiveness, not revolutionary change.

The effects of political culture on the coverage of domestic conflicts may be more subtle, but equally significant. Consider the comments of Paletz and Entman (1981) on the political orientation of American journalists:

Journalists are not innocent. They are disproportionately white, male, middle-class, and middle-aged. Avowedly nonpartisan, American reporters, especially those employed by the major metropolitan dailies and television networks, tend to traditional values. They are sympathetic to the poor, object to the principle and practice of segregation, espouse a modified welfare statism at home and international cooperation abroad. They almost all unilaterally reject "extreme" ideological positions from the dismantling of the welfare state urged occasionally by Ronald Reagan to socialist solutions. The overt bellicosity of Barry Goldwater and the cynical racism of George Wallace were equally unappealing. (p. 14)

The minute we accept the notion that there is such a thing as a "mainstream media" we are making a statement about the importance of political culture in the construction of media frames. The range of opinions within a particular country's news media is likely to reflect the range of political parties represented in the formal political structure. Because journalists rely on political elites as news sources, one must look first at the range of opinions considered legitimate by each political system. This may partially explain why critics of the news media in the United States and Britain complain about the difficulties progressive groups have in promoting their frames to the news media. Perhaps at least part of the problem lies with the two political systems that ensure a very small number of political parties in the legislature. One suspects that in multi-party systems such as Italy and Germany one would find a wider range of opinion in the news media.[6] This is yet another example that illustrates the importance of looking beyond the news media to the influence of the underlying political structure on the nature of coverage.

The competition over media frames

There are, then, three major elements that contribute to the construction of media frames of conflict: the nature of the information and events that are being processed, the need to create a good news story, and the need to create a story that resonates politically within a particular culture. Now we turn to the second part of the discussion that examines the implications of this process for the competition between authorities and challengers over frames.

A central premise of this work is that political power offers important advantages in influencing the news media but that many challengers can overcome these obstacles and successfully employ the news media to achieve political goals. This principle also applies to the promotion of frames. As Gamson et al. (1992) put it:

[6]   Nevertheless, even in those countries with a multi-party system one would still find that most of the debate within the news media reflects the opinions of the largest political factions. It is also true that the news media in every country still have an obligation to collect ideas and information from outside the formal political structure.

That actors differ in their resources and access and that some have enormous power advantages in such contests does not make it part of the natural or hegemonic realm. Even an uneven contest on a tilted playing field is a contest. (p. 382)

A good deal of the information about political conflicts used by the news media comes from outputs generated by political actors. Outputs refer to all actions, information, and interpretive frames produced by political antagonists. These outputs are not created specifically to influence the news media nor are they all planned in advance. The notion of incoming information refers to the sum total of data about antagonists and the conflict that are available to the press, including outputs. The success of antagonists in promoting their frames to the news media will depend on their ability to ensure that the incoming information and events offer a good narrative fit with their preferred media frames.

The political power of any antagonist has an important effect not only in the struggle over access, which was discussed in the last chapter, but also in the battle over meaning. Political power provides one with a large arsenal of weapons that can be used in this contest. The same factors that increase the politically powerful's level of access to the news media also increase the professional and political resonance of their outputs. Accordingly, it is necessary to go over some familiar ground in this part of the discussion. Hopefully, however, this strategy will serve the additional purpose of clarifying some of the ways in which the structural and cultural dimensions overlap.

The relationship between political power and control over media frames runs through several paths. The first has to do with the distinction between "front gate coverage" and "back gate coverage" which was alluded to in the previous chapter. Antagonists with political power are much more likely to gain access to the news media through the front gate as legitimate players in the political process, rather than through the back gate reserved for social and political deviants. Those with political power and resources are more likely to be treated with respect by the news media (Blumler and Gurevitch, 1986; Paletz and Entman, 1981). Assumptions about the inherent importance of such groups, and their ability to produce acts that enhance their legitimacy, lead to more dignified frames. Antagonists with less political power are more likely to come to the public's attention through what Gans (1979) has called "disorder news."

A second reason political power leads to cultural advantages has to do with the creation of news beats. Beats not only provide routine access to particular sources they also serve as a means of cultural inculcation. Just as a social scientist spending a good deal of time in a particular culture runs the risk of over-identification, journalists – who are selected for a particular beat because they have the appropriate education and background – often adopt the language, customs, and perspective of the host culture (Molotch, Protess, and Gordon 1987). Editors are very aware of the dangers of reporters "going native" and often try to rotate them.

Journalists who cover the Pentagon offer a good example of this phenomenon, and one that is particularly relevant to the issues at hand. Most of the major media outlets are given offices and facilities within the Pentagon complex. This allows journalists the luxury of being close to the scene of action and to exploit the technological infrastructure established for the dissemination of information. However, when journalists spend so much time within the military environment the line between expertise and co-optation becomes blurred.

I am reminded of an interview I conducted in the Pentagon with a senior reporter from a major television network. His major claim at the time was that he had trouble understanding all of the complaints by other journalists about the difficulty in obtaining information from the Pentagon during the Gulf War. He argued that he had no such trouble and that he could operate independently during the war. His claims of independence sounded somehow discordant with the scene of the interview. His office was located inside the Pentagon, where he was on a first-name basis with the officers in the surrounding departments. The pictures on the wall were typical battle scenes, his bookcase filled with books about the military including many publications by the Pentagon, and both his sweater and his coffee cup carried the emblem of the Joint Chiefs of Staff.

It is much rarer for challengers to be considered sufficiently valuable to be designated for a beat, and thus they usually have fewer opportunities to socialize reporters into their own culture. More often editors will assign one of their less experienced journalists to cover an unconventional story or even assign a different journalist to each such event. There are, however, exceptions to this rule. In the coverage of Tiananmen Square, for example, journalists spent a considerable amount of time with the protesting students, and had very few contacts with Chinese officials. This may be one reason why so many reports adopted the students' perspective of the conflict (Joan Shorenstein Barone Center, 1993). A similar process occurred during the protests in Israel over the evacuation of the Sinai town of Yamit (Wolfsfeld, 1984a, 1984b): journalists and protest leaders spent a good deal of time working together and a symbiotic relationship developed which went beyond the normal source–reporter relationship. Goldenberg (1975) offers yet another example by showing how the *Boston Globe*, in response to a successful mobilization by resource-poor groups, changed some of its news beats to give more coverage to these activists.

Another important reason for the relationship between political power and success in the cultural domain can be explained by examining those production assets that increase an antagonist's ability to plan, execute, and package information in ways that are easier to absorb by the news media. Effective public relations demands knowledge, experience, talent, and money. Professional spokespeople – sometimes described now as "spin masters" – are experts in inter-cultural communication who translate political information into newspeak. Bennett (1990) discusses some advantages authorities enjoy in this area:

Public officials have the resources to script and stage well-produced political performances. Most high officials have writers, media directors, costume consultants, readily available dramatic settings, and an attentive press corps ready to cover official announcements and events ... Through the careful preparation of messages, public officials often succeed in controlling the *scene*, the status of the *actor*, and the motives or "ends" the political action is to serve, the "means" through which the action will accomplish its ends, and the significance of the political *action* itself. (p. 46)

Challengers can rarely afford to hire such professionals and usually do without official spokespeople or depend on spokespeople who are much less knowledgeable and experienced. The communication between the challengers and the news media becomes more difficult and the culture gap more telling. Those challengers who do mobilize some of these resources will be in a much better position to compete with the authorities in the cultural realm.

The ability to control the political environment is another benefit that political power brings to those who want to promote their frames to the news media. Each of the three elements said to be important for determining the quantity of news coverage also has an influence on the quality of coverage. The ability to initiate and control events allows one to carefully prepare the story in advance; the ability to regulate the flow of information allows one to take control of the story line; and the ability to generate consensus among elites assures that most frequent sources will all be telling the same story.

Political power in Western countries, however, is a variable rather than a constant; it is limited rather than absolute. The political process is a dynamic one and the ebbs and flows of political control provide many opportunities for challengers to promote their frames to the news media. Some of these opportunities emerge from the political failures of the authorities, others arise out of the actions of outside forces or unplanned events, and yet others from the actions of the challengers themselves (Staggenborg, 1993).

The fact that the authorities are never able to take absolute control of events and the fact that their best laid plans often go astray provide important opportunities for challengers to promote alternative frames to the news media. The best way to understand the relationship between events and the promotion of ideological frames is to suggest that certain events give advantages to certain frames. When journalists have to choose between alternative ways of placing the events within a context, some frames make more sense than others. The nuclear accident at Three Mile Island gave important advantages to *anti-nuclear* frames (Walsh, 1988); the decision by "Bull" Connor to use attack dogs and fire hoses on civil rights demonstrators gave advantages to *civil rights* frames (Garrow, 1978); the IRA attacks on London civilians offers advantages to the *terrorism* frame; and the collapse of the Soviet Union offered important advantages to those promoting *anti-communism* frames.

In each case the events serve as vivid demonstrations of some underlying political claim. The resonance of such events is very plain to see. One side appears to be attempting to ride the wave for all its worth, while the other finds itself speaking in terms of "damage control." Having defined the context of the event, journalists look for other sources and stories which fall under the same heading.

Challengers who are able to produce outputs that resonate within the professional and political culture of important news media can compete with their more powerful adversaries. The news media maintain a large store of anti-authority frames that can be taken down and applied when circumstances warrant.[7] The *power corrupts* frame described above is just one example of such a construction. The fact that leaders are considered inherently newsworthy is a dual-edge sword. From a journalistic perspective a negative story about someone in power is often valued even higher than a positive one. Challengers often perform symbolic judo by turning the celebrity of authorities to their own advantage. Thus, under varying circumstances journalist culture can either reinforce political power or set limits to it.

A very detailed example of such a campaign is provided by Paletz and Entman (1981) who talk about the exceptional ability of the American interest group Common Cause to promote their frames to the news media. Although the authors were attempting to illustrate why this group was more successful at "manipulating the news media" than

---

[7] For a British example of this phenomenon, readers should see the research carried out by Deacon and Golding (1994) on coverage of the conflict over the poll tax.

more "marginal" groups, Common Cause also illustrates how a challenger can successfully compete with the authorities in the construction of media frames. Paletz and Entman discuss why they believe the *New York Times* was so willing to pass on the group's message:

Common Cause was covered because it connected with the *Times*' concepts of news. Its targets were "big" names: Presidents, campaign finance chairmen, and the kind of congressmen whose length of tenure is usually commensurate with their arrogance, pomposity, and sense of security. These public targets were approached in the newsworthy terms of their derelictions, duplicity, and malfeasance, their efforts to conceal information which might lead to investigation and, perhaps, exposure. Individuals were attacked, accusations leveled, demands made. There was the tincture of scandal, of corruption. The press did not have to be cajoled; this is the stuff of daily journalism and its headlines.

Thus part of the success of Common Cause can be attributed to their ability to produce outputs that resonated with the existing frame *power corrupts*.

Ryan (1991) provides an example of a much less established challenger who was able use journalistic norms to promote successfully their frame to the news media. The New Bedford (Massachusetts) delegation to Nicaragua was organized with no staff and few resources to protest against the US government's role in Nicaragua during the 1980s. Ryan talks about the careful planning that went into the media campaign of the New Bedford delegation that allowed them to have a good deal of success in passing their frame to the news media:

Interest was the strong suit for the New Bedford group. The delegation itself was a *good story*: amidst the rumors, lies, and self-serving misspeakings of Washington bureaucrats, a group of average Americans, with no political axe to grind, had ventured into a war zone and come back to speak the truth as they had seen it with their own eyes. (p. 34)

Their presentation to the news media had all of the elements of a good news story that resonated with existing media frames of conflict. It included human interest (delegates crying during the press conference), good visuals (pictures of victims taken during the trip), and cultural resonance (ordinary citizens had gone to see for themselves). The New Bedford group was also very conscious of the need to present a well-structured frame of the Nicaraguan story that could compete with the dominant frame that was being promoted by the Reagan administration. The government was promoting *East–West conflict* frame as a way of describing what was happening in Nicaragua, and this well-known concept was given a good deal of play in the news media. Nevertheless, the New Bedford challengers put forth a *human cost of war* frame, and this also resonated well within journalist culture; it was a familiar media theme and one that had a good deal of cultural resonance within the general society. The fact that both frames were very familiar to the news media facilitated genuine competition between the two interpretations.

While many challengers are forced to enter the media through the back door, others are able to promote a more sympathetic frame to the media. The principle of political resonance tells us something important about which challengers will be most successful in their attempts to promote competing frames to the mainstream news media. Groups whose members appear to come from the elite, whose goals are more reformist than revolutionary, and whose actions fall into what the news media regard as reasonable dissent, will find it much easier to promote their frames to the media than those who violate these norms. This helps explain why the group Common Cause had such success in this area.

Many challengers are interested in significant changes and they face several dilemmas. How can they tailor their message to resonate within the political culture of the mainstream media without altering them beyond recognition? If they do attempt to promote a more moderate frame, how can they remain newsworthy? How can they achieve both political resonance and journalistic resonance?

One option is to work for long-range change in the society that will then lead to changes in media frames. The ways in which the news media relate to political movements are especially likely to reflect such changes in political context. Consider changing media frames about the women's movement in the United States (Danielian, 1988; Tuchman, 1978). The fact that media frames about this movement changed so radically from the mocking notion of "bra-burners" to the current level of legitimacy is more than anything else an indicator of the changes that occurred in the general society. The concept of sexism may have been reinforced and popularized by the news media but the creation of the term and its cultural resonance are better traced to changes in the American political culture.

In a similar vein, some scholars have suggested that the environmental movement in the United States initially had trouble obtaining media coverage, because the press did not have any ready-made categories for dealing with this issue (Strodthoff, Hawkins, and Schoenfeld, 1985). The American news media no doubt played a role in raising public consciousness about this issue, but there were larger political processes at work that affected the political culture of the press.

Social movements can be important here. As Gamson (1988) shows, until the 1970s there were no anti-nuclear power frames appearing in the American news media, because such frames were so rare within general society. This helps explain why a serious nuclear accident that occurred in 1966 in the Fermi reactor, thirty miles south of Detroit, was barely mentioned in the American press. Later, environmental and anti-nuclear movements played an important role in changing the nature of media discourse about this issue by successfully promoting anti-nuclear frames to compete with those being promoted by the authorities. This led to a very different framing by the news media of the subsequent accidents at Three Mile Island and Chernobyl, and in the more general discourse about this issue.

Promoting frames internationally

Opportunities also exist for international challengers to promote their frames to the outside news media. Authorities will find it much more difficult to promote their frames of conflicts to the news media of other countries due to differences in political culture. International challengers may in certain circumstances find that their frames resonate much better abroad than they do at home. The political implications of this process may depend on the relative power of each country involved. The key for challengers is to find political resonance within the news media of the most powerful third parties they can find.

When the United States is not the authority in question, the American news media becomes a critical target for both sides in the conflict. Antagonists will often attempt to package their messages in ways that resonate within the American political culture. The use of signs, speeches, and materials in English employed by international challengers and the conscious use of symbols that resonate within Western societies tells us something about the search for third-party help. The student demonstrators in Tiananmen Square quickly realized the importance of the American news media and adapted their media strategy accordingly (Joan Shorenstein Barone Center, 1992). A good deal of their attention was devoted to mobilizing the American television networks to their cause by using the appropriate signs and interviews. When the Chinese authorities decided to suppress the protest, they prevented the American cameras from covering the event.

When the United States is directly involved in a conflict, on the other hand, foreign challengers will find it especially difficult to find any sympathy within the American news media. They may be able to promote successfully their frames to other countries but the realities of power in the international community suggest that this may not prove important. To compete successfully against the American authorities within the United States, challengers may have to find domestic sponsors for their frames.

Thus, there are two major factors that set important limits on the ability of authorities to totally dominate media frames. The first is that they often lose control over the political environment and this offers important opportunities for challengers to promote alternative frames to the press. Secondly, there are many influences within the professional and political culture of the news media that work against the authorities. Those challengers who can overcome the obstacles of entrance to the central arena will be given a genuine opportunity to fight.

Three framing questions

I want to suggest three framing questions that should make it easier for researchers to apply these theoretical principles to actual conflicts. The focus on these questions helps clarify how journalists construct media frames for news stories about political conflicts, and how they attempt to find a narrative fit between incoming information and existing frames. I am not suggesting that editors or reporters actually ask these questions every time – or even anytime – they cover conflicts, but rather that they behave *as if* they were asking these questions. The three questions are:

1. How did we cover this conflict in the past?
2. What is the most newsworthy part of the conflict?
3. Who are the good guys?[8]

The use of these questions serves two purposes. First, it forces us to think like journalists who are attempting to build a news story. Secondly, it allows us to understand better the influence of the events and the professional and political inclinations of those who must cover them. The first question helps us to define the political *context* of the conflict, to understand the range of frames that are available at a particular time and place. The second question, concerned with newsworthiness, focuses on the most important *professional* consideration facing journalists. Focusing on newsworthiness also reminds us of the importance of the events themselves. The final question centers on *political* influences as journalists find themselves allocating blame.

How did we cover this conflict in the past?

The most natural tendency in producing frames is to continue to use an existing construction. News in this sense is a misnomer. Most news

---

[8] I regret the use of the term "guys," which some may find sexist. But there is no better way to express what journalists are asking.

stories deal with ongoing conflicts, or with conflicts covered in the past. Pro-choice demonstrations, troubles with Libya, the Middle East conflict, and the ongoing conflict in Northern Ireland all have routines and frames established through previous coverage. Thus, coverage will normally attempt to tie them to what is already "known" about this conflict.

The construction of media frames for new conflicts will revolve around finding as close a parallel as possible to something that is familiar. The question will then be: "How did we cover this *type* of conflict in the past?" An attempt will be made to *label* the conflict: is this a demonstration, a protest, a disorder, political violence, a riot, terrorism, guerrilla warfare, a rebellion, a revolution, tribal conflict between "war lords," senseless bloodshed, civil war, war, or genocide? There are established rules for covering these different types of conflict that will have an effect on everything from the quantity and quality of journalists sent out, to the types of information and images they will be expected to bring back.

Having established the mode of reporting, journalists then attempt to find historic examples which best appear to fit the circumstances. Are these protesters like those of the 1960s? Will this war turn out to be another Vietnam? Is this a case of "naked aggression" which invokes the "lessons of Munich"? Is this a struggle like that of the American civil rights movement?

Indeed, questions of which historical example offers the most appropriate frame often become a matter for public debate. The framing of the conflict in Bosnia is a perfect example of this process. Initial coverage talked about a civil war that resulted from the breakup of Yugoslavia. Soon, however, the major story line revolved around the aggression being carried out by the Serbs against the Muslims in Bosnia. The *genocide* frame soon began to dominate coverage and no story was complete without referring to "ethnic cleansing" by the Serbs.

The political elite in the United States was not quite sure how to frame this conflict. Consider, for example, a *New York Times* story concerning the debate within Congress about whether the United States should intervene in the conflict between the Serbs and Muslims in the spring of 1993.

Many in congress, citing Vietnam, oppose attacks

While many advocates of tougher American action against the Bosnian Serbs have drawn parallels to the origins of World War II and the appeasement of Nazi aggression and brutality, the dominant analogy in Congress today was Vietnam. (*New York Times*, April 28, 1993, p. A10)

The question of whether the conflict is really a case like Nazi aggression or another Vietnam will determine how the conflict is covered and what the United States should do about it. Several weeks later, when President Clinton was attempting to avoid intervening in Bosnia, the administration tried to return to the initial *civil war* frame by suggesting that "there are atrocities on all sides" (*New York Times*, May 19, 1993, p. A10). If both sides are aggressors and both sides have victims, there is no need for American intervention. Yet, it would be difficult for any but the most persistent of citizens to learn about any actions against the Serbs. Indeed, many Americans would be surprised to learn that the Muslims had a military force fighting the Serbs. Once the frame of *genocide* had been created, it was very difficult to even suggest that Bosnia had any active part in the conflict. The dominant frame of *Serbian aggression* was even less likely to be challenged after NATO took a firm stand against Serbian actions in that part of the world. None of this is meant to suggest that the Serbs did not carry out atrocities or that they were not the major aggressors in this conflict. The point is methodological rather than political: researchers should remember that there are always other frames available for dealing with any conflict.

What is the most newsworthy part of the conflict?

To ask this second question is to ask how to build the best possible news story. The answer has a major impact on the collection of information. It determines where to send reporters, whom they should interview, what types of questions they should ask and what types of pictures the camera people should look for. The fact that there is so much similarity in the headlines of newspapers, television, and radio illustrates how most journalists not only carry out similar news-gathering routines but also have a fair amount of consensus about what constitutes a good news story.

The answer to this question also tells us a good deal about how the story will be "sold" to the public. One of the first lessons in journalism is to construct news stories as a pyramid by leading off with the most important part before spreading out to give background and details. The answer is conveniently found in the headline or lead:

- Fourteen protesters killed by police
- Ten thousand march in pro-life demonstrations
- Fierce debate on Capitol Hill over Contra support
- Terrorists kill 5 at CIA headquarters
- Fifth day of Serbian bombing of Sarajevo
- Libyan leader tells President – Stay out of my face

The substance of each of these headlines is constructed primarily to attract attention and interest. Most headlines could probably be written before the editor sends a reporter out of the newsroom.

Antagonists often find it difficult to remember that journalists are looking for information that is dramatic enough to compete not only with the information being brought by other reporters on the same topic, but with all of the other stories that are competing for the same space. The newspaper, radio, or television editor must then decide which of the many possible stories has sufficient news value to be run. This means that at every stage of the process the news industry is selecting and promoting those aspects of the conflict that make the best news story, and this has a critical influence on the construction of frames. Thus, when analyzing the framing of an ongoing conflict it is helpful to begin by asking what aspects of the conflict seem most newsworthy at different points in time.

Who are the good guys?

Conflict is considered bad news and the resolution of conflict is considered good news, even if the professional interests of journalists run in the opposite direction. Thus, one way to place the conflict in context is to decide which side is at fault. The proportion of blame that will go to each side in a conflict can be understood by looking at two sub-questions:
1. Is the challenge/challenger legitimate?
2. Is either the challenger or the authorities using an "excessive" amount of force?
The ways in which journalists answer these questions are closely tied to the cultural base of each news medium.

Questions about whether the challenge is legitimate focus on whether the demands or behavior of the group appear "reasonable." Challengers who make what are deemed by the press to be unjustified demands will be framed as either weird or dangerous. The mainstream media have a basic belief in the need for reform and an abhorrence for radical change. The distinction between the two can only be understood in terms of the political culture of each news media. A demand for better schools in the inner cities will be treated very differently in the news than a demand for unilateral disarmament. A demand of a colony for independence from France will be treated very differently by the American press and the French press as would a similar demand for independence from the United States. Some political demands will be deemed extreme or ridiculous from a cultural point of view and this will determine how they are framed by the news media. A march by the American Nazi party will be framed differently than a march of Mothers Against Drunk Drivers. The mainstream news media of any country serve as a fairly accurate map of what is considered by a given society to be the range of legitimate opinions.

The second sub-question deals with the level of force used by authorities and challengers. The higher the level of violence in a conflict, the greater the need for the news media to allocate blame. One common method for deciding fault is to focus on the *victims*. Victims are a central element in most good news stories about political conflicts and once the victim (or potential victim) has been identified, so has the aggressor. In some conflicts of course both sides are victims, and such confrontations are usually framed as *senseless violence*. An illustration of this type of frame can be found in the coverage on CNN of the violence in Rwanda that began in April 1994:

Reporters for Reuters news service in what has been described as rebel-held territory came across a horrific scene just south of Kigali. They found at least one hundred rotting corpses strewn over a wide area and more bodies spilling out of nearby dwellings. Efforts to establish a truce between Rwandan government and rebel forces over the weekend failed. Both sides declared unilateral cease fires, but heavy fighting was reported on Sunday. Representatives of the international relief group "Doctors without Borders" estimate that 170 patients and doctors were massacred during the past three days at a hospital in the Rwandan town of Butare ... [Voice of Dr. Romy Zacharias] "It is very difficult to say who exactly is doing this, we have bands of militia and people with uniforms, green uniforms. I would say it's a combined sort of action. Everyone seems to be responsible." (CNN *World News*, April 25, 1994, 11.00 am, GMT)

Nevertheless, there is often a tendency in unequal conflicts, especially ones that involve some form of violence, to frame one side as an aggressor and the other a victim. Victims and threats serve as central themes in many news reports and any attempts to explain the roots of a conflict must include at least a partial allocation of blame. This is a critical stage in the framing process for antagonists because the answer to this question, more than anything else, will decide the extent of their legitimacy in the media.

Here too, what is considered an excessive amount of force will vary within different political contexts. A leftist militant hijacking an American plane to Cuba will be framed as a terrorist in the American news media while a Cuban hijacking a plane to arrive in America will be framed as a hero. In general, however, the greater the level of violence used by the challenger the more likely the news story will center on the victims of that violence, because that is the most newsworthy part of the story. Challengers who resort to violence against property and civilians will normally be framed as a threat to law and order. News stories will focus on the damages and the victims as well as the attempts of the authorities to restore law and order. Here too, the news media are both reflecting and reinforcing a social consensus about what are considered acceptable means of action.

Critics of the press often ignore the fact that evaluations are also made about whether the authorities are using an excessive amount of force to deal with a challenge. There are certainly enough frames that come under the headings of police brutality, military atrocities, torture, and human-rights violations. The construction of such frames depends primarily on the ability of journalists to obtain reliable information about victims. It is sad but true that stories of those who are tortured and killed behind closed doors are almost never reported in the news media. By contrast, when victims have been found and especially when they can be filmed, the search for culprits begins. If it is the authorities who are found at the other end of the stick, then it is they, rather than the challengers, who find themselves in an uphill battle for legitimacy.

The struggle over media legitimacy in political conflicts often begins then with the identification of victims and threats. This is the center of most conflict stories and the allocation of blame quickly follows. The blame may fall on both sides or only one, and it can change in the course of the conflict. The assignment of blame is a critical part of the framing process that determines which side prevails in the struggle over meaning.

Summary

The cultural dimension of analysis attempts to explain the role of the news media in the struggle over meaning which characterizes every political conflict. The media serve as *public interpreters* of events and as *symbolic arenas* for ideological struggle between antagonists. News stories about political conflicts are a form of social construction, in which some frames are more likely than others to serve as the underlying theme of news stories.

The construction of media frames of conflict is an interactive process in which the press attempts to find a narrative fit between incoming information and existing media frames. While the scope of incoming information is limited by both inside and outside forces, the data that do come in have an important influence on the construction process. The professional and political culture of each news medium also plays a significant role in this procedure by directing the search for relevant information and defining the range and tone of existing frames that can be applied to a given conflict.

As in the structural dimension, authorities have important advantages over challengers in the promotion of their frames to the news media. Their political power can be translated into cultural power through their ability to socialize journalists, and through their ability to plan, execute, and package events in ways that resonate within the professional and political culture of the news media. Challengers, however, can and do compete in the cultural realm. The news media have a large variety of frames waiting on the shelf for those activists who are skilled enough to construct an effective package and lucky enough to be promoting them at a time when the authorities are vulnerable to attack. In these cases the news media can play a critical role by legitimating oppositional frames that increase the status, resources, and power of challengers.

The struggle within the news arena is more than a simple test of raw force. The ability to survive and succeed also depends on the ability of each antagonist to demonstrate honor and achieve respect. The struggle over media frames is primarily a battle for political legitimacy, and the results of that contest have important consequences for the political process.

3   Media influence and political outcomes

The first two chapters dealt with the attempts of antagonists to have an influence on the news media. This chapter looks at the opposite direction of power: the influence of the news media on antagonists. Here too, however, it is critical to understand this process within the more general political context. The relationship between antagonists and the news media is analogous to the relationship between wind and fire. The outcome of this fire depends on the direction and power of the wind, the characteristics of the fire itself, and the surrounding environment. A small fire can be extinguished by a large wind, while a more moderate blaze can become an inferno. How antagonists will react to the news media depends on the direction and power of the news media involved, the ideology and goals of the antagonists, and the political context of their transactions.

The discussion will be divided into four sections. The first will build on the structural analysis developed in Chapter 1 to explain why some news media are more likely than others to have an influence on political conflicts. The second section will talk about the major types of political outcomes that are likely to result from media influence. Next, a "continuum of influence" is put forth with three possible roles for the news media in political conflicts. The final segment presents some criteria for assessing the extent of media influence.

The power of the news media

Just as some political antagonists are more likely than others to have an influence on the news media, so some news media are more likely to have an influence on antagonists. The key to understanding these differences is to focus again on the notions of value and dependence. The greater the value of a given news medium to a particular antagonist, and the smaller the medium's dependence on the information being provided, the more powerful the antagonist's influence. This point is

56

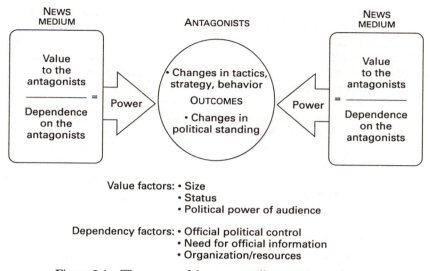

Value factors: • Size
               • Status
               • Political power of audience

Dependency factors: • Official political control
                    • Need for official information
                    • Organization/resources

Figure 3.1   The power of the news media over antagonists

made in graphic form in Figure 3.1, which provides the reverse perspective to the figure presented in Chapter 1.

A hypothetical example will help illustrate the dynamics of this process. Let us assume that the Teamsters union in the United States has called for a nationwide strike against a decision by the administration to impose an especially heavy tax on gasoline. This is a major story that will be covered by a variety of news media each attempting to get as much information as they can from both the Teamsters' leaders and administration sources.

Newspapers such as the *New York Times* and the *Washington Post* will have tremendous advantages in covering this story over smaller, less prestigious papers such as the *Des Moines Register* in Iowa. First, both the Teamsters and the administration want to get their message to as wide and important an audience as possible. Thus, each of the spokespeople will make a much greater effort to meet with reporters from the newspapers that can provide that service. Secondly, the *Times* and the *Post* have many resources that provide them with the independence to collect information about the strike from a variety of sources. The editors of major papers can assign many more journalists to cover the story and send them to different locations to obtain a variety of perspectives. Thus, the power of these newspapers comes from their high level of value to the antagonists and their low level of dependence.

Similar to the weak antagonists that were described earlier, the *Des Moines Register* suffers from a multitude of disadvantages. Poorer news media often have to depend to a large extent on the wire services which limits their ability to cover the story independently. Even if they have a reporter in Washington, that journalist will find it much more difficult to obtain interviews with the major players. The only advantage the Iowa newspaper will have is that it is in a better position to cover some local aspects of the story such as how the strike will affect local industry.

The point is that to understand the balance of power between a particular antagonist and a particular news medium one must consider the *relative* level of value and dependence. Only then can one understand the relative willingness of each side to adapt to the other in order to attain needed services.

The value of the news media to antagonists

The value of a given news medium to antagonists can be understood by focusing on its audience: its size, its political and social status, and its level of political power. This is the major service that antagonists need to achieve their political goals: to communicate with the largest and most important audience possible. The reason the *New York Times* will be given more access by leaders than a more local paper is because it is believed that the *Times* is the most effective means of communicating with an important segment of the public. The *Times* is seen as an important outlet because it is read by a large, elite audience. Television journalists often have more influence over antagonists than newspaper reporters because of similar assumptions about the size of their audience.[1]

The value of these services can be illustrated by thinking about how the news media sell themselves to advertisers. A sales manager will typically call a prospective advertiser and tell them about the size of their readership or the number of viewers who tune in to their news programs. They will also stress how the newspaper or the television news program offers the most effective means of reaching specific segments of the population, for example young educated consumers.

The transactions between antagonists and the news media are more subtle but run along similar lines. Decisions by the White House or the Pentagon about the allocation of offices to the press are based on comparable considerations about the importance of the competing news

[1] The power of television may also be related to assumptions about the *impact* of that medium. It is, however, a much more difficult variable to evaluate than the nature of the audience.

media. Those who make such decisions must consider not only audience size but also the status of the news medium and its assumed impact on various segments of the population.

It is again important to extend these principles to the transactions between antagonists and the news media that characterize international conflicts. The power of CNN comes from the size and status of its audience. The fact that leaders from around the world make a point of monitoring these news broadcasts means that antagonists compete for its attention. Activists know that cases of famine and slaughter ignored by CNN are unlikely to get much attention from anyone else, while those who are "discovered" by CNN will have a very different type of career. Getting access to CNN has become a major priority for any antagonist hoping to reach an international audience.

The political power of a given country is directly reflected in the respect accorded to its news media. The ability of a program such as *Nightline* on ABC television to gain access to the most important leaders in the world during times of crisis – despite the time differences – tells us something important about the value of this medium to these leaders. Nobody in Eastern Europe is going to get out of bed for an interview with the Brazilian news service. It is critical for international antagonists to communicate with American leaders and the American public because of the potential impact the United States can have on every conflict.

It is true that antagonists rarely need to focus their attention on only one news medium. A press release, for example, can be sent to hundreds of news media simultaneously. Nevertheless, choices often have to be made – at least by the more newsworthy of the antagonists – about how much time and attention to devote to various reporters, and the value of each news medium will certainly be considered in making these decisions. Such choices are analogous to the decisions made by editors about which conflicts to cover.

To evaluate the power of a news medium, however, one must also consider its level of dependency, and thus the discussion turns to this part of the equation.

The independence of the news media

The notion of value becomes meaningless if the news media are unable to achieve independence. The concept of independence as it is used here refers to the extent to which the press is *willing* and *able* to make genuine *choices* about how to collect, process, and distribute information.

This notion of independence implies that press freedom can just as easily be surrendered as taken away.

In an unequal conflict, the most important question is the extent of independence from the authorities. This is because the authorities are usually in a much better position to take control of the press than most challengers. Challengers rarely have the organization and resources to become the exclusive source of information for the media. It may sometimes be helpful also to look at the overall level of dependence of the news media on certain challengers, but this would normally be a less central issue.

The model suggests three major factors that determine the level of media independence:

1. the level of *official political control* over the news medium;
2. the *need for official information*;
3. and the level of *organization and resources* at the disposal of the news medium.

The first factor reduces the level of independence while the second increases it.

The *level of political control* refers to the extent to which the authorities have the power officially to regulate the news media. In the non-democratic world such control is quite blatant. The government usually owns a good part of the broadcast system and newspaper editors understand what kinds of stories can get them in trouble. Questions of news value become secondary and would-be challengers find all gates closed.

The political controls in many European countries are more subtle but these differences also offer important lessons about the relative amount of media independence. Thus, in those countries where the broadcast system is under tighter control than the newspapers, one would expect to see significant differences in the coverage of political conflicts. In October of 1988, for example, Prime Minister Thatcher could place a ban on live interviews with IRA activists on all of the broadcast networks (Irvin, 1992). There can be little doubt that such controls led to important differences in the coverage of the IRA that appeared in newspapers and television.

While the level of political control remains fairly constant over time it is likely to vary in times of "crisis." The quotation marks around this word indicate that it is often the authorities who decide what does and does not constitute a "crisis" (Raboy and Dagenais, 1992). When a crisis frame has been accepted by society, it becomes much easier for the authorities to use emergency orders and the like to impose a greater level of control on the news media. Not only is the public more likely to favor such controls, but the press itself may prefer a certain amount of censorship to protect itself from charges that suggest that coverage is either "risking lives" or "unpatriotic."

The second variable that increases the dependence of the news media is the *need for official information*. The need for such information is often related to the amount of public demand for a particular story among a particular audience. Local journalists, for example, may be more dependent on official sources within a particular community because they have a larger "news hole" to fill about that issue than the national or international press. When many journalists have a similar need, the authorities can exploit such competition for their own benefit, which gives them greater power over the press.

One can assume, for example, that British journalists had a greater need for official information about what was happening in the Falklands than the American journalists covering the conflict. The British public wanted to know everything they could about the conflict; competition among journalists for scoops at times like this gets especially cut throat. The fact that the British maintained a tight lid on information about the war was especially difficult for the British journalists because they had a much higher level of need for the information.

The final set of variables which influences the independence of a news medium is its level of *organization and resources*. The wealthier news media are in a much better position to gain access to alternative sources of information. In the previously discussed example of the Teamsters strike, the fact that the *New York Times* had the luxury of stationing journalists around the country lowered the paper's dependence on any one source. News media with less organization and resources are almost completely dependent on official sources of information and the services offered by larger news agencies such as Associated Press and United Press International.

Here too, hard resources such as money lead to softer resources such as knowledge, experience, and talent. The ability to hire the best journalists results in greater independence, for one of the most important attributes of a talented journalist is the ability to find information which others cannot. Journalists who have both prestige and knowledge are in a much better position to solicit more significant information from superior sources; those lower down on the totem pole are more like students and their sources more like teachers.

Knowledge about a particular conflict is one of the factors that can vary over time and circumstance and with it the level of media dependence. As noted earlier, this is especially true when the news media are called upon to cover foreign conflicts where they lack language skills, a basic understanding of the culture they are covering, and a selection of sources for information. This often leads to some exceptionally poor coverage. In the coverage of the Romanian revolution in 1989 in which Nicolae Ceausescu was deposed, for example, all of the news media accepted widely exaggerated counts about the loss of life in the country. Initial counts stated the number of dead was over 70,000 while the final number turned out to be about 700.[2] When the press has to depend on rumors, and cannot distinguish between reliable and unreliable sources, it is in no position to cover the conflict. The longer the story continues, the higher is the level of knowledge and contacts, the higher is the level of media independence, and presumably the higher is the level of accuracy.

Thus, media independence depends on three major factors: the level of official political control over the news medium, its need for official information, and its level of organization and resources. When combined with the value factors one obtains a fairly thorough understanding of the power differences among news media. As with antagonists, there is little justice in the distribution of advantages. Within Western countries, independence is directly linked to the size and prestige of each news organizations. While large news services, such as UPI, offer a minimal amount of compensation for these differences, there is no substitute for exclusive coverage. Mostly, the relationship between antagonists and the news media consists of one elite talking to another.

Political outcomes

What then are the results of all these forces? What types of influence do the news media have on antagonists and on political conflicts? As communication scholars have learned over the years the notion of media influence is never simple. Four clarifications are necessary before answering these questions.

The first concerns the use of the term "outcomes" rather than "effects." The term "effects" is problematic for it suggests a form of influence that is both automatic and inevitable. Transactions between antagonists and the news media are carried out by two or more goal-seeking actors who are continually making decisions about the form and extent of mutual accommodation. Thus, many "effects" are in fact self-imposed changes rooted in political self-interest.

[2]   It is not surprising that the mistakes in this area are almost always in the direction of more casualties rather than less. The more the casualties the better the story and when the picture is ambiguous it is only natural for reporters to see it as being more dramatic than it is. Such conflicts often serve as the perfect Rorschach test for journalists.

Consider, for example, the issue of whether the presence of the news media increases the level of political violence among antagonists. Antagonists react to the news media according to their collective norms and goals (Wolfsfeld, 1991). There are some protest groups who want to send a message of militancy; the arrival of the television cameras serves as a trigger for carrying out dramatic acts of violence intended to send that message. There are other antagonists, however, who hold ideologies that negate the use of political violence. While such groups are unlikely to ignore the arrival of the news media, their reactions will be very different. Adaptations to demands of the news media are, to a large extent, a matter of choice. Here again, political considerations set important limits to the seemingly involuntary imposition of power.

The same differences can be found when looking at the influence of the news media on political leaders. As discussed in Chapter 1, differences in the relative dependency of political leaders provide us with a set of predictions about which of them is more likely to invest time and energy in finding ways to attract media attention. Nevertheless, every political leader must make a personal decision about how and when to adapt to the needs of the media. One political leader will be willing to engage in an endless series of media stunts while another will continue to carry on important committee work even if it means less attention in the press.

The fact that many political outcomes are based on antagonist decisions does not mean that all such outcomes are either intended or expected. Authorities and challengers carry out a variety of acts only some of which are directed at the news media. The fact that the news media cover such events may lead to unintended political outcomes. Challengers who carry out acts of violence to receive publicity, for example, may not always realize that such attention in the press can lead to a drop in membership.

The discussion in this study will focus, therefore, on transactional outcomes rather than effects. This formulation places antagonists on a more equal footing with the news media and serves to remind us that many outcomes are based on deliberate decisions made by the parties involved. The term "influence" is also preferable to the term "effect" because it too leaves more room for choice by those who are being influenced. In addition, while the term "outcomes" is a superior theoretical concept, the word "influence" is much easier to use in a sentence.

A second clarification deals with when and where media influence is likely to occur. Many commentators first think of the simplest form of influence, when antagonists react to the *presence of the news media*. The fact that protesters and politicians act differently when the cameras come out is hardly surprising. People rarely act in public the way they would in private, and having a large audience for one's behavior makes one even more self-conscious of one's actions.

There are, however, other types of outcomes associated with the news media that are more subtle. Antagonists are just as likely to react to *coverage in the news media*. Political actors spend a good deal of their time monitoring the news media, in part as a barometer of success. Too little coverage may lead to greater attempts to achieve publicity and too much negative coverage can lead to a change in strategy to change one's image. It would also be a mistake for researchers to attempt to understand this process by looking exclusively at how antagonists *react* to the news media. Many important types of adaptations are carried out in *anticipation of media coverage*. Even inexperienced antagonists quickly learn what the news media expect of them and some of them act accordingly. Those who carry out case studies on political conflicts should attempt to ascertain the centrality of the news media in the ongoing decision-making process of leaders. While some events are staged by actors almost exclusively for the news media, the news plays a more marginal role in others.

A third clarification returns us to the issue of media independence. While this question will be even more central in the second part of this chapter, it is also relevant to the present discussion about whether the news media have an influence on antagonist transformations. It is important to differentiate between those cases where the news media have played a *passive* and *transmissional* role in bringing about changes among the antagonists and those in which they have played an *active* and *independent* role.

Say a political leader makes a particularly inflammatory speech that leads to riots in a particular city. The fact that the news media reported on the speech or even the fact that they chose to emphasize the more sensational aspects of it could not be considered as convincing evidence of media influence. The news media merely served in this instance as a reliable channel of communication between the leader and the public. These political outcomes are best attributed to the event itself rather than how it was reported.

If, on the other hand, the politician made the comments in what he or she thought was a closed meeting of friends and colleagues and a particularly industrious reporter managed to get hold of the information, that would be something different. Here, it is the active participation of the news media that led to the subsequent riots.

It is only fair to point out that the distinction between independent and transmissional influence is much easier to make in theory than in practice. As with most variables it is much better to think of the notion of media independence as a continuum; the job of researchers is to learn where a given case falls between the two poles. I shall have more to say about this issue below.

The final clarification has to do with an important difference between the influence of antagonists on the news media and the flow of influence that runs in the other direction. The distinction has to do with the issue of *intent*. Whereas antagonists have every intention of influencing the news media, journalists normally do not have the same goals concerning antagonists. Their goal is to obtain as much information as possible and to produce the best news stories. The influence of the news media on the conflict are *usually unintended* by-products of behavior designed to achieve these goals.

There are of course exceptions to this rule. When the news media emphasize the victims in a conflict, they are issuing a call to stop the bloodshed. The press also sometimes puts pressure on the authorities to intervene in a conflict, usually for the side that is losing. When journalists uncover government incompetence or brutality, the underlying message is that "something should be done" about it. Normally, however, journalists are in the business of constructing news stories rather than influencing politics.

Having weeded through these clarifications, it is time to deal with the essence. There are two major classes of political outcomes that can be attributed to the news media. The first set can be placed under the rubric of *antagonist transformations*. Changes in tactics, strategy, group solidarity, and the status of various leaders would all be included in this category. The second class of outcomes has to do with *changes in political standing* of the antagonists. The most dramatic cases of such influence are those where the news media serve as equalizers by increasing the political status of challengers or by mobilizing third parties into the conflict.

Antagonist transformations: adapting to the news media

All political actors must adapt themselves to the news media. Political leaders have to plan their speeches and actions in ways that can be easily turned to news, avoid having embarrassing information leaked to the press, and consider which personalities are best suited to serve as public spokespeople. The question which concerns us is the *nature* and *extent* of adaptation by various antagonists. The greater the level of adaptation by antagonists, the more central the role of the news media in the conflict.

The most common forms of adaptation to the news media are changes in *tactics, strategy,* and *behavior.* As discussed in Chapter 1, weaker challengers are especially likely to alter their behavior to achieve access to the news media. These tactics can range from dramatic gimmicks such as carrying out mock funerals to terrorist attacks whose time and place are planned to ensure the maximum amount of publicity. Authorities also adapt and react to media coverage. When news stories focus on the amount of force used by the police or military, leaders are likely to be especially careful about how they deal with future incidents.

Political authorities have another important option: to change policy. It is especially difficult to isolate the role of the news media in such cases but this is no reason to deny media influence. A change in policy is more likely to occur with respect to smaller conflicts where public benefits of concessions far outweigh the cost. The ability of the news media to set the public agenda is an important part of such processes and a major reason challengers depend on the news media to achieve political goals.

A second pattern of antagonist transformation comes as *internal changes* within the organization, group, or country. Transactions with the news media can lead to changes in the legitimacy and status of leadership and the level of collective solidarity. A good example of such changes can be found in Gitlin's (1980) study of the influence of news media on the Students for a Democratic Society. Gitlin found the media's tendency to focus on the more radical elements of the movement increased the status of these activists and they thus become the most important leaders within the movement.

The direction of internal changes may be difficult to predict in advance. The fact that a group leader frequently appears in the news media, for example, may either enhance or diminish his or her position within a particular political structure. While such exposure is an important asset in building public recognition, others may resent that exposure, especially if there are questions about the pecking order. This is true among both authorities and challengers. Those who work for mayors, presidents, and prime ministers constantly monitor media images and they are all aware of the impact such coverage can have on political status and power.

The most extreme form of internal transformation that can occur is the disbanding of an organization. While it is unlikely that the demise of any group can be attributed solely to the news media, there are cases in which the press can be considered an important agent in such transformations. Here too, the key is to assess the impact of news coverage – or even more likely the lack of coverage – on group strength. Small, *ad hoc* groups who depend on the news media for their organizational sustenance can easily starve to death without the manna of publicity.

Changes in political standing

The news media can also have an important influence on the political standing of antagonists. Political standing refers to the relative level of political status and power of the two rivals. This type of influence can have a dramatic impact on the balance of power among antagonists.

The most common such influence occurs when the press *raises the political standing of the challenger.* Challengers who obtain a significant amount of media coverage usually enjoy a significant rise in political status. Those who are recognized by the news media as serious political players become serious political players. As discussed, this is usually part of a broader cycle in which political success leads to media success that brings on more political success. Nevertheless, the news media can play an independent role in this process by devoting a disproportionate amount of attention to some challengers while ignoring others and by exaggerating and accelerating existing trends.

A rise in political standing normally leads to a wide range of benefits. Political standing can be translated into a much higher level of organization and resources and easier access to the political elite. A greater level of political standing also increases the pressure on the authorities to make some type of response to challenger demands.

One of the most important benefits of increased political standing is the increased likelihood of third-party intervention. The significance of this can be understood by considering the strategic needs of each side in an unequal conflict. The weaker side in the conflict – the challenger – must find a means of bringing third parties into the conflict on its side to create a more equal balance of power. The authorities, on the other hand, have less need for third-party intervention, and certainly not those aligned against them.

The news media, especially in recent years, often play a critical role in this process: they are the only means for bringing the case of the weaker side to light. Those challengers who successfully promote their frames to the news media are in a much better position to bring third parties into the conflict. The rebels in Chechnya hope to use the pictures on CNN to stop the Russian onslaught. The Zapastista rebels in Mexico stopped government troops dead in their tracks by sending out faxes that the army was "killing children, beating and raping women" (*Newsweek*,

1995, p. 18). As their leader put it: "What they [the government] should really fear is a communication expert" (*Newsweek*, 1995, p. 18). When political conflicts become part of the public agenda, political actors are under pressure to "do something": to react, to mediate, or to come to the aid of victims.

The more powerful side in such conflicts approaches the news media from a very different strategic perspective. The authorities attempt to dominate the political environment: they either neutralize the role of the news media by keeping the conflict off the public agenda or, in more serious challenges, ensure that the official voice drowns out all others. In these cases, the conflict takes its normal course, with the powerful defeating the weak.

Thus, when the news media, by choice or by compulsion, adopt the frame being promoted by the more powerful antagonist, they are less likely to play a central role in political conflicts. As an analogy, consider a conflict between a rich landlord and a group of poor tenants. If a large sum of money were given by an interested party to the wealthy landlord it would be unlikely to have much of an effect on either the behavior of the parties or the course of the conflict. The landlord would probably invest the money in some stocks or bonds and continue with his or her normal routine. If, on the other hand, that same amount of money were given to the poor tenants it could have a dramatic impact on both their behavior and on the balance of power. The tenants can carry out a much more sophisticated mobilization effort and hire professionals such as lawyers and public relations people to aid their cause.

The same principle holds for the distribution of favorable media coverage: the more positive attention given to resource-poor antagonists, the more dramatic its effects. Even a balanced type of coverage will offer the weaker antagonist important opportunities to challenge dominant frames. Resources given equally to both parties will still be a more significant development for the weak than for the powerful.

The news media can also *lower the political standing of the authorities*, which will also mean a change in the balance of power. When the authorities are portrayed in the press as incompetent, cruel, or simply misguided, it lowers their level of political status and power. Critics suddenly become more vocal, supporters start looking for cover and the gap between authorities and challengers begins to narrow. Political failures are soon considered the norm and any successes become exceptions that prove the rule. The authorities become more vulnerable to attack, the news media become more willing to carry such attacks, and the playing field begins to level.

A continuum of media influence

It is useful to think of the role of the news media in political conflicts in terms of a continuum of independence. At one end of the continuum one would place those cases in which the news media serve as *faithful servants* to the authorities, constantly publicizing official frames of the conflict and either ignoring or discrediting challengers. The middle of the continuum would be occupied by those conflicts in which the news media act as *semi-honest brokers* by offering challengers a significant amount of time and space to air their views against the authorities. The most interesting end of this continuum is occupied by conflicts in which the news media play the role of *advocates of the underdog* by amplifying the claims of challengers against authorities. These are the conflicts in which the news media play the most independent role, and it is the authorities who find themselves in an uphill battle for legitimacy.

The news media are most likely to play the role of faithful servants in times of national crisis and war, especially in the early stages of such conflicts. The news media in these incidents rely almost exclusively on official sources for information about the conflicts and there is a close, cooperative relationship between government officials and journalists. This process is often called the "rally round the flag" phenomenon as journalists display their patriotism by supporting the state against its enemies. Enemies can be either other countries or challengers whose actions or goals violate central norms within the society. Groups defined as terrorist organizations would be obvious examples of such challengers.

The British coverage of the Falklands war offers a good example of this mode of reporting. The research on the news coverage of that war (Glasgow Media Group, 1985; Morrison and Tumber, 1988) demonstrates how a combination of government restrictions and a sense of patriotism among British journalists provided the government with very supportive media frames for the war. Once the enemy had been defined and engaged, the news media became a passive transmission belt for official frames intended to build up domestic and international support.

The news media are most likely to take the role of semi-honest brokers within domestic debates over controversial issues. The term "semi-honest" is used because authorities still enjoy important advantages over challengers in these situations, but the challengers are given a significant amount of time and space to air their views. The news media attempt to identify the major players in the conflict and offer them a public platform for debate. As discussed in Chapter 1, only the more powerful challengers are likely to be represented in these debates. Rival political parties are likely to be the most frequent sources of oppositional views. Nevertheless, the news media do exhibit independence in these cases and government critics can be heard.

The American news media often adopt this mode of reporting in the debates that *precede* the decision by a given administration to carry out some form of military action. One will find evidence of this mode of reporting in looking at American coverage of the debates over policy in Nicaragua, the Persian Gulf conflict, Bosnia, Somalia, and Haiti. The debate itself becomes the news story and the "pro" and "con" arguments become the leading format for reporting about the issue.

The news media play their most independent role when they become advocates of the underdog. The most telltale sign of these situations are *injustice* and *victims* frames whose underlying theme is that "something must be done" to rectify the situation. Official frames are never completely absent, but they occupy a much less significant amount of time and space. Political leaders begin to speak of "damage control," "circling the wagons," or "bracing for the storm." There is a clear shift in the balance of power and third-party intervention becomes a real possibility. The poodle, who had been so willing to serve and obey, has been transformed into an attack dog, intent on killing its former master.

The role of the news media in the conflict over civil rights in Birmingham, Alabama in the early 1960s offers a good example (Gamson, 1990; Garrow, 1978; Paletz and Entman, 1981). The stories and pictures of the Birmingham police using dogs, clubs, and water hoses on the protesters resonated around the world. These stories remained on the front pages of the *New York Times* and the *Washington Post* for almost two weeks in May of 1963 (Garrow, 1978). President Kennedy reportedly said that the photo of dogs attacking the demonstrators had made him "sick" (Garrow, 1978, p. 141). The civil rights leaders were well aware how important this publicity was to their cause.

The distinction among the different roles of the news media presented here has a certain amount of theoretical overlap with the three "spheres of opinion" put forth by Hallin (1986). His three categories are: the sphere of consensus, the sphere of legitimate controversy, and the sphere of deviance. Journalists only feel the need to exhibit balance and neutrality, Hallin argues, when issues fall within the realm of legitimate controversy, such as the debates between the major political parties in the United States.

There is, however, an important difference between Hallin's perspective and the one being advanced in the present work. Hallin's model excludes the possibility of the news media serving as advocates for challengers. This may be the exception, but it is a particularly significant exception in which the press becomes a full participant in the conflict.

Assessing news media influence

It is impossible to assess precisely the degree of media influence in a given political conflict. The major reason for this is the difficulty in isolating the influence of the news media from other factors that affect such struggles. Nevertheless, there are several methods and strategies that can provide important evidence about the centrality of the news media in a given conflict.

The first goal of such research should be to establish the extent of media independence. As argued earlier, the question of independence in unequal conflicts refers almost entirely to the question of independence from the authorities. It is possible to examine the course of a conflict and establish whether the news media take an independent role by asking about:

1. The extent to which the news media use exclusively official sources for information.
2. The extent to which non-official stories and frames appear in the coverage of the conflict.
3. The extent to which the authorities appear to be surprised, frustrated, or angered by the coverage they are receiving.

The answers to these questions come from interviews with journalists, officials, and political leaders and from content analyses of the news media.

The fact that the news media exhibit a certain amount of independence in their coverage is not a sufficient indicator of media influence. While it does allow us to move the case beyond the faithful servants section of the continuum, further tests are needed to determine the centrality of the news media in a conflict. This part of the analysis focuses on two central questions:

1. To what extent do the antagonists appear to be adapting their behavior to better promote themselves to the news media?
2. To what extent does the balance of political power between authorities and challengers appear to have changed due to the news coverage of the conflict?

The first question refers to the amount of adaptation by both the authorities and challengers. Only qualitative methods allow researchers the type of understanding they need to analyze these processes. The power of Gitlin's (1980) work on the Students for a Democratic Society comes from his intimate knowledge of this group and how they were continually transformed by the news media. In-depth interviews and participant observation enable researchers to come in close to examine how political actors struggle and cope with the news media in the midst of a political conflict.

Interviews with leaders and journalists should focus on several key questions. To what extent did the topic of press coverage come up in planning sessions? How central was the role of the spokesperson within the leadership? To what extent was the news media coverage of activities used as a barometer of success? How did political actors react to the presence of the news media? Were any tactics or strategies changed because of coverage?

Political leaders often attempt to downplay the centrality of the news media in their decision-making process. This tendency may be related to a belief by both authorities and challengers that use of the news media to achieve political aims is somehow cheap or tainted. Distinctions are often made between those who carry out the "real" work and those who deal with "public relations" (Cook, 1987). Nevertheless, the use of direct and indirect questions should allow for a reasonable appraisal of the importance of media considerations in collective planning.

Assessments about changes in political standing should begin with a content analysis of news media. If challengers receive a significant amount of space and time in major news media, it represents a *prima facie* case that the news media had an influence on the conflict. The greater and more sympathetic the coverage of challengers and their cause, the more central and independent the role of the news media in altering the balance of power. Whereas challengers have no official standing, any unofficial standing they achieve makes them stronger. Changes in the public agenda should be considered a *bona fide* political outcome.

The weaker the challenger the more significant the influence of such publicity. The news media's role as equalizer becomes most obvious when a weak, previously unknown challenger is suddenly thrust into the public's eye. Antagonists who are portrayed in the central arena as significant challengers are then considered significant challengers and the authorities are compelled to respond publicly. The response may often be superficial or symbolic but this need to respond tells quite a bit about the public status endowed by the press.

A similar strategy can be used to examine the relationship between media coverage and the intervention of third parties. There are many reasons besides media coverage why a particular group or government decides to become involved in a conflict. Interviews with challengers, authorities, and third-party leaders should attempt to focus on the centrality of news media coverage as a source of information and persuasion for those not directly involved. Another tactic would be to compare the amount of third-party intervention and reaction to a well-publicized conflict, to a similar confrontation that received much less publicity.

Researchers who are uncomfortable with a qualitative approach to this issue will remain skeptical about our ability to measure accurately the amount of media influence on political conflicts. While some questions in this area are simple and direct, others are more subtle and subjective. One can never "prove" that the news media played a central part in a political conflict. The goal is to collect as much evidence as possible, from as many sources as possible, in order to make an informed assessment about the extent of media influence.

A comparison of different conflicts makes this task easier. While a good deal of previous work in this field has focused on a particular movement or war, only a comparative approach allows one to look at the ways in which the role of the news media changes. In-depth knowledge of each case allows one to build a fairly accurate picture of the quantity and quality of transactions between antagonists and the news media. The pictures that emerge from this work may not be totally accurate representations of what occurred. But they are usually sufficiently different from one another to provide convincing conclusions about the varying role of the media.

This is the goal of the second part of this work.

Part 2

The contests

4 Political movements and media access: the struggle against the Oslo Accords

Protest movements are the classic challengers. They provide the best examples of the principle of cumulative inequality: they have a tremendous need for the news media but little to offer in return. Few are well organized, and most are resource poor. Their opponents are huge and powerful. The David and Goliath analogy – however hackneyed – is usually appropriate in such contests. Nevertheless, David did defeat Goliath, even without CNN.

Movements need the media for three major purposes: mobilization, validation, and scope enlargement (Gamson and Wolfsfeld, 1993). They need the media for mobilization because more primitive means of communication such as mailings and phone calls severely inhibit their ability to grow. Movements also need the mass media for validating their existence to members, supporters, and the authorities. For members media coverage provides a sense of accomplishment, which can be especially important in a long campaign, when inducements for participation are few and far between. For supporters and the authorities such coverage defines the movement as a recognized voice for a particular constituency – it provides political standing. Finally, movements depend on the news media to bring third parties into the conflict. Only outside support can alter the tremendous inequality that characterizes the political balance of power between movements and the authorities.

Turning to the upper part of the ratio, movements can produce events that appeal to the news media. They provide drama, conflict, action, and a wealth of photo opportunities. The problem is that such events are expensive and few movements can afford to stage them repeatedly. Movements are rarely considered important enough to justify a beat. They must prove their newsworthiness every day. Finally, as discussed, those movements who do obtain publicity, must often pay with violence and disorder which works against the very goals they are trying to achieve.

The picture, however, is not always bleak. Political and non-political events sometimes change the rules of entrance to the central arena. A nuclear accident can serve as a cultural explosion that opens the arena to a plethora of anti-nuclear challengers who under normal circumstances would be left out. When a doctor is killed for carrying out abortions, journalists look for activists from both pro-choice and pro-life movements to react to the event. When the threat of war hangs in the air, the value of peace group sources rises.

Such critical events not only increase the dependency of the news media on movement sources, they also make it much easier for movements to mobilize for action (Staggenborg, 1993). Citizens become impassioned about their causes, when the smell of crisis is in the air; phones begin to ring again and volunteers are everywhere. Movements that had found it difficult to gather a quorum for their bi-weekly meetings are suddenly overwhelmed with supporters. All of this dramatically increases the movements' ability to initiate newsworthy events.

These political waves rise and fall and with them the ability of movements to ride them to shore. The same waves, however, also serve the authorities and the government is much better equipped to deal with them. Also, times of crisis are rarely a time of celebration for movements. They are usually periods of threat and disaster such as nuclear accidents or wars. Most movement leaders would prefer to meet the news media under happier circumstances. But when things are going well, both supporters and journalists are very hard to find.

The struggle over the Oslo Accords

The Israel–Palestinian Declaration of Principles signed in September of 1993 was just such a political explosion. It was a critical event in the history of the Arab–Israeli conflict and there were many political actors who had a real need to get their views to the news media. Among the most important were the Israeli government, the leadership of the PLO, the political opposition in Israel, and the political opposition among the Palestinians. I shall focus on the conflict between the Israeli government and the many political movements that organized to stop the Oslo agreement. Other actors will emerge, however, for they too played important parts in this drama.

The right-wing opposition in Israel saw the agreement as a national disaster. This was especially true for the Jewish settlers who live in what they feel is the heart of historic Israel. Many other Israeli citizens were concerned that this was simply a new tactic in the Arab war against Israel. The Rabin government had been elected with an extremely thin majority and opposition to the Accords often approached the 50 per cent mark within the Israeli public (Katz and Levinsohn, 1994). Many groups mobilized to oppose the Oslo Accords and protests began immediately after the news broke in late August. Collective action against the Accords included large and small demonstrations, the setting up of a "tent city" near the Prime Minister's office, vigils that lasted for weeks and months, a variety of media gimmicks, illegal disorders such as blocking roads and establishing new settlements, and even one terrorist attack, the infamous massacre in Hebron.

This set of events offers many benefits for those interested in understanding how the role of the news media changes over time and circumstance. First, there were many different movements active against the government, all with a definite deadline for their activities. This offered a rare opportunity to observe and compare a variety of transactions among a diffuse set of protest leaders and journalists. Secondly, while many previous studies of this topic have looked at peace movements, this will be the first study to look at how "anti-peace" movements cope with the news media. It is important to examine whether the same rules developed regarding leftist movements can also be applied to movements of the right. Finally, while most previous studies have looked at movements in either North America or Britain, looking at the relationship between movements and the news media in a very different country increases the likelihood of developing a more comprehensive explanation for these phenomena.

This case study focuses on the period from August 27, 1993 to May 5, 1994. This period spans the time from when the first stories were published about an impending agreement between Israel and the PLO until the day after the signing of the Cairo Accords on May 5, 1994. In-depth interviews were carried out with a total of thirty-five individuals, including movement leaders, journalists covering the story, and several government spokespeople responsible for promoting official frames of the conflict. Several direct observations were also carried out at protests and public meetings held by the groups. A content analysis of the coverage of the conflict in two Israeli newspapers was also conducted. Details about both methods can be found in the methodological appendix.

Competition between the Rabin government and the opposition over the news media ran, for the most part, along the usual lines. The government used its vast power, organization, and resources to promote its version of events to the news media, while the movements were continually forced to provide collective actions to remain on the public agenda. Nevertheless, several groups made a significant impact on public discourse, and the emerging picture was certainly not one of political consensus.

There were also several periods in which the Rabin government lost control over the political environment and this provided important opportunities for the challengers. The most important events were the terrorist attacks that began very soon after the signing of the Oslo Accords and offered important opportunities for those opposed to the agreement to promote their views in the media.

The discussion will be divided into three sections. The first part will look at the central competition over access between the government and the Settlers' Council, which was the major political movement that organized against the Accords. The notions of value and dependency help explain the contest between these two antagonists. These same principles also help explain the competition for media space *among* the different challengers, and this is discussed in the second part of the chapter. The focus in this section is on the attempts of weaker protest movements to get into the news media. Having established the basic rules of the game in the first two sections, the third is devoted to demonstrating how quickly political events can change these routines. Neither the Rabin government nor the mainstream settlers' movement were ever in complete control of the political environment and some of these lapses led to dramatic changes of which voices became the loudest.

Struggles over public space

The opening moves of the Rabin government caught the Israeli news media and the public by surprise. The ability to keep the Norwegian talks away from the news media was probably a primary reason for their success. This complete control over events, and over the flow of information in the first week or so when the story broke, placed the Israeli and international news media at the mercy of the Rabin government. Here was one of the most dramatic events in the history of the Arab–Israeli conflict and reporters and editors were almost totally dependent on the government for every crumb of information. The Israeli government had managed to keep the entire story secret and there were no alternative sources available. The competition among journalists for details was fierce and the power of the government over the news media in this initial stage could only be compared to that exercised by public officials during wartime.

The Israeli government devotes a considerable amount of organization and resources to dealing with the news media. Four major offices were responsible for promoting the government's stand on the peace process:

the Prime Minister's office, the Foreign Ministry, the Defense Ministry, and the Government Press Office. Each of these offices employs full-time, experienced staffs who are responsible for ongoing relations with the press. Naturally, all these sources are considered essential for journalists who cover the peace process.

The government increased its already high value as a source through a steady flow of dramatic information and media events. Information included stories about the intrigue and suspense surrounding the Oslo talks, the negotiations toward diplomatic relations with Third World and Arab countries, the tremendous benefits that peace would bring to the Israeli economy and society, and a constant infusion of optimism about the ongoing talks with the Palestinians. As pointed out by an official in charge of promoting these stories to the media, it was not a very difficult assignment.

There's demand. The minute there's demand, you can dictate conditions, you can establish some sort of direction. When there isn't, and you have to run after the news media, then your situation is much more difficult.

Elaborate ceremonies were carried out in Jerusalem, Washington, and Cairo to mark each stage of progress. Access to these ceremonies was a coveted prize awarded to the elite of the news media from each country. The press promoted these events well in advance because such marketing opportunities are rare, even in Israel. Television and radio commercials inundated the airwaves, encouraging audiences not to miss the great milestones in Israeli history. Production of the actual events was, in many ways, a joint effort by the political leadership and the journalists. The signing ceremonies were the type of media events (Dayan and Katz, 1992) that most political leaders can only dream about. The setting, the drama, and even the music could all be meticulously planned, and journalists treated the events with reverence.

The Israeli journalists also received plums to keep their attention in focus. For the first time in history they could be invited to Arab capitals and be given exclusive interviews with the Arab leaders. A fascinating element of this process had to do with the interviews carried out with Arafat and other PLO leaders in Tunisia. Whereas many researchers have talked about the "demonization of the enemy" by the news media, suddenly the news media were being used to legitimize the former enemy. Competition for these interviews was intense – these were not sources that any reporter would want to lose. People who had only recently been framed as terrorists by the Israeli media were now being treated as respected political leaders.

Lest the reader misunderstand the theoretical implications of all this, I am not suggesting that the power of the government over the news media at this time was a matter of clever public relations. The opposite is the case. The Rabin government had something very real and valuable to sell the news media: the first breakthrough with the Palestinians in the history of the conflict. Given the value of this information, journalists had little choice but to wait for whatever information their official sources deemed appropriate for public consumption. It is a clear case of political success leading to success in the media. The triumphant coverage may very well have led to even greater political success, but that is a more difficult question to answer.[1]

It is also important to remember that the government was also dependent on the news media during this period. Continued public support for the peace process was an essential element in the general political plan. The Rabin government was initiating a dramatic change in the Israeli political reality and the role of the news media was a central tool in that effort.

The movements against the agreement were faced with all of the dangers and opportunities that characterize a critical event such as the Oslo Accords. On the one hand, the political explosion had opened the news media as never before. As the primary victims of the Accords, the settlements in the West Bank and Gaza were swarming with Israeli journalists looking for interviews that would describe "how settlers felt about all this." In addition, the threat created by these dramatic political developments brought out thousands of new recruits for collective action. Thus, the opposition had something to sell the media and something the news media was very interested in buying. On the down side, however, their need for the media had risen as quickly as their value. The threat was immediate and unless they could quickly mobilize the public to stop the government, they'd be run over by the peace train.

The Settlers' Council

The most powerful extra-parliamentary movement to mobilize against the agreement was the Council for the Settlements in Judea, Samaria, and Gaza. Judea, Samaria, and Gaza are the historic biblical terms for the areas known to the rest of the world as the West Bank and Gaza. The Council was less involved in protest during the years when the right-wing Likud party was in power, although there was a good deal of collective action concerning the security of the settlements during the *intifada*. The election of the Rabin government in 1992 dramatically

---

[1]   A counter-argument might be that the enthusiastic coverage only made matters worse when the difficulties in implementing the peace process became more apparent.

increased their need for news-media coverage in two ways. First, Rabin had run on an election campaign promise to "change priorities" in the country: to stop spending money in the territories and to use the funds for meeting needs within Israel proper. The Oslo Accords only served to intensify this threat. Secondly, under the Likud, the settlers had direct access to an administration that was sympathetic to their cause, and now the doors had slammed shut.

Many journalists pointed to the change that took place in the settlers' attitude toward the news media. For many years the settlers had scorned the press, believing that only action "in the field" mattered. They also considered the news media hostile to their cause, and this lack of affection went both ways. The change, according to at least one reporter, can be traced to the 1991 Madrid conference in which the Likud government began direct negotiations with the Arabs:

Then the game turned around. They just didn't think that they needed to generate public sympathy. Then they realized that the game had turned around and they had blown it. They need to get their message out, to have it expressed. Before that it was very hard to get any information at all from them ... now the settlers are very sensitive to the news media and they report to us about every incident, positive or negative.

This need to mobilize public support created a greater need among settlers for the services being offered by the news media. Unlike many challengers, however, the Settlers' Council had something to exchange for those services. Their assets are impressive and while they cannot be compared to those of the Israeli government, the Council maintains a sophisticated system for the manufacture of newsworthy information and events. The Council is made up of representatives from twenty-one regional councils who have responsibility for the maintenance and development of these areas where approximately 130,000 Israelis live. This offers them a large pool of financial and human resources for carrying out extremely large protests on an ongoing basis.

Interviews with the leaders and spokespeople of the Settlers' Council and with the journalists who cover this area all point to the fact that the Council has dedicated a tremendous amount of resources to public relations. The Council has three full-time spokespeople, two of whom work with the local and one with the foreign press. They also have a special public relations committee to plan media strategy, an advertising firm that works contractually, and several full-time support staff who help maintain daily contact with journalists around the country. This information-distribution system is extremely effective. The staff sends announcements to dozens of beepers simultaneously. One journalist reported that he sometimes received eleven or twelve announcements from the Council on a single day.

The experience and sophistication of these spokespeople rivals that of any government office. The senior spokesperson worked for five years in the field and his knowledge and understanding of the news media would put many communication professors to shame. In direct contrast to most of the protest leaders I have talked with over the years, these spokespeople felt confident in their ability to get the movement's message out to the news media. While they share the basic belief among the right wing in Israel about the "leftist bent" of the news media, they believe that they can overcome such preferences by providing good stories. The Council served as the major organizing body of the first two protests against the agreement in September 1993. These were possibly the largest demonstrations ever held in Jerusalem. The number of participants was a matter of public debate, but it is seems that at least 100,000 people participated in the first protest and only a slightly smaller number at the second.[2] That was only the start of a long series of collective acts that continued throughout the period.

The organization and resources of the settlers' movement not only assured a large turnout, it also provided the expertise for exploiting those events to achieve the maximum amount of exposure. The media tactics employed for publicizing the first major demonstration offers a good illustration of these advantages. The Israeli news media are often reluctant to offer free publicity for such events by talking about them in advance. One of the spokespeople found a clever way to overcome this obstacle by announcing that all of the schools in the settlements would be closed during the day of the demonstrations to allow the young people to attend. As he expected, this initiated a major debate within the country about the ethics of closing schools for political purposes. The newspapers, the talk shows on radio and television, and the television news were filled with government attacks on the decision to close the schools and rebuttals by the spokespeople. It would be hard to calculate the cost of all this publicity if the Council had to pay for it.

---

[2] I attended both protests as an observer. The numbers game is always interesting to watch at such events but this particular episode was especially intriguing. At the rally itself the organizers announced to the crowd that the police had estimated the number at 250,000. The police became angry at this fabrication and in retaliation released an estimate of 50,000 which was then reported on television and radio. The BBC reported the 250,000 figure the next day under a story which claimed that the police had intentionally underestimated the number in order to help the government. As an observer I can tell you that it is almost impossible to know just how many people were there, and standing with the journalists watching the event it was clear that one reporter's guess was as good as any other's.

Media expertise was also very helpful during the actual demonstration. The fact that the protest was planned to coincide with the evening news is hardly surprising. What was impressive was the manipulation of the evening news during the event. The organizers had threatened to lay siege to the Prime Minister's office and this story dominated coverage in the days leading up to the demonstration. The spokesperson described how he got the best possible television coverage for the event:

We made sure their camera operator got the best position. He was on the actual stage instead of standing with all of the other reporters. He was so happy that he signaled me when we were going on the air [with live coverage]. We made sure we had someone serious up there talking. We were off the air in about three or four minutes. Our goal was to get into the news broadcast as often as we could. Soon as we went off the air I told them [the organizers] to start moving the people toward the Prime Ministers office . . . Immediately Gadi Sukenic [Israeli television political correspondent] broke into the broadcast and said "they're starting to move," and we were on the air again. So I said: "stop them." As soon as they stopped the live broadcast, I got the crowd to move again. We broke into the news four times in one half-hour broadcast.

Although they may use different terminology, the notions of value and need which were developed in Chapter 1 are very familiar to both the leaders and the journalists who constructed these stories. The leaders talk about making sure that the journalists have everything they need – not only information but also more prosaic needs such as food, shelter, and even protection from some of the more hostile elements in the crowd. One spokesperson put it all rather graphically: "When they eat from your hand, they're not going to shit on your head."

The Council also had extremely good control over the flow of information. The increased sensitivity of the settlers to the need for the news media brought tremendous amounts of information into the central office that was then distributed immediately to all of the journalists. Another spokesperson talked about the importance of this system:

Every event that happens, I usually hear about much faster than either the army spokesman's office or the police. I let all the journalists know right away – everything by beeper. This creates a circle: they get something from me and they have to give me something in return. And that's good work. They get from me reports of everything that happens in the field: everything from terrorist attacks to events that happens in the settlements like the founding of a new school, every three people that are moving from here to there. It takes about a minute to distribute it to all the beepers with one message . . . and when I ask them to come to cover a protest, to get my reaction, I come as a media power, because they get a tremendous amount of information from me.

One journalist confirmed the fact that it was much easier and faster to get information from the Council than from the army spokesperson's office.

The Council's high level of production assets allowed it to exhibit a large amount of exceptional behavior and to compete with the government for control over the political environment. The most important accomplishment of the Council was to achieve *standing*. They received both standing in the news media and in the political system because they were considered representatives of an important constituency that was directly affected by the peace process. This tended to lower the costs of access to the news media and the Council was often able to have their announcements and reactions covered in the news media without resorting to media gimmicks.

It would be a mistake, however, to suggest that access to the Council was in any way equal to that of the government. Government access was much more automatic, immediate, and effortless. Unlike the peace process, the newsworthiness of protests lasts for a day or two and then disappears. Even a large movement such as the Settlers' Council is politically incapable of carrying out massive protests on an ongoing basis. After two or three major demonstrations, the movement was forced to resort to smaller, more irritating types of actions such as blocking streets and the like. Collective action is expensive and this is a major reason time often works to the advantage of the authorities.

The small protest groups: you gotta have a gimmick

There were also many small protest groups that organized against the Oslo Accords. Assessments vary but a conservative estimate would place their number at over 100. Their members came from a variety of social, educational, and geographic backgrounds. Some were organized in reaction to the peace agreement while others had existed for years before. The protest groups also varied with regard to the radicalism of their ideologies and their willingness to break the law. Some came from the territories while others were based within the "Green Line" (the border between pre-1967 Israel and the "occupied territories"). What they shared was a low level of status, organization, and resources. Very few of the groups could afford an office or any paid staff, and there was usually only a handful of volunteers in charge of the operation. This lack of assets assured that the vast majority of groups would never get to compete in the central arena. Some groups, however, were more successful than others; they made up for their lack of resources by being novel enough to obtain news coverage. The moral of the story is that if you cannot get in by being important, you have to compensate by being interesting.

Three groups will serve as examples of many protest groups that were active against the agreement. The first is a group known as "The Professors Circle" (Hug Ha'Professorim), a group of academics who organized several years earlier to serve as a right-wing voice within the academic community. The second group is called "This is Our Land" (Zeh Artzainu) and is composed of settlers who organized a plan that became known as "Operation Double" in which they would create 130 new settlements to torpedo the peace process. The third and final group is "Kach" which was the right-wing movement founded by Meir Kahane who had been killed in New York several years before. Following the paths of each of these groups offers important lessons about alternative routes to the news media.

The Professors Circle

The Professors Circle is composed of academics from around the country who organized about six years before the Oslo Accords in an attempt to promote right-wing positions on the topic of the territories. A primary motivation for starting this group was to combat the wide spread assumption within Israel that all academics were leftist. The group started with about 20 members and grew to about 500 at the time of the protests against the Accords. Their resources were meager and all work was carried out by volunteers except one part-time secretary.

This lack of organization and resources made it very difficult for them to carry out any newsworthy activities. They carried out several demonstrations, issued a multitude of press releases, and tried every way they could to get coverage, all with very little success. Interviews with the leaders are full of frustration and anger about their inability to make a dent. An interview with one leader that took place several days after the Hebron massacre provides a good illustration of this feeling:

Access to the media is very difficult. This morning is a classic example. No matter how much you phone, I'm sitting here hoping that despite it all somebody will get back to me. You explain to people: "look what happened Friday morning [the massacre], maybe this is the time to show that there is another way to express dissent." But if every time you bring it in another way they don't relate to you, then you understand why people take more drastic action ... The media wants to see the action ["action" said in English]. They did it during the *intifada*, they did with the Jews. If I want to be cynical I'll say that what happened on Friday was abnormal. You know how much they profit from that, in the sense of selling newspapers, selling televisions?

The Professors felt that they were always losing in the competition over media space, not only to the government but also to other groups that are willing to carry out more radical actions. The Professors had a certain sense of decorum that they were unwilling to undermine to gain access to the news media. Scholarly position papers could hardly compete with political violence.

The Professors tried to carry out gimmicks, but they were subtle and dignified. One of their leaders, for example, walked out of a speech by Foreign Minister Shimon Peres opening an umbrella, intending to symbolize Chamberlain's appeasement to the Nazis. Even this failed to get a picture on the evening news. The leader commented that the only way to make it to television was to get arrested. This same sense of frustration led the Professors to carry out a demonstration *against* the television. They had hoped that the demonstration would somehow increase their standing with the news media. But even this protest was mostly ignored and apart from an apparently futile meeting with the head of the television news department, nothing changed.

The Professors' general approach to the news media is typical of such weak groups. On the one hand they realize their tremendous need for the news media to expand their influence. One professor compared it to a piece of research that remained in the drawer – it has no significance unless it gets publicized. Yet they were incapable of producing anything that was newsworthy. They had no one in charge of dealing with the news media, they had no strategy for handling the media, and their understanding of how journalists operate was extremely limited. What they did understand is that their lack of organization and resources had a direct impact on their ability to compete with the government. One leader's comments reflect that understanding:

I just don't have the strength. When it comes down to it, I'm just a working person. I have my obligations to my students, my obligations to my work. I can't run around all the time, it's a full-time job ["full-time job" said in English] to do that. So I just don't think that we will make changes. Because we all, in the final analysis, do it in our free time. With a great deal of good will, but it's not professional. Us against such a well-oiled machine, we don't have a chance.

This is Our Land

The second group, This is Our Land, had a similar lack of organization and resources but they managed to overcome these limitations by providing the news media with a wonderful story. The leadership was composed of three people and a mere thirty people were active in the organization. The group was organized by an *ad hoc* collection of settlers who felt that the best way to oppose the government's peace plan was to double the number of settlements in the territories, making it even more difficult to achieve a compromise with the Palestinians.

The group was in many ways created by the news media. The initial idea for "Operation Double" was sent by fax to many settlements and discovered by the press. The major newspaper in Israel published it as a "secret plan" and framed it as a major scoop. A leader of Our Land was asked why he felt the plan created such excitement in the press:

It really kept them in suspense. Actually what we had here was the first time there was a practical plan of opposition to what was happening. In other words, it was not your standard protest. Rather an attempt, I defined it as a plan, an attempt to put the government in a situation that it can't deal with . . . a situation that will halt the process and maybe bring down the government . . . It is a conflict that goes from being a conflict of ideas or shouting to a power struggle. Not teasing but definitely a question of power: who will coerce whom? Till now people talked about the dogs barking as the convoy moved on. Now we are talking about an attempt to stop the convoy and the press was fascinated.

There is, till today, a serious question about whether "Operation Double" was intended as a media gimmick from the very beginning or a sincere attempt to carry out an authentic challenge to the peace process. The initial reports were given a good deal of credence because the plan was attributed to the powerful Settlers' Council instead of to the weak group of individuals who were the real force behind the plan. Nevertheless, even the most naive of observers, and certainly the journalists themselves, could hardly believe that any group could create 120 settlements within such a short period.

The idea, however, had a life of its own and the actions designed to implement the plan provided the news media with all of the components of a good news story: drama, action, and violence. The group would take a couple of dozen people out to vacant land, set up a few tents, put up a flag and declare it a settlement. The Israeli government contributed to the drama of the story by making two mistakes. First, they ordered every new "settler" arrested which provided dramatic footage at each site. Secondly, they declared the confrontation areas "a closed military zone," presumedly to prevent granting any free publicity. As often happens, this latter decision had a boomerang effect by increasing the value of the story and creating a bond between settler leaders and the press.

Whatever the initial intentions of the group, "Operation Double" soon turned into a huge media gimmick. As one leader put it: "For those who watch CNN all you need is a tent, a fence and a generator to call it a settlement. They can't tell the difference between that and Ariel [a major Jewish city in the territories]." The medium was the message for this operation and the fact that not one settlement was ever created was of little significance. Here was a visual conflict between settlers and the army over the building of new settlements that provided a vivid illustration of the more general struggle over the Oslo Accords. One leader described the technique he developed for making sure these "settlements" received the proper coverage before they were torn down by the army.

The most important thing when you are setting up a settlement is that people will see it. What do I mean that it will be seen? That the [Israeli] people will see it, not that we'll see it. Now I have a problem. The minute that people come to a settlement, the army comes and takes it down. I must have the settlement established and photographed before it's taken down. So I take the cameras there before I take the people there. Or I take the hard core of people and then have the cameras come ... Another problem. The army is smart. It doesn't follow the people, it follows the photographers. They know that the photographers will bring them to the right place. So what I would do is take the photographers that I don't care about, like the foreign photographers whom I don't care about anyway and leave them with all the other people. I personally took the photographer from *Yediot* [the newspaper with the highest circulation], put him in a cab and sent him to the right place.

This story offers lessons not only about the centrality of the news media in such events, but also about the ways in which the relative value of each news medium has a direct influence on its ability to collect information. *Yediot* offered the widest possible audience and thus it was given access to the best pictures, while competitors were left in the dust.

How do we reconcile the seeming sophistication of this group in dealing with the news media with their lack of organization and resources? Digging deeper one finds that it is probably more realistic to suggest that This is Our Land stumbled into fame rather than planned it. As noted above, it was actually the press who discovered the "secret plan," and it turned out that this drama met all of the standard definitions of news.

There are several bits of evidence that support this notion. First, the leaders themselves talk about how "green" they were when it came to the news media, how little they understood it. The impression one gets is that they were simply swept away by all of the publicity and tried to ride it for as long as they could. Secondly, none of the journalists are very proud about the extensive coverage they gave to "Operation Double." In hindsight, most admit that they too got carried away by the drama and gave far too much attention to what proved to be an unimportant side show.

The journalists did, however, get their revenge on the movement. After the large buildup, several journalists turned on the group, writing scathing attacks about how the whole "operation" was a big fake. The most damaging article was entitled "Operation Bluff" [Mivtza Awanta] and was written in the style of an exposé.

Group leaders decided to boycott the journalist who wrote that article but it is safe to assume that he did not lose too much sleep over it. This offers another illustration of the ways in which value and need influence the transactions between journalists and sources. Journalists have little trouble writing such stories about weak groups, but they would be much more worried about burning a valuable source. The boycott probably hurt the group much more than the journalist.[3]

The leaders of This is Our Land soon learned one of the most important lessons in this field for weak antagonists: the higher you rise, the steeper you fall. There is something ironic about the fact that the same journalists who blew up the balloon were also responsible for popping it.[4] The press represents a powerful but dangerous type of weapon; many of those who use it end up getting hurt. One of the group leaders put it this way:

We just didn't realize that it is a fire and one should be careful. You should get warm from the light but don't get too close. The closer we got and the closer we let them get to us, the more we got burnt.

This is Our Land took over a year to recover from their bitter experience with the news media. They then returned to the protest scene with an entirely new set of provocations, many of which received a considerable amount of publicity. The most important acts were a number of nationwide highway blockings designed to bring traffic to a halt. Pictures of police dragging supporters off the roads provided the same level of drama as the previous images of soldiers dispersing would-be settlers. The group called for massive civil disobedience claiming that they were following in the footsteps of Martin Luther King and Gandhi. As in the past, however, their ability to stay in the news depended

---

[3] Group leaders also suggested that if they had to do it all over again, they would be much more careful about using rewards and punishments as a means of punishing journalists. I believe that such an attitude is another sign of a lack of understanding of how the news media works. I have never met a professional spokesperson who believed that the use of rewards and punishments was, in the long run, an effective means of managing the news.

[4] There are certainly other examples of this phenomenon. Journalists can build up unknown candidates for office and then use that fame as a hook for tearing the candidates down. They can dramatize stories of terrorism, then write exposé pieces on how the news media help terrorists. The news media often creates their own news peg.

entirely on their ability to carry out newsworthy forms of political deviance.

Kach

The Kach movement represents the prototypical back-door challenger. Kach is the most radical of the right-wing movements in terms of both its ideology and its tactics. Its ideology calls for the "transfer" [expulsion] of the entire Palestinian population from the territories, and their tactics allegedly include "reprisal raids" against Arab villages that, at the very least, involve considerable property damage. Baruch Goldstein, who was responsible for the Hebron massacre, was a member of Kach. Although there is no evidence that the movement itself was behind the murders, movement leaders made no secret of their support for Goldstein's actions and this was one factor that led to the Rabin government's decision to outlaw the organization and place its leaders under administrative arrest.

Their role as political deviants within Israeli society, however, goes back long before the Oslo Accords (Sprinzak, 1991). The height of the Kach movement's success came when its leader, Meir Kahane, was elected to the Knesset in 1984. He was considered a social outcast in the Knesset and the country went through a long period of soul-searching to try to explain how a racist party could have gotten elected.[5] The Kach list was banned from running in subsequent elections when both major parties declared it a racist movement.

The news media was an important agent in this process of condemning Kahane and his beliefs. One radio station devoted an entire day of broadcasting to the issue of racism after Kahane's election. Kahane's followers point out that their leader was not even allowed to respond to the charges made against him during that broadcast. There was also an official decision taken by the national radio and television networks to boycott Kahane to prevent him from using the news media to gain more supporters. This policy was later overturned in a precedent-setting decision of the Supreme Court. Nevertheless, in the entire period when Kahane was a Knesset member, he was never invited to participate in a single talk show on either radio or television.

The Kach movement does have some important advantages over the other protest movements. Its organization is larger, better financed, and much more experienced than any other groups except the Settlers' Council. Kach has branches all over the country and can carry out

---

[5] It is perhaps useful to point out that due to the rather unusual electoral system in Israel, Kahane only needed 1 per cent of the total vote to win a Knesset seat.

collective actions at a moment's notice. They are also a well-known group and have developed long-term relationships with many journalists who cover their activities. In addition, unlike groups such as the Professors Circle, their statements and their behavior are almost always considered exceptional. Thus, their inherent news value is much greater than any of the other small protest groups.

Nevertheless, they also have a high level of dependency on the news media, and the press was always a central element in movement strategy. Kahane was a master at creating publicity stunts and was often able to steal the limelight from much larger and more organized movements (Wolfsfeld, 1984a). The news media became even more important after the leader's death in order to prove that they could carry on without him.

There are several indicators that point to the centrality of the news media in their general strategy. They send faxes and beeper messages to reporters every day, their spokesperson plays a major role in the planning and execution of events, and they maintain an immense archive of media material that includes clippings not only of their own exploits but also those of their enemies. It is also revealing that Kach leaders refused to sign an agreement that would have let them out of prison if they promised to avoid the press.

There is an interesting argument between Kach and the other protest groups about the amount of media attention given to Kahane's followers. While Kach leaders claim that the media boycott continues, other leaders complain that Kach gets a disproportionate amount of press attention. The other groups find it difficult to compete with Kach's natural appeal. The comments of the founder of the Professors Circle are typical:

I'm trying to tell the public that there is a center, a sane right, that wants to use the proper means to bring a different opinion and it just doesn't work. I personally have been at demonstrations in which the Kach people came. I brought a big banner ... to try to hide Kach. So you come to the demonstration and Kach goes and takes a picture of Prime Minister Rabin, burns it, and all the cameras and all the print reporters run for it. You're standing there like a poor slob [Misken], uninteresting because you're sane, you're normal. It's a difficult struggle and we don't manage to overcome it.

The comparison of four different movements, each of which was attempting to achieve a similar set of goals provides a better understanding of the alternative strategies available for breaking into the news media. Those who have done research in the field will have little trouble recognizing similar movements in other political settings.

The Settlers' Council was in some ways more of an institution than a movement. It had the status, organization, and resources to be considered a major player. Its strategy was to use massive demonstrations, a series of smaller, more annoying type of collective action, and to flood the news media with information. The Settlers' Council is the strongest of challengers, with recognized political figures who enjoy regular access to the news media.

The Professors Circle was mostly an *ad hoc* group that did not really have a media strategy. Their political ideology and their sense of decorum ensured a continual frustration over their inability to break in. They represent the challengers who always find the gate to the central arena permanently locked and bolted.

This is Our Land is a movement which specialized in civil disobedience. This type of strategy is one way to overcome the inherent dilemma of weak groups who have to choose between obscurity and negative news stories. Such groups attempt to find the exact place in the escalation curve where provocation comes to be considered violence. The advantages of sit-ins and blocking roads and the like is that one is in a much better position to be framed as a victim, rather than an aggressor. Such groups achieve drama without paying too high a price in terms of legitimacy.

Finally there is Kach, the bad boys. Their claim to fame is being more radical than anyone else, by making outrageous statements and threats. They are given almost automatic passage through Deviants' Gate while groups like the Professors Circle must stand outside in the cold, gnashing their teeth as Kach passes by. Like the Settlers' Council, Kach is allowed to compete regularly for media space. However, as detailed in the next chapter, the condition of their entrance is that they remain in costume during filming.

The struggle for political control

Having met the contestants, we can move on to the battle itself. In keeping with the major theme of this work it is important to look at the struggle over the media as part of a larger and more significant contest over political control. The major goal of the Rabin government was to keep the peace process moving forward and to convince the Israeli public that any concessions would bring genuine peace between Israel and the Palestinians. The goal of the opposition was to stop the process before the final agreement could be signed in Cairo, and to persuade Israelis that the Declaration of Principles would bring nothing but more bloodshed.

Government control over the political environment tended to waver during this period and this had a direct and immediate influence on the contest over the news media. This becomes clearer when one considers the three variables discussed in Chapter 1: the ability of the authorities to initiate and control events, their ability to regulate the flow of information, and their ability to mobilize elite support.

The government could exercise a fair amount of control regarding the peace process itself. While the talks did stall from time to time, progress was being made and they commanded a great deal of public interest. From the very beginning, however, it was clear that terrorism would continue. Every terrorist attack placed the government on the defensive and provided important opportunities for challengers to express their own views on the Oslo Accords. The massive protests organized against the agreement were another indicator of the government's lack of political control.

The level of government control over the flow of information was dictated by the fact that this was a crisis over peace rather than over war. While the public and journalists are willing to suspend certain freedoms during times of war, they insist upon full disclosure in times of peace. One reason for the initial breakthrough in Oslo was that the discussions were kept secret until the agreement was signed. The interviews with government officials revealed that the presence of the media made subsequent negotiations much more difficult. The public was kept fully informed of every concession made by Rabin and any snags in the talks. The press also had no trouble gaining access to the site of every terrorist attack or protest. In short, the flow of information during the debate over the Oslo Accords was typical of those that characterize public controversies in Western democracies.

The Rabin government also had little chance of mobilizing a broad level of political consensus around the Oslo Accords among elites. The government held a slim majority in the Knesset and most of the population opposed any recognition of the PLO. While early polls showed most of the population in favor of the agreement, the continuing terror attacks chipped steadily away at that figure and a year after the signing only 25 per cent of the Israeli public believed that the PLO would keep its end of the agreement (Levinsohn and Katz, 1994). Debates in the Knesset over the Accords were fierce and frequent.

The struggle for political control over the Oslo Accords was a genuine contest. The Rabin government had the upper hand, for it was carrying out a major policy initiative and the challengers were forced to react to these developments. Nevertheless, the challengers had plenty of soldiers and ammunition of their own and anyone who followed the confrontation could be assured that they would see a first-rate match.

To get some sense of how this struggle for political control was reflected in the news media, I conducted a content analysis of articles that appeared in two important Israeli newspapers: *Yediot Ahronot* and *Ha'aretz*. *Yediot* is the most popular newspaper in Israel. It has the largest circulation in the country and while it does not sink to the level of some tabloids in other Western countries, its marketing strategy does emphasize drama and human interest over sophisticated analysis. *Ha'aretz* is considered the elite paper in Israel and generally adopts a more serious, reflective, contextual approach to the news.

The analysis was carried out on fifty days of news articles that appeared during the period under study: August 27, 1993 to May 5, 1994. The fifty days were selected at random and the analysis looked at all news articles about the peace process that appeared in the first three pages of each newspaper.[6] The results of this analysis offer a closer view of the struggle over media space that characterized this critical period in the Israeli–Palestinian peace process.

There were four major news stories that dominated this period. The first major set of stories focused on the peace process itself. This included reports about the initial breakthrough at Oslo, the signing ceremonies, stories about the amount of progress in negotiations leading to the Cairo Accords, and the economic and political benefits that could come from peace with the Palestinians.

The second major news story looked at the opposition to the Accords, especially by the movements discussed above. These stories included mostly reports of the actual protest actions, actions that were being taken by the government to control the illegal and violent aspects of the protest, and statements by protest leaders against the agreement.

The third major set of news stories dealt with the terrorist attacks. These stories focused mostly on the attacks themselves, the funerals of the victims, and what measures the government was taking to prevent terrorism.

The last major news story in this period was the Hebron massacre in which Baruch Goldstein murdered thirty-nine Palestinians. The stories centered on the attack itself, the victims, government condemnations, analyses about who was responsible for allowing it to happen, implications of the attack on the Israeli–Palestinian negotiations, and government actions against right-wing movements such as Kach designed to prevent further incidents.

The proportion of stories and space given to each of these news stories are presented in Figure 4.1. These results offer a helpful summary of the

---

[6]   For more details see the methodological appendix.

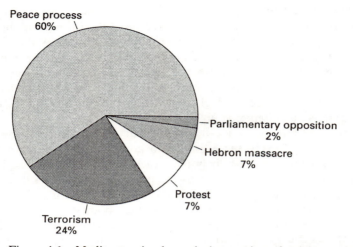

Figure 4.1   Media attention by topic (proportion of articles appearing on pages 1 to 3 on sample days in *Yediot Ahronot* and *Ha'aretz*)

amount of media attention given to each of these topics. Note that this first analysis does not say anything about the tone or direction of these articles, only about the amount of media attention given to each topic.[7] I shall deal with the quality of coverage in the next chapter that analyzes the contest over media frames.

A quantitative analysis says nothing about the *impact* of the different stories. A thousand words that report about the state of the peace talks are unlikely to have the same impact as a similar amount of space devoted to describing the death and destruction from a terrorist attack. This analysis does, however, provide some insights into which voices were heard the most. The subject titles also offer a rough indication about which antagonists received the most benefit from each set of stories.

The picture that emerges reflects much of what has been said until now. The Rabin government did indeed have the upper hand in setting the media's agenda. Reports about the peace process were especially likely to dominate the front pages of both newspapers and they also took precedence in terms of the number of articles written and the amount of space devoted to the topic. The news value of these events was indisputable.

The government, however, paid a heavy price for their lack of control

---

[7]   The results are very similar when one measures the amount of space given to each topic or the number of front-page stories.

over terrorism. The terrorism stories occupied a major portion of media space that the government would have preferred to exploit for other purposes. It is also reasonable to assume that the impact of these stories far outweighed their numerical proportion. This would be especially true in the more popular newspaper *Yediot Ahronot*. Not only did *Yediot* devote much more attention to terrorism than *Ha'aretz*, but the coverage of these incidents included glaringly large red headlines and horrific photographs that often took up an entire page.

There was also news about protest, but the numbers suggest how difficult it was for the these groups to compete with the government agenda. Surprisingly, this analysis revealed even fewer articles devoted to the *parliamentary* opposition to the peace agreement. In this case at least, the movements were much more successful than the Knesset members in obtaining media attention. The settlers were considered the major victims of the peace process and, combined with their ability to generate a variety of collective actions, proved to be more newsworthy than than the elected opposition.

The right-wing movements, however, had their own problems of event control. As with the terrorist attacks, the impact of the Hebron massacre was far greater than suggested by a simple comparison of the amount of space devoted to the subject.[8] The interview material show that the Hebron massacre placed the settlers' movement on the defensive; it offered movement critics a convenient vehicle for portraying settlers as violent fanatics.[9] Many events planned by the Settlers' Council scheduled for those weeks had to be canceled until the political waves generated by that incident began to abate.

The final analysis looks at the competition over access among the various movements. The ability of a movement to achieve access to the news media is one of the most important indicators of political standing. The question of which movements achieve standing in the news media has important political consequences not only for the future of the movement itself, but also for the opposition as a whole. If the more radical movements can get more media attention than moderate ones, it undermines opposition attempts to achieve public legitimacy.

Analyzing this competition is not as simple as one might think. First, many news articles about protests describe several different groups and activities within a single piece and this makes it difficult to look at the

---

[8]   It should also be remembered that the content analysis is based on a random sample of fifty days which runs throughout the period. The Hebron massacre occurred on February 14 and the days which fell into the sample are February 21, 25, and 28.

[9]   The inability of the Rabin government to prevent the Hebron massacre also created serious problems for Israel in their negotiations with the Palestinians.

number of articles and space devoted to a particular movement. Secondly, it is not always clear just who has organized each action. This is especially likely to occur regarding small protests carried out by settlers. Some are spontaneous and *ad hoc*, others are coordinated with the Settlers' Council, and yet others are planned and managed by the Council.[10] In addition, the Council itself often prefers to remain in the background because a multitude of spontaneous protests produces a more authentic image than if those same actions are attributed to an institution.[11] Even the journalists who covered these events were unable to tell us about the extent of Council involvement.

The analysis will focus on the number of articles that mentioned one of the four groups described above: The Settlers' Council, Kach, This is Our Land, and the Professors Circle.[12] A fifth category was constructed containing those articles that referred to settlers without mentioning any specific organization.[13] While it can be assumed that those who participated in these actions have some type of relationship to the Settlers' Council, there is no way to know if the Council was directly involved in planning or executing these events. I shall use the term "settlers" or "settlers' movement" to refer to all actions by settlers, and "Settlers' Council" when speaking specifically about that organization. It should also be noted that some articles are counted more than once when more than one group is mentioned in a single piece. The results are presented in Figure 4.2.

The findings generally confirm the more subjective evaluations of the leaders and journalists. The two major movements which dominated coverage during this period are the settlers and Kach. Both have higher levels of organization and resources than any of the other movements and Kach has the added "advantage" of being considered extremist. It is true that many settler actions were not attributed directly to the Council but as noted the benefits of this confusion probably outweighed the

---

[10] Even the notion of "coordination" is somewhat complicated. Most of the various movements set up a "United Headquarters" which was responsible for coordinating the overall campaign against the government. The Settlers' Council supplied most of the organization and resources for this body but each group had its own representative sitting on the steering committee.

[11] The Council also sometimes receives "credit" for acts it doesn't carry out. Thus, "Operation Double" was initially treated as a secret plan of the Settlers' Council which may have led to it getting much more credibility than it deserved.

[12] A small splinter group called "Kahane Chi" (Kahane Lives) was included in the Kach category. This group was founded by Meir Kahane's son and it merged with the larger group when both organizations were declared illegal movements after the Hebron massacre.

[13] There are two ways to refer to settlers in Hebrew: "Mityashavim" and "Mitnachlim." The second term is considered more controversial for it refers only to those settlers who live in the territories.

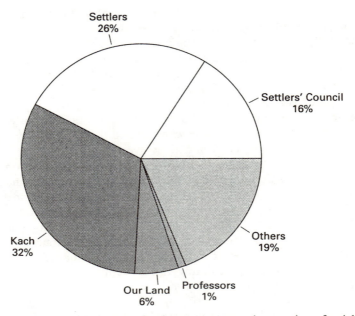

Figure 4.2   Media attention by protest group (proportion of articles in which each group is mentioned in *Yediot Ahronot* and *Ha'aretz*)

costs. The media gimmick of "Operation Double" provided This is Our Land with advantages over the dozens of other groups competing, but it can hardly compare to the media status achieved by the Settlers' Council and Kach. Finally, these results also show that the sense of frustration expressed by the Professors Circle was well founded. Months of activity and efforts produced very little coverage.

A closer look at the competition between the settlers' movement and Kach offers an important demonstration of how political events can change the amount of access granted to various antagonists. The critical event during this period was the Hebron massacre. The results presented in Figure 4.3 show the number of articles devoted to the various movements before and after the massacre.

The first period, before Hebron, can be considered "politics as normal." The settlers could use their organization and resources to become the major voice against the Oslo Accords. Kach was considered a fairly marginal group, mentioned in only 13 percent of these articles in this period. After Hebron, Kach was transformed into a major player and received 45 percent of the references.

Critical events, such as the Hebron massacre, change the political

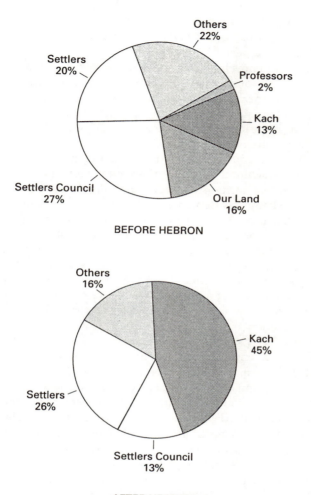

Figure 4.3   Media attention by protest group before and after Hebron massacre (proportion of articles in which each group is mentioned in *Yediot Ahronot* and *Ha'aretz*)

context. They do so because the perceived importance of such events forces political actors to stop and reassess their positions and behavior. The news media are especially sensitive to such changes due to their professional interest in novelty. The change in context creates news pegs as journalists look for sources and stories linked to that event. Baruch Goldstein was a member of Kach and Kach's importance rose accordingly. The government also contributed to this process by outlawing the Kach movement in reaction to the massacre. Quite of few of the references to Kach were official references about what would be "done" about Kach. News media amplified and reinforced this change in context by moving Kach to the foreground of public attention. This was hardly the image the opposition wanted, but all they could do was wait until the tidal wave known as Baruch Goldstein began to subside.

The massacre also had an important effect on the government's efforts to promote the peace process. There were no articles about the peace negotiations because they had been halted. There were no articles about the benefits of peace, because for several months after Hebron many believed that peace was impossible. Losing control over Baruch Goldstein was in some ways as big a problem for the Rabin government as it was for the right-wing opposition. Both paid for that mistake, politically and in the news media.

As this book was being completed, the world received a tragically vivid illustration of the influence of critical events on the role of the media. Prime Minister Rabin was assassinated on November 4, 1995. The press turned on the right-wing with a vengeance and the movements were forced to take cover. Those who had opposed the government, especially those who had broken the law, were publicly vilified and "right-wing incitement" was the dominant frame for explaining the murder. Movement leaders were asked about their sense of responsibility and whether they had done any "soul-searching" after the assassination. A frantic search was carried out to find file footage of protests which included pictures of Rabin as a Nazi and of chants calling him a traitor. All protests were cancelled. Leaders from This is Our Land and Kach found themselves faced with criminal charges for their previous actions and news stories focused on their crimes. The political environment had changed once again, and with it, the role of the news media.

Summary

To understand the struggle among antagonists over media access one begins by constructing the base line and then looks to the struggle over political control to explain how the battle unfolds. The base line is determined by the status, organization, and resources of each player and the ability and willingness of each to carry out exceptional behavior. It is the struggle over political control, however, which often generates the most important deviations from that base line, in part because journalists love surprises.

Movements that hope to overcome the natural advantages enjoyed by the government must wait for the right political wave to bring them into the arena. This wave usually comes as a major disaster or threat and this is exactly how the Israeli right-wing viewed the Oslo Accords. Here too, organization and resources established the base line and the Settlers' Council enjoyed significant advantages over the dozens of other movements that were struggling to find a way to be heard. They remained the major players for the first few months until Baruch Goldstein changed the contest for everyone.

Similarly, the initial breakthrough at Oslo presented the Rabin government with a powerful vehicle for dominating public discourse. The novelty, the pageantry, and the political significance of that story combined with the routine access granted to authorities provided the government with a wonderful opportunity for promoting the peace process through the media. But the government's control over the political environment was far from complete, and this provided important opportunities for the opposition. The continued terrorism in Israel was especially damaging to Rabin's plans. Public attention was diverted and momentum was lost.

The struggle over media access can only be understood by looking at both the characteristics of the players involved and the political dynamics that distinguish each conflict. It was the political breakthrough at Oslo that provided the Rabin government with such an attractive package to supply. It was that same political process that brought thousands to demonstrate in anger, increasing the ability of the right-wing movements to carry out newsworthy events. These political changes also led the news media to assign special reporters to cover the settlers, due to the radical change these citizens were about to endure. It was also politics as much as resources that determined the obscurity of the Professors Circle and the fame of Kach. Finally, it was a political assassination which ensured that those who supported Rabin would be given unlimited access to attack those who had opposed him.

The contest over media space, however, is only one part of the story. Gaining access to the news media is only the first stage in the struggle for public legitimacy. The second is to achieve the type of coverage that furthers one's political goals. The discussion turns then to the struggle over meaning.

5 Competing frames of the Oslo Accords: a chance for peace or a national disaster?

The contest between authorities and movements over media frames usually centers on two types of issues. The first competition revolves around ideological issues such as the American debate over abortion. The second issue has to do with frames of the movement itself, about whether it can be considered a legitimate representative for those who oppose the government. One of the most effective ways of undermining a movement's claims is to have it framed as unimportant, weird, or dangerous.

Journalistic routines for covering movements often facilitate such frames. The news media often focus on the most radical elements within a movement and demand continual drama as an entrance fee for entering the arena. In addition, journalists feel obligated to place movements on a continuum of respectability that runs from crazy extremists to law-abiding citizens with a legitimate grievance. The challenge for movements is to produce events that are novel enough to be considered news, yet moderate enough to be considered legitimate.

A study of the struggle over the Oslo Accords demonstrates that these principles can be applied to right-wing movements just as well as to those on the left. The Israeli news media were much more interested in what the settlers' movement would do, rather than what they had to say. The news media is interested in events, not ideology. The fact that the settlers opposed the agreement could hardly be considered news. The important news question centered on how far they would go to stop it. This meant that the settlers spent just as much time struggling over news frames about the movement as they did trying to promote their frames about the Oslo Accords.

Here too, political events had a critical impact on the outcome of this struggle. Major events can change the reference points that are being used by activists, authorities, the press, and the public. The breakthrough at Oslo, the continuation of the terrorist attacks, and the Hebron massacre all had important effects on the ability of the two antagonists to promote their frames to the Israeli news media.

104

A more comprehensive understanding of the variations in these cultural contests requires a closer look at both the events themselves and the ways in which journalists use events to produce news.

A chance for peace or a national disaster?

The analysis begins by looking at the frames being promoted by each side in the conflict, and then attempts to evaluate their successes and failures. The frames of the government and the opposition are summarized in Table 5.1 using the signature matrix developed by Gamson and Lasch (1983) as an analytical tool. I have added one additional component, that of "meta-frames," which allows us to link these particular frames with deeper cultural frames.

The frame contest between the right and the left in Israel goes back years before the establishment of the state, but the most relevant battles began after the 1967 Six-Day War and continue till today. The right-wing position is that the territories captured in the war are part of the historic "land of Israel" and therefore should be annexed. The left wing promotes the idea of territorial compromise, arguing that peace can only be achieved by giving back some of the territories taken in 1967.

The frames being promoted by each side came directly from these two ideologies. The left was attempting to show that the PLO was a genuine partner for reconciliation. The PLO, they argued, is the most moderate faction among the Palestinians and is willing to compromise and accept Israel's right to exist. Further, Israel cannot and should not rule over another people; the price of occupation is far too high. The only real solution to the problem of terrorism is a political settlement. The PLO, they argued, can deal much more effectively with terrorism that we do.

Peace with the Palestinians, the Rabin government claimed, will move us closer to peace between Israel and its Arab neighbors, and will bring increased prosperity to the entire region. Israel will have diplomatic relations with the vast majority of the world and the Middle East can become a major economic power. The government contended that those who oppose this agreement are destroying an excellent opportunity to achieve Israel's most important aspirations. They are fanatics who insist upon looking backwards at the old conflicts and hatreds rather than forward to the endless possibilities provided by this dramatic breakthrough. Too much blood has been shed over the years, and it is time to stop the cycle of violence.

The right-wing opposition, on the other hand, considered the agreement to be a national disaster. They argued that the Palestinians never gave up their goal of destroying Israel, only changed their tactics.

Table 5.1 *Competing frames of the Oslo peace agreement*

Meta-frame	Territorial compromise	The complete Israel
Package	A chance for peace	National disaster
Core frame	The issue is whether we can achieve peace with our neighbors through compromise.	The issue is whether we are willing to surrender our national rights to our enemies and risk the destruction of Israel.
Core position	Israel must give up land in order to achieve peace with our neighbors. The Israel–PLO agreement is just such a compromise.	Israel's agreement with the PLO constitutes a grave danger to Israel's existence. Israel should cancel the agreement.
Metaphors	Dove/Time bomb	Suicide
Historical exemplars	Peace with Egypt/Algeria	World War II (Chamberlain/Vichy Government)/Yom Kippur War
Catchphrases	Give peace a chance/Enough blood, enough tears/Let the sun rise/Peace is my security	The Land of Israel is in danger/The Land of Israel is not for sale/Rabin is a traitor
Depictions	PLO as the more moderate force among the Palestinians/The settlers as opponents to peace/Israel as a democratic country who cannot rule over another people	The PLO as terrorists who kill woman and children/The left as stupid, naive, or traitorous for giving up Israel's security
Visual images	Signing of accords in Jerusalem and Washington/Palestinians celebrating peace accords	Dead and wounded from terrorist attacks/Arafat's face/Palestinians wearing kefiyahs as masks/Rabin in kefiyah
Roots	New willingness of Palestinians to accept Israel's right to exist	A Palestinian state/Destruction of Israel
Consequences	Peace and prosperity for the entire Middle East	A Palestinian state/Destruction of Israel
Appeals to principle	Israel's eternal striving for peace/The end of oppression of another people.	The right of the Jewish people to the Land of Israel/The survival of the Jewish state

The PLO national charter continued to call for the destruction of Israel. The Palestinians had long ago settled on the "Stages Plan" for the destruction of the state. The opposition contends that the Palestinians intend to use any land given up by Israel as a beachhead for taking the rest.

Arafat and his cronies, the right argues, have never kept their word about anything, including their promise to stop terrorism. The PLO has a very convenient division of labor with the Hamas – Arafat gets diplomatic recognition, and Hamas terrorists continue to do the dirty work. The Gaza Strip will become a safe haven for terrorists and Israel will be unable to do anything about it. The Oslo agreement is a complete surrender by Israel that will inevitably lead to a Palestinian state that can threaten Israel's very existence.

The settlers are the true pioneers of Israel, the right wing argued. Israel must continue to create settlements in Judaea, Samaria, and Gaza. If Israel had given in to the Arabs in 1948, there would never have been a Jewish state. We won't go back on the experience of Yamit, they argued. No Israeli government will ever be allowed to uproot people from their homes again.

These then are the frames each side was attempting to promote. The contest over media frames of the Oslo Accords should be seen as part of a more general political contest between the Israeli right and the left. The debate over territorial compromise was always an intensive contest between two fairly equal sections of the population. The news media always served as the central arena, and it was clear from the beginning that the stadium was being prepared for a genuine battle.

As suggested, the struggle between the settlers movement and the Rabin government revolved around two issues: the viability of the peace agreement, and the legitimacy of the movement's actions in opposing it. The movement's success and failures in these two areas can be best understood by organizing the remainder of the discussion around the three framing questions discussed in Chapter 2:

1. What do we know about this conflict?
2. What is the most newsworthy aspect of the conflict?
3. Who are the good guys?

What do we know about this conflict?

The goal of the Rabin government during this period was to frame the PLO as a partner and to frame the settlers as obstacles to peace. The settlers' movement's goal was just the opposite: to discredit the Palestinians by having them framed as terrorists and to increase their own legitimacy as patriots struggling to save the country from disaster. It is important, therefore, to begin this discussion by considering the previous frames of each of these groups. While existing frames of the PLO worked to the movement's advantage, their own public image before Oslo can be considered a definite point against them.

Before Oslo, the Israeli media frame of the PLO was one reserved for enemies. The PLO was seen as a terrorist organization and there was a national consensus against recognizing the organization. Until the elections of 1992, it was forbidden even to interview Palestinian leaders from any organization on television or radio. Thus, such figures as Feisal Husseini and Chanan Ashrawi – who were already media celebrities in the United States – were totally ignored by the Israeli broadcast media. The Palestinians most likely to be featured in the Israeli press were either terrorists or rioting mobs appearing in *intifada* coverage. The more independent newspapers carried many stories about PLO political developments and announcements, but interviews were rare.[1]

It was also illegal for any Israeli to meet with any member of the PLO. Abie Natan, a left-wing activist, was put in jail for such a meeting and this act of civil disobedience became a major news story. Those who supported talks with the PLO were considered leftist extremists. Thus, during the 1992 election campaign, when Rabin was accused by his opponents of considering negotiations with the PLO, he vehemently denied the charge. Upon election, Rabin also refused to bring members of the Arab Israeli parties into his government, in part because of their close relations with the PLO. In short, before Oslo the PLO was considered the enemy and the Israeli news media covered the organization accordingly.

A thawing in the political environment was reflected in the media coverage even before Oslo. The Israel Broadcasting Authority changed its policy regarding interviews with Palestinians soon after the Rabin government took office. Feisal Husseini and other Palestinian leaders soon became regulars on Israeli news shows, although due to legal restrictions they could never officially claim membership of the PLO. The law banning contact with the PLO was one of the first to be repealed by the new government, an additional sign of changing norms. Here again, we see the ways in which political developments lead to significant changes in media frames.

Nevertheless, the transformation of Arafat from terrorist to peace partner was an uphill battle for the Rabin government. An illustration of these cultural difficulties can be found by looking at the brouhaha that developed at the time of the first official meeting between Rabin and Arafat at the signing in Washington on September 13, 1993. The major issue was whether Rabin or Foreign Minister Shimon Peres would have to shake Arafat's hand, a task that all agreed would be odious. Even commentators on the left side of the political spectrum acknowledged the difficulty in shaking the hand that "had so much Israeli blood on it," but most felt it was a necessary "sacrifice" for peace.[2]

Many advantages enjoyed by the right wing due to the PLO's

---

[1]   It is also important to recall that the PLO itself was reluctant to give such interviews to Israeli journalists for it was considered a sign of recognition.

[2]   The importance of political context can be illustrated by pointing to the fact that there was no similar controversy when Rabin shook King Hussein's hand. While the Jordanian army killed a lot more Israelis than the Palestinians, Hussein was considered an "honorable enemy."

negative media image were offset by the settlers' own image problems. The settlers were often framed in the Israeli media as trouble-makers and religious fanatics. The images of the settlers as extremists began early, in part because some early settlements were illegal and their establishment was often marked by fierce confrontations with the Israeli army. This media frame was given more salience in the violent struggle against the evacuation of the town of Yamit given back to the Egyptians in 1979 (Wolfsfeld, 1984a). This frame was given further support during the *intifada*, when several settlers were brought up on charges for shooting and killing Arabs in what they claimed were acts of self-defense.

The lowest point in the settlers' media image before Oslo was the discovery of the Jewish underground in 1984 (Sprinzak, 1991). Although the Israeli press was understandably reluctant to use the term, the underground was a group of Jewish terrorists who carried out several attacks on Palestinian civilians and were arrested just before they were going to blow up an Arab bus. Thus, the settlers had been framed as violent extremists long before Baruch Goldstein carried out the Hebron massacre.

It is also helpful to remember that settlers had some very significant enemies. The United States, most of Europe, and the United Nations had all framed the settlements as obstacles to peace. The fact that most of the settlers were religious and that some of the more conspicuous leaders claimed to be on a messianic mission, also made it easier to label them as deviants. Finally, one of Rabin's central messages in the 1992 elections was that it was time to stop wasting money on the "spoiled" settlers and start spending it in the rest of the country where it could be better put to use. Thus, not only were the settlers often framed as political extremists, they were also portrayed as economic parasites living off handouts from the rest of the country.

The settlers' problems with the news media then, go back much further than the Oslo Accords. Their normal activities of building settlements and expanding their communities were rarely considered newsworthy. Although about half of the Israeli population supports the establishment of settlements in the occupied territories, the settlers only become prominent in the news as law breakers and extremists. It is no small wonder that most of the settlers feel hostility towards the press.

In summary, it can be said that the previous frames of the PLO worked to the advantage of the settlers' movement, while the settlers' own image made it easier for the government to discredit them. It is important to understand this starting point for it offers an important insight about the contest to follow. The settlers found it much easier to promote a negative frame of the Palestinians than to promote a positive frame of themselves.[3]

What is the most newsworthy part of the story?

After the signing of the Oslo Accords, the Israeli media focused on two central questions:
1. Was the peace process working?
2. What was the opposition doing to stop it?
While there is some overlap between these two issues, it is helpful to discuss media frames about the viability of the agreement within this section, and deal with the more specific issue of how the settlers' protest was covered in the next.

Journalists attempted to answer these questions by focusing on the most newsworthy information and events they could find. Some of these events provided important advantages to the *chance for peace* frame while others seemed to demonstrate the validity of the *national disaster* frame. The journalists, however, were simply trying to use those events to produce news stories that were both professionally rewarding and culturally familiar.

The best way to sum up the media frame in the Israeli press during this period is with one word, set in capital letters, followed by a question mark: "PEACE?" The word "peace" set in this way represented the most important issue facing the country since its creation – whether Israel could have peace with the Palestinians and its Arab neighbors. The question mark points to the fact that the peace frame was always being contested, and that the issue of who was "right" remained in doubt.

The ambiguity of the Oslo Accords had been a central part of public discourse from the very beginning. The government itself had promoted the "Gaza and Jericho first" plan as a "test," as an "attempt" to see if Arafat could deliver what he had promised. In its simplest form the deal was sold to the Israeli people by saying that Israel would grant autonomy to Gaza and Jericho in exchange for an end to terrorism. If this worked out, then the negotiations would move on to the second stage in which the Israeli army would pull back from the major population areas in the West Bank, elections would be held, and autonomy would be extended to the rest of the territories. Only then would negotiations begin on the

---

[3] Those who study political communication may suggest that this principle holds more generally. The spread of negative political advertising may very well be related to the fact that the press is much more willing to accept negative stories about candidates than positive ones. It would not be at all surprising (or unrelated) to find a similar propensity among citizens.

final settlement that would deal with the thornier issues of Jerusalem and Palestinian statehood. It was only natural then that the Israeli press would constantly focus on the question of whether the agreement was working, whether terrorism was under control, and whether the agreement would lead to peace.

The government was attempting to keep the peace process moving forward while the opposition was attempting to kill it. It is ironic but true that the Islamic fundamentalists proved to be the opposition's greatest allies in promoting challenger frames.[4] The ability of Hamas and other Palestinian groups to continually carry out terrorist attacks provided the most important evidence that the agreement was not working. The media frames constructed during this period focused on the most newsworthy aspects of each move and counter-move and what emerged was a cultural contest between the oracles of peace and the prophets of doom.

The competition between these two frames of the peace process was an important story from the very beginning. Consider the first-page story that appeared in *Yediot* on September 13, 1993 as Rabin was flying to the historic signing ceremony in Washington. The major headline was "With hope and with concern" (B'Tikvah VB'Daaga). Above it was the following secondary headline:

Rabin to Yediot Ahronot, in the plane on the way to Washington: Today there will be four funerals, and I will stand on the White House Lawn. Despite the pain, there is no choice but to continue to fight against those who want to damage the agreement.

The headline that appeared on the same day in the less sensational paper *Ha'aretz* provided a similar ambiguity: "Israel–PLO agreement will be signed today, a wave of attacks in the country."

These conflicting themes remained an important part of coverage throughout the period. The newspaper *Yediot* sometimes provides those who are interested in studying media frames with an important gift. Stories are sometimes placed within actual frames, complete with borders and a colorful icon to ensure that everyone recognizes the frame. The frame is used to connect several different news stories that all relate to the same general topic. One such frame used a thick red border with an icon that had in Hebrew the words: "Peace in the shadow of terrorism." A knife, dripping with blood, was drawn over the word "peace".

---

4   Hamas provides another important example of a challenger who is able successfully to promote their frames to the news media. While future work will deal will this aspect of the issue, this particular analysis focuses on the interactions between internal movements and the news media. Hamas is, therefore, considered here as an outside agent.

The content analysis described in the previous chapter offers important evidence about the direction of the most newsworthy parts of this story. The headlines were divided into sixteen categories according to subject.[5] I then divided these subjects into three smaller categories: those that could be considered good news for the government, those that could be considered bad news for the government, and those that fell somewhere in the middle.

Articles that offered an optimistic frame about the peace process included reports on progress being made in the negotiations with the Palestinians, the ceremonies associated with the peace process, economic benefits that could come from the agreements, international support and acclaim for the agreement, changing relations with other Arab countries related to the signing, optimistic statements being made by the government and others about the peace process, and other (non-economic) benefits that could result from the agreement.

A much more pessimistic picture of the peace process was provided by stories about terrorism, difficulties in the negotiations with the Palestinians, dangers related to the agreement, parliamentary opposition to the agreement, and protests against the government.

The mixed news stories included articles about what was happening in the negotiations, similar stories about negotiations with Syria, developments among the Palestinians, negotiations with Jordan, discussions in the Knesset about the peace process, and stories relating to the Hebron massacre.[6]

The results of this analysis are presented in Figure 5.1. They show that there is a major difference between gaining access to the news media and controlling media frames. The peace process remained on the front page for the entire period but much of this news was negative.

As noted, the impact of the stories about terrorism was probably even worse than these figures suggest. There were graphic color pictures of the blood and the gore, interviews and coverage of funeral after funeral, and pictures of weeping children who had just lost their parents and parents who had lost their children.

The terrorist attacks provided an important political and cultural springboard for promoting oppositional frames. Public anger was intense and protest leaders had no trouble mobilizing people to take to the streets. A Kach leader referred to these post-attack protests as

---

[5]   For details see methodological appendix.
[6]   Some might question whether such incidents as the Hebron massacre should be considered neutral. I preferred, however, to be conservative and only include in the positive and negative categories those stories with a very clear direction.

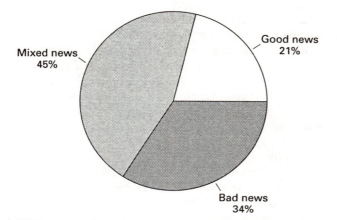

Figure 5.1   Good news and bad news about the peace process (proportion of articles in which each is mentioned in *Yediot Ahronot* and
Ha'aretz from August 27, 1993 to May 5, 1994)

"organized spontaneity." As he put it: "All you have to do is make sure
it flows in the right direction."

It was especially important for the settlers to include Israelis from
"inside the Green Line" in the protests for journalists were constantly
attempting to evaluate the breadth of the opposition to the Accords. The
protests that followed terrorist attacks made it much more difficult for
the press to marginalize the opposition. The journalists themselves
talked about this dynamic:

They [the settlers] were looking for a common ground with the population.
People that weren't settlers or religious or belonged to the National Religious
Party ... It was much easier to bring these people out after a terrorist attack.
Because terrorism happens everywhere: in Tel Aviv, in the Jordan Valley,
everywhere ... It's an issue that speaks to everyone, which brings everyone pain.
It's not exclusive to the settlers.

The fact that terrorism continued after the peace process offered
significant advantages to those promoting the *national disaster* frame. It is
important to remind ourselves that neither the peace process nor the
terrorist attacks were carried out for the media. They were authentic
moves and counter-moves that were part of an ongoing struggle between
two political forces each attempting to achieve specific goals. If the
government and/or the PLO had managed to stop the terrorism by the
fundamentalists, there would have been more icons of doves and fewer
of bloody knives.

Nevertheless, these news stories represent a journalistic interpretation of political reality. The emphasis on the most dramatic aspects of the peace process, which is rooted in the professional culture of all journalists, has a critical impact on the construction of media frames. The negotiations carried on between the Declaration of Principles and the signing in Cairo may have made for dull reading, but they ended in success. Some would argue that all of the ups and downs that preceded the signing of the agreement should be considered small deviations in a trend line that was moving steadily upwards. By definition, however, news stories focus on the here and now with only marginal attention to the past or the future.

This shows why it is important to examine both the events themselves and the ways in which the news media interpret those events. The fact that Israelis were being killed after Oslo greatly affected the settlers' movement's ability to promote its frames to the Israeli media and to the public. The media frames, however, tended to exaggerate the importance of terrorism and to understate the importance of progress being made at the negotiating table.

The role of the news media in such situations is to exaggerate and accelerate political successes and failures. One frame dominates media discourse while the other is hard to find. Experienced movements learn to anticipate such cycles so they can minimize the damage associated with government success and seize the opportunities that come from official failures.

Who are the good guys?

The last framing question relates to the question of movement legitimacy. In order for a movement to promote successfully its frames it must be considered a legitimate spokesperson. When movements are framed as extremists, they find it difficult to mobilize public support and to promote their frames.

The settlers' movement faced several difficulties in this area. Some are typical of those that every movement faces while others are specific to the struggle against the Oslo Accords. A typical dilemma was how to remain novel enough to obtain media coverage to express their outrage, without paying too heavy a price in terms of legitimacy, how to convey intense anger and still appear reasonable.

As noted, a central question during this period was what the opposition would do to stop the Accords: how far would they go? From a journalistic perspective the major question concerns the size of the threat. Would the settlers confine themselves to peaceful protest and minor acts of civil disobedience, or would opposition take the form of a violent rebellion in which people would be killed? Media frames inevitably focused on what settlers would do rather than what they had to say.

A useful example of this phenomenon can be illustrated by looking at the first major demonstration described in the last chapter (pp. 84–85). The demonstrators announced that they would "lay siege" to the government buildings; they would surround them with hundreds of thousands of citizens so that the government could not sign the Declaration of Principles with Arafat. The news stories leading up to the demonstration focused on the prospects for violence, on how many police officers would be needed, and whether the mass of people who were coming could bring the government to a halt. The issue of protest thus became a question of law and order. Consider, for example, an interview with a police reporter that appeared on a television news program about five hours before the event.

Q: What's going on in Jerusalem now?

A: Thousands of protesters and potential protesters are moving towards the Prime Minister's office and there are more than 2,000 police officers getting ready for a full night and a morning of continual protest.

Q: Is the city full of traffic jams?

A: The city is not yet full of traffic jams because the protest hasn't started yet. The police are directing the traffic, but no traffic jams yet ... I suspect that the traffic jams will start in another hour, hour and a half because there are more than 2,000 buses flowing towards Jerusalem ...

Q: They haven't laid siege to the Prime Minister's office?

A: Not yet, because the protest hasn't started, but that is definitely their intention. There was an official announcement that they would lay siege for the whole evening ... They have one goal: to stop the government from meeting tomorrow morning.

Q: Have you seen many children among the protesters?

A: Yes there are many children coming. There are whole families coming. There are some settlements near Jerusalem that are completely empty ...

Q: Now this is the first time that Habad – which is a spiritual, religious movement – announced that they are taking a political stand and coming to the demonstration. Can you see that in the field?

A: That is indeed an interesting point. This is the first time that the Habad people received an order from their rabbi to come out in full force ... That of course will increase the number of protesters by quite a large amount. The Habad people come together as one for this struggle for the land of Israel. They already published the slogan: "The land of Israel is in danger," which perhaps reminds some of slogan "Get ready for the coming of the Messiah," almost with just as much determination. (*A New Evening*, Israeli television, September 7, 1993)

The construction of the frame begins by interviewing a police reporter whose job is to give the police perspective on the protest. How many police are assigned to deal with the protest, what kinds of traffic jams are expected, and what is the probability for violence? The message being sent to the television viewer – especially if he or she lives in Jerusalem – is that there is trouble on the way and the best thing to do is to stay inside.

The questions and answers undermine the legitimacy of the protest by focusing on children and the participation of the messianic movement Habad. Young people are usually an important element of such protests and editorial decisions about how much to focus on them has important consequences for the final framing. Camera shots of smiling children often serve as a particularly effective technique for mocking protesters. The mention of Habad, the rabbi giving orders and the slogans about the coming of the Messiah all imply that anyone that comes to the protest is either a religious fanatic blindly following their leader or a fool.

The most important lesson, however, is that journalists are interested in action, and that news stories inevitably focus on the threat being posed by protesters rather than their demands. On the other hand, this demonstration provided some of the most positive coverage the settlers received in this period. Although they failed to stop the government from meeting the next morning, the large number of participants generated a tremendous amount of radio, television, and newspaper coverage. This left considerable room for quotes from the various speeches given, a luxury rarely afforded to protest leaders.[7]

As pointed out in the previous chapter, however, the settlers' movement was unable to sustain that type of momentum. Subsequent protests tended to be more spontaneous and unorganized and the Settlers' Council began to lose some of its central control, especially when settlers were being killed on a daily basis. A lack of control leads to a more radical frame for a movement because the news media tend to focus on the more violent elements (Gitlin, 1980). This is just as true about coverage of right-wing movements as it is regarding news stories about the left. News reports soon focused on settlers carrying out retribution raids, destroying classrooms, damaging property, and shooting at Palestinians.

By the end of October *Yediot* had developed a new icon and a new frame: "The Jewish *intifada*." The term was based on a random

[7] Most of the important speeches were given by the leaders of the parliamentary opposition, such as Binyamim Netanyahu. The settlers were responsible for most of the organization of these protests but having the big names come and speak provided that much more publicity.

statement by one settler and the icon featured the word *intifada* being surrounded by smoke from burning tires.[8] Despite the intended irony of the concept, it signified that the settlers had become a genuine threat to the State. The new frame provided a convenient way of selecting, organizing, and distributing information about the settlers. The question of whether there would be a "Jewish revolt" in the territories quickly became a major political issue. The government apparently had a special meeting about it and the newspapers felt obligated to write editorials condemning the settlers for "taking the law into their own hands."[9]

Everyone wants peace, no one wants terrorism

The settlers' movement also faced another difficulty in promoting its frame that was more specific to the fight against the Oslo Accords. As mentioned earlier, it was extremely difficult to avoid the impression that they were fighting against peace. The press kept talking about the "peace process" and the "peace agreement" and the movement was clearly against it. I myself realized the power of this frame when I mistakenly asked an activist about their goals concerning the peace process:

First, let's get our terminology straight. It is not a peace agreement. It's an agreement but not a peace agreement. It's a terrorist agreement, a murder agreement in my opinion. But that's part of the government's marketing in the media, to convince us that this is a peace agreement. It's an agreement for repression, not peace.

This provided the Rabin government with an important advantage in their attempts to delegitimize the opposition to the agreement. Rabin and other ministers kept speaking about "those who want to prevent the peace" and "the enemies of peace." There were several editorials and cartoons that appeared in the news media that featured the ironic alliance between the settlers and the Hamas terrorists.[10]

One of the movement's strategies for overcoming this dilemma was to adopt slogans that would co-opt the cultural resonance of the term "peace." Signs appeared calling for "A *different* peace," or "Peace in exchange for peace," and "Peace *with* the Golan Heights." The first

[8] Burning tires are a traditional component of protests in both Israel and the occupied territories.

[9] One article proved to be eerily prophetic. On November 8, 1993 one settler was quoted as saying: "Another murder and another murder and someone is going to take the law into his hands and then we'll have 30 killed. For God's sake: do something!" (*Yediot Ahronot*, p. 2).

[10] A political turmoil erupted when Rabin himself lumped the two groups together. He then corrected his statement by saying that there was a difference between "opponents of peace" and "enemies of peace."

slogan proved especially effective when the government flooded the country with posters of doves with the word "peace" written on them. A few dozen activists and many magic markers turned the entire operation into a wonderful vehicle for the promotion of opposition frames.

These problems of cultural resonance that characterized the settlers' campaign against the Oslo Accords are similar to those that peace movements often face in their attempts to protest against wars. While the settlers' movement was constantly attempting to avoid being framed as war mongers, peace movements must constantly "prove" that they are patriots. Movements attempting to prevent the Gulf war in the United States, for example, always made a point of emphasizing their support for the troops. Patriotism and peace are equally powerful symbols and thus the ability of the authorities to package their policies within such wrappings puts movements on the defensive in the battle over meaning.

Here too, however, the changes in the political process greatly affected the competition over media frames. Protest and violence that would be considered wrong in the context of a peace process were considered more justified within the context of terrorism. As discussed, terrorism was the one issue that united all Israelis. A news editor who was interviewed talked about these differences:

If you look at what the settlers were yelling after the agreement, there were three elements. One was terrorism, and they were right about that, because terrorism will have a major influence on what happens. I mean to say, even on the election of the government. So here they chose correctly. In the second thing they were mistaken, because they came out in principle against the peace. And here they made a mistake. I think that people, whatever their political views, have an immense and deep yearning for peace in our country. And the third thing was that they didn't succeed in explaining why the agreement itself is bad ... I mean they talked about all sorts of things that looked to those who didn't live there as marginal: weapons, Palestinian police, so that people didn't quite understand what is going on there.

The settlers' movement received their most sympathetic coverage as victims. The stories about the families of those who were killed were compassionate and understanding. The protests that followed such attacks were given a very different frame than the usual coverage of violence. The following story was typical of this genre:

Friday night dinner, followed by a hail of bullets

Friday night, 11:30 at night. The Sasson family traveled in their Mitsubishi. The parents, Tzipi and Roni, and the girls, Nateli and Inbar, were on their way to their house in Ariel after having dinner with Roni's parents in Petach Tikvah. At a turn in the road, behind an embankment, waited two Hamas terrorists. They opened fire. Fifteen rounds from a "Kalatchnikov" hit the car. Tzipi, in her eighth month of pregnancy is killed. The murderers get away. Last night hundreds of Ariel residents went on a retaliatory raid in Arab villages in Samaria. The police didn't succeed in dispersing them. (*Yediot Ahronot*, February 20, 1994, p. 2)

The story was accompanied by a picture of Tzipi's mother crying. This is an Israeli story written for an Israeli audience. The cultural influence here is just as important in the construction of the final frames as the professional one. The violence against the Arab village has a very different meaning when it is placed within the context of the murder of a pregnant mother.

The cultural influence on the construction of media frames is best understood by talking to the reporters who covered these stories. All of them talk about how different it is to cover a protest that follows a terrorist attack than other protests. One television journalist described one particularly memorable experience.

Usually every protest is the same protest. But then there's the coverage of the families themselves. The coverage of the families is very different. Because when you cover families, you can't help but be empathetic ... Such as Sarit Frigel who was with her father in the car, that was such a sad story. The whole time I was interviewing the father, I was crying. I just couldn't help it. It was so sad. Here was a very poor family who came to live in Kiryat Arba [a major town in the territories] mostly so their financial situation would improve. You know, the kind that can barely afford to buy their girl a notebook for school. She finally grows up and she takes a bullet sitting next to her father which drops her head on to his lap and he's telling me all this and you just can't help it. It's not a question anymore of peace and all that, it's a story about a father who lost his daughter.

Finding victims is a central method journalists employ for defining "the good guys." As one protest leader pointed out, the entire Middle East conflict is a struggle over who is the bigger victim. He also pointed out that when settlers are murdered the press is much more willing to listen to what they have to say, and when Arabs are killed, Palestinians are given a chance to speak. Victim frames represent important opportunities for challengers as long as they remain in character.[11] As that same leader put it: "Weakness is often strength."

---

[11] The need to stay in character is an important part of this process and many challengers have difficulties using the legitimacy they have gained when they become more active. Abused women, for example, get much more sympathetic coverage than feminist movements who fight for women's rights.

The Kach movement and the Hebron massacre

The settlers' struggle for public legitimacy was also made more difficult by the tremendous amount of coverage dedicated to Kach. It was easier for the government to marginalize the settlers' movement as Kach rose to prominence, especially after the Hebron massacre. The settlers were continually attempting to distance themselves from Kach; any association with them would undermine the movement's attempts to project an image of rationality and moderation. Kach, however, made for much better copy. One leader put it this way:

> We don't coordinate anything with Kach, quite the opposite. Our problem is that they're always trying to hitch a ride from us. We carry out a protest with fifty thousand people, and they come with fifteen, with their yellow shirts and their yellow flags, and they know where the cameras are. The news media looks for them. A demonstration that we worked on for three weeks, and we spent 200,000 shekels [$67,000] and in the end there is one minute on television and during that minute all you see is Kach.

Media frames of Kach are quite different from those used concerning the settlers' movement. Here the coverage leaves what Hallin (1986) has called the sphere of legitimate controversy and moves into the sphere of deviance. The coverage often takes the form of an exposé in which the reporter is uncovering an embarrassing scandal. The police reporters are often the ones who receive the assignment for covering Kach and this was true long before Kach was declared an illegal organization in Israel.

The coverage that appeared in *Yediot* in December 1993 is typical. Three Arabs had been killed a few days before and as often happens in such cases an anonymous caller contacted the press claiming that Kach was responsible.[12] There were then calls in the Knesset to outlaw Kach. The following article was published on the first page of the "color" section of Yediot with a large picture of police grabbing a young Kach protester holding the movement's yellow flag:

The yellow time

> The yellow flag of "Kach" has become lately the symbol of Jewish terrorism in the territories. Is the "Kach" movement really dangerous? Are Kach activists storing illegal weapons? Who is behind the announcement of the murder of the three Arabs in Turkomia? The Kach people are actually very pleased about the demand to make them illegal: they love to be in the headlines.

When movements are covered as deviants, it usually takes two forms: they are either treated as a serious threat to public order or as ridiculous.

[12] The police are often suspicious of such calls because Kach (or those claiming to belong to Kach) sometimes takes "credit" for acts which had nothing to do with them.

The article itself combines both elements. It talks about how well they manipulate the news media with various stunts, but then goes on to frame them as dangerous fanatics. There are pictures of three of the leaders set in black borders which look very much like mug shots.

The Kach leaders have an ambivalent attitude about the coverage they get. They complain about being framed as terrorists and criminals and they are convinced that the Israeli news media serve as a forum for government propaganda. The interviews, however, also reveal that what might be considered negative coverage for many groups is perceived very differently by Kach.

A good example is a series of stories published about a Kach "summer camp." These stories were also written as exposés, showing young children being taught to shoot at Arab targets. A leader was asked why he invited journalists to cover the camp story when he realized how they would deal with it:

Because it has value. First of all you have to realize that it doesn't hurt our image. You have to understand. A reporter wants to slander Baruch Marzel [leader of Kach]. What will he say? Baruch Marzel hit an Arab that threw stones at him. And people sit on Shenkin street [yuppie hangout] and say "Yuk, what a violent person." But most of the people of Israel say: "That's great, finally there's someone that gives it back to them." That's most of the country. One of the things the media don't understand is what the public likes and what it doesn't like. That's why they don't do so much damage. The try to curse us and in the end they bless us.

One reason Kach receives a more militant image than the settlers' movement is because it sees itself as more militant. As with many radical groups, Kach leaders talk about the need to remain "pure" and "real" and reject any suggestions of compromise designed to project a more reasonable image. They also apparently have very different perceptions about the distribution of opinion in Israel that would alter their evaluations about the cultural resonance of their message. In a sense, Kach is not exactly conceding the middle ground, it is simply redefining it.[13]

As discussed, the greatest blow for the settlers' attempts to achieve public legitimacy was the Hebron massacre. Media frames again focused on victims, only this time the victims were Palestinian and the murderer was a settler living in Kiryat Arba. The damage to the settlers' image was magnified by many interviews with the extremist elements within the movement who not only justified Baruch Goldstein's actions but declared him a hero. Rabin himself said that his subsequent decision to

---

[13] Kach leaders generally tend to exaggerate their support among the public. It is very difficult to tell how much of this is sheer rhetoric and how much is a genuine belief in their own popularity.

outlaw Kach and initiate a crackdown in Kiryat Arba was related to these reports, especially the television interviews.

These interviews were collected by the press to illustrate the *massacre* story line, just as the previous piece with the grieving father were carried out to further illustrate the *terrorism* frame. The initial event has a narrative fit with a certain frame that then sets in motion a search for specific types of information that are consistent with the story line. Here too, it is important to understand both the characteristics of the event itself and the journalistic norms that define how that event will be used to construct a coherent story line. While the subsequent search for suitable information is driven by earlier framing decisions, this does not take away from the significance of the initial event in directing that search.

Although the Hebron massacre was a serious setback to the settlers' attempts at legitimacy, there is another side to this story. Many journalists who were interviewed argued that the long-term effect may have been quite different. After Hebron, a much more conscious effort by reporters and editors was made to distinguish between what was called the "extreme right" and the right. A radio correspondent commented on this change in framing:

I think that the Hebron massacre was in some ways a significant turning point . . . We learned to make a distinction between the different types of right. It's impossible to come and call the right a "people." There's the radical right, which includes the Kach movement and Kahane Chai [another group led by Kahane's son] that were made illegal organizations, and you have to give them their slant [Kivun]. Then you have the core of 150,000 settlers, and you have to distinguish between them.

The Hebron massacre proved to be a double-edge sword. In the short term it tended to marginalize the settlers' movement and undermine their efforts for public legitimacy. In the long run, however, the massacre may have had the opposite effect of underscoring the difference between themselves and the more radical groups. In some ways, the existence of Kach actually helped the Settlers' Council by establishing new end points on the continuum of legitimacy. The influence of critical events such as the Hebron massacre on media frames is not always as clear as one might think.

Summary

The frame contest between the Rabin government and the anti-Oslo movements can only be fully understood by considering three central factors: the nature of the political events that marked the period, the professional norms that determined how these events would be turned into news, and how these events resonated within the political culture of the Israeli media. The influence of all these factors tended to vary over time and circumstances and so did the resulting media frames.

The period was marked by a genuine contest between two frames: the *chance for peace* frame put forth by the Rabin government, and the *national disaster* frame being promoted by the right-wing opposition. Neither side could dominate public discourse in part because neither side could take complete charge of political events. Some events such as the breakthrough at Oslo gave important advantages to the *peace* frame; others, such as the terrorist attacks gave advantages to the *disaster* frame. There were also many events – such as the Hebron massacre – whose ultimate meaning remained ambiguous.

While the obstacles and the opportunities that confronted the settlers may have been more intensive than those experienced by other movements, the pattern was familiar. They were confronted with balancing the need for publicity with the danger of being framed as extremists, the difficulty of using actions to promote ideas, frustrations over the news media's fixation on the more radical elements within the movement, and the difficulties of attempting to ride the political waves flowing in the right direction while ducking under those that could drown them.

Despite all this the settlers' movement did enjoy a significant amount of success in promoting their frames to the Israeli news media. They were certainly not the only force working to keep the debate alive, but they were one of the most important. After the signing in Cairo, the movement returned to a more usual level of activity, with selected appearances in the news media, made possible by some smaller waves such as Arafat's arrival in Gaza. The Rabin assassination proved to be the most important event of all. Whatever legitimacy the movements had achieved over their long months of activity was instantly destroyed when Yigal Amir murdered the Prime Minister. But during that critical time between the signings in Oslo and Cairo, the settlers' movement was able to wage a fierce cultural battle whose outcome was far from clear.

6 Controlling the media in insurrections and wars: the *intifada* and the Gulf war

The battles over the news media that characterize insurrections and wars are very different from the ones that have been described up to now. These conflicts constitute a genuine threat to the state, a threat that can neither be ignored nor dismissed with symbolic gestures. Powerful antagonists can ill afford to lose such battles either on the ground or in the realm of world opinion; such contests constitute a direct challenge to their power and legitimacy.

While movements generally recognize the political authority of those in power, challengers engaged in insurrections and wars would prefer to kill those in power. Such threats become defined by the political leadership as a crisis and the news media – or at least the domestic news media – normally adopt that definition (Raboy and Dagenais, 1992). Reporting about the battle against enemies of the state is a radically different news genre. The domestic media may ask questions about the wisdom or efficiency of certain actions taken by the authorities. The press may even take issue with the amount of force being used against the challenger, but no one could doubt their patriotism.

The best hope for the challenger is to expand the scope of the conflict. Many insurrections and wars become international conflicts, and challengers attempt to use the international news media as a means of promoting intervention. This strategy was also employed in less recent conflicts. During the American Civil War, Knightley (1975) reports, the South hired a Swiss immigrant to give out cigars, whiskey, and cash to any British correspondent willing to place favorable articles and editorials in the London newspapers. In 1876, the Turkish government used Kurdish troops to suppress a Bulgarian revolt. The *London Daily News* commissioned a reporter to cover the atrocities and the press coverage led to a massive intervention by Russia (Knightley, 1975). The Soviet invasions of Hungary in 1956 and of Czechoslovakia in 1968, on the other hand, went unanswered by the West. Whether things would have gone differently if American television had been able to cover these events remains an open question.

The competition over access to the news media takes on a different form in insurrections and wars. Challengers want to gain access to a variety of news media especially those from powerful countries who can help them. In the present era it is the Western press more than any other which sets the international agenda. Since the fall of the Soviet Union and the Eastern Block, challengers must turn to the West for their salvation. This puts those who confront the West in an especially difficult position, and those who challenge the United States in an almost impossible one. Their only hope is to create divisions within that block, or to convince the domestic press in each country that the risks of military conflict outweigh the benefits.

The authorities' level of control over the political environment is the most important variable determining the role of the news media in these more intensive conflicts. There are a number of reasons for this which can best be understood by considering the three facets of political control: the initiation and control of events, the regulation over the flow of information, and the ability to mobilize elite support.

First, news coverage of military confrontations often centers on what is happening on the ground, on who appears to be winning. The ability to initiate and control events is one of the most important determinants of which voices will be heard. When it is challengers who take the initiative, it is they who set the media's agenda, a fact that can be especially embarrassing for the military. The use of civil disobedience, guerilla warfare, and terrorism all offer a powerful demonstration of authorities' vulnerability.

Secondly, the government and the military are given a much greater degree of latitude in controlling the flow of information in more intensive conflicts and the news media are much less likely to achieve autonomy. While democratic norms would inhibit the authorities from limiting press access or carrying out censorship with regard to internal political movements, such acts are considered legitimate during times of crisis. When governments close media access to challengers they maintain a monopoly on the supply of information.

Finally, the ability of the government to mobilize national and international consensus in support of the government will also have critical influence on the independence of the news media. A lack of alternative sources leads to a united front against the enemy; the news media are understandably reluctant to be cast as traitors. When, on the other hand, challengers have had success mobilizing elites to their cause the news media will have little trouble presenting oppositional sources.

This is not to say that production assets and exceptional behavior do not also play a role in the struggle over the news media. These factors are especially important in the early stages of such conflicts when challengers are attempting to achieve international standing. There are hundreds of conflicts going on around the world which are ignored by the Western news media. The lower the international status of the challenger, and the further the conflict from the Western cultural realm, the more exceptional the behavior needed to break into the Western press. Challengers from Africa and Asia have to kill thousands, take some Western hostages, or invade another country before they can achieve standing as a serious player.

Production assets and exceptional behavior are also important in helping the challenger break the authorities' domination over the political environment. As noted in Chapter 1, organization, resources, and international status allow one to initiate and control events, to break through government restrictions on the flow of information, and to mobilize oppositional support. Nevertheless, the key variable to monitor in the course of insurrections and wars is the authorities' level of political control, and this will serve as the organizing principle for this chapter.

The two conflicts

In the next three chapters I shall use the political contest model to analyze the role of the new media in two very different conflicts: the Palestinian *intifada* that began in December 1987 against the Israeli occupation, and the Persian Gulf conflict which began in August 1990. At first glance, it would seem that the conflicts have little in common. The *intifada* was a low-grade uprising against one specific country while the Persian Gulf conflict developed into a major war involving twenty-three different countries.

These differences can be seen as an advantage. A major goal of this work is to develop a dynamic model which helps explain how the role of the news media can change over time and circumstance. The utility of the theoretical model is best demonstrated by applying it to cases as divergent as possible.

There are also enough similarities between the conflicts to ensure that the comparison will also be coherent. Both conflicts were unequal confrontations in which the stronger side had a significantly more powerful military force than the weaker challenger. In addition, the *intifada* and the Gulf war were both considered significant international conflicts which were given a good deal of international news coverage. Thus, both challengers were granted international standing. Finally, in both conflicts the stronger side attempted to justify suppressing the challenge in the interest of maintaining *law and order* while the challenger was promoting a frame of *injustice and defiance*.

The most important reason for choosing these conflicts is that they provide near-perfect examples of two cases which stand at opposite ends of the continuum of influence described in Chapter 3. While the role of the press was that of an independent advocate in the *intifada*, its role in the Persian Gulf conflict was that of a faithful servant to the United States and her allies. The reasons for this difference are best understood by examining the structural and cultural factors that characterized the struggle for political control.

The *intifada*

The Palestinian *intifada* began in December 1987. The role of the news media in this conflict quickly became a major controversy both in Israel and abroad. At the beginning of the uprising many Israelis felt that the media presence was the major cause of violence, and they called for banning the press from the territories. A great deal of the initial debate within the Israeli government centered on what should be "done" about the media (Schiff and Ya'ari, 1990).

The argument here is that the news media did play an independent role in the *intifada* due to the particular nature of the conflict. It is critical to emphasize, however, that this does not mean that the news media "caused" the *intifada*. The central reasons for the uprising are best found by examining the social and political history of the Arab–Israeli conflict: Palestinian violence came from a genuine sense of anger and frustration. Nevertheless, the nature, direction, and intensity of this particular stage of the conflict were certainly affected by the media presence, the reports which were filed, and international reactions to that coverage.

Initiation and control of events

The *intifada* offers an almost textbook case of how a seemingly weaker challenger can shatter the authorities' domination over the political environment and successfully promote their frames to the news media. During this period, the Israelis were unable to initiate or control events, they were unable to regulate the flow of information to the press, and they were unable to generate national or international consensus in support of their suppression of the *intifada*. The news media served the role of equalizer, dramatically changing the balance of power between the two sides.

The events that defined the news story in the initial months of the *intifada* were massive protests of unarmed Palestinians defying the Israeli army. While riots of this type had often occurred in the past, they had never been as massive or as sustained. The Palestinians had developed an impressive organization within the territories which afforded them a good deal of control over the events. As pointed out by Lederman (1992), during the *intifada*, the Palestinians were transformed from a "media event" to a press beat. Their most important resource was the willingness of the Palestinian people, especially the youth, to take to the streets and defy the Israeli soldiers on a daily basis. The duration and scope of this commitment was far beyond anything witnessed in the past.

The organization and resources of the Israelis were far superior to those of the Palestinians. The government invested millions of dollars and thousands of soldiers in their attempt to contain the rebellion, all to no avail. The confrontations were controlled by the protesters, and the spokesperson's staff struggled to keep pace. The major news stories centered on incidents in which Israeli soldiers were accused of brutality in dealing with Palestinian rioters. The story that came out in subsequent trials was one of general confusion. Soldiers in the field were never sure how much force to use and this contributed to the government's lack of control. In addition, while responding to charges of brutality is never an agreeable task, it is made especially difficult because of the military's need to investigate each story before issuing a response. These investigations usually take days and the news media are not in the business of waiting.

Regulating the flow of information

The Israeli military also found it extremely difficult to regulate the flow of information to the news media, for both political and geographic reasons. The army initiated a number of policies designed to gain control over the flow of information about the *intifada*. The press were often prohibited from entering certain areas and the army shut down the Palestinian Press Service (PPS).[1] The PPS had been providing beepers to journalists to alert the reports about the time and place of each new protest. Closing the PPS offices, however, probably had only a minimal influence on the reporters' ability to arrive at the protests.

Israel is an open society, where any attempts to limit the flow of

[1]   The army justified the bans by arguing that the presence of reporters tended to increase the level of violence. Indeed, most of the television reporters who were interviewed acknowledge that the cameras did have an effect on the level of protest violence.

information from the territories is both politically and geographically impossible. It is especially difficult to close off physical access to the West Bank. Journalists can normally take an Arab taxi from East Jerusalem to anywhere in the West Bank, cover a story, and be back a few hours later to send the reports overseas. Another reason why the Israeli authorities were reluctant to seal off completely the territories was their fear that the news agencies would then supply the Palestinians with video cameras. Such cameras could produce footage that would not only be more damaging to Israel but would also be more newsworthy because it had been smuggled out past the Israel censor.[2]

The army spokesperson talked about the development of military policy on how to handle the news media during the *intifada*:

It was a process, perhaps an evolution ... There was no decision by the senior staff which said that on this day of the riots we will act this way and on another day differently. I must say that when the issue of the media came up in the first days of the discussion, I insisted that the areas will stay open, and that's for three reasons. First, because of the principle. I believe in the principle that we must have freedom of the press in a democratic country, and one has to pay a price for that ... Secondly, if we close the area we are only making it worse for ourselves, because as it is there is very unsymmetrical reporting. This would give complete advantage to the Palestinian side and they [the media] wouldn't be willing to hear our side if we closed the area. The third reason is practical, we have no way to hermetically seal the area, and we'd have to use a large amount of forces to close it.

There was another important reason why the Israeli government was unable to control the flow of information to the international press: the extremely high international status of the Palestinians as challengers. In Table 6.1 a comparison is made of the number of stories which appeared in the *Washington Post* about the Palestinians and about a number of other challengers in the year *before* the *intifada* (December 1, 1986 to November 30, 1987). It is amazing that a group as distant as the Palestinians was mentioned almost daily during that year. As can be seen, no other challengers even come close to receiving the amount of coverage given to the Palestinians.

There are, of course, a variety of reasons for these reporting differences. One is the tremendous news interest concerning Israel and the Middle East. In that same period for example, there were 1,302 news stories which mentioned Israel. It is ironic but true that Israel's high level of media status is a major advantage for the Palestinians, for it offers a convenient springboard for making their demands to the international community. The Palestinian beat is an important part of

---

[2] Such cameras were in fact distributed to Palestinians during later stages of the *intifada*.

Table 6.1 *The publicity of challengers in the* Washington Post[a] *(December 1, 1986 to November 30, 1987)*

Challenger	Number of stories
Palestinians	352
Belfast	43
Basques	29
Kurds	15
East Timorians	1

Note: [a] Counts are based on Nexis search using the challenger name as the search word. In the case of East Timorians the word "Timor" was used as the search word.

the work the large number of journalists stationed in Israel are expected to cover. Secondly, the PLO had spent years building up an international reputation with exceptional behavior, starting with terrorist attacks against Western targets in the 1970s (Lederman, 1992). This was accompanied by extensive diplomatic work in the 1980s; the PLO was recognized as a legitimate political entity by dozens of countries and in the United Nations. Third, those same logistical factors which were so important during the *intifada* were also in play long before the uprising. While journalists might have difficulties getting into East Timor or the Kurdish area of Iraq, reporters never had any trouble gaining access to Palestinian sources.

Thus, there was a huge demand for the information about the Palestinian uprising because of the high level of political and media status achieved by the Palestinians in previous years. The amount of attention brought the ombudsman of the *Washington Post* to criticize his own paper for giving a disproportionate amount of attention to this particular conflict while ignoring other, equally newsworthy events. After reviewing the massive amount of coverage given to the *intifada*, the ombudsman concluded:

Even for the Post, that is quite a quantity of verbiage. On the scale by which we ordinarily evaluate wars, revolutions and domestic fratricide, what was happening in Israel was a relatively low grade civil conflict. By the end of last week (after nearly six months), the death toll was fewer than 200 ... Earlier this month when 65 Shi'ites were killed on a single day in one of the brotherly battles in Beirut, the 600-word story in the Post appeared on page 15. (Harwood, 1988)

The high level of demand for the story made it that much more difficult for the Israelis to control the flow of information about the uprising.

Mobilizing elite consensus

The third problem facing the Israeli authorities was the lack of political consensus surrounding their actions in the territories. The subject of what to do about the territories has been the major political issue dividing the Israeli polity since the early 1970s, and the major source of friction between Israel and the rest of the world.

On the face of it, the period when the *intifada* broke out should have been a time of political consensus among Israeli elites for the country was being ruled by a "national unity government." The two major political parties, Labor and Likud, had decided to join together in a single government. The Minister of Defense, Yitzhak Rabin, was from the Labor party while the Prime Minister, Yitzhak Shamir, was from Likud. Nevertheless, Israel has a multi-party political system, and the smaller parties from the left and the right formed a vocal opposition to government policy in the territories. While right-wing Knesset members were demanding a much tougher stand towards Palestinian rioters, the left was talking about the brutality of the Israeli army and the need to end the occupation. The fact that many Israeli opinion leaders were themselves condemning the actions of the military created an ideological environment which was as open as the geographic one. News sources of varying political views were all pressing to be heard, holding press conferences, and staging demonstrations. When the issue became an international one it allowed for an even greater diversity of news sources as leaders from around the world and the United Nations were all expressing their views on Israeli behavior. If there was any international consensus it was against Israel's policies in the territories.

In summary, three factors led to Israel's inability to control the political environment: its inability to control or initiate events in the field, its inability to regulate the flow of information to the news media, and the lack of consensus about the conflict among the elite in Israel and abroad. All of these factors provided the Israeli and international news media with a tremendous amount of independence in the collection and dissemination of information, and an unusual opportunity for the Palestinians to make their case to the Israeli public and to the world.

It is important to remember, however, that it was the actions of the Palestinians who made all of this possible. The PLO had spent years building an organization, mobilizing resources, and achieving the international status which made their challenge viable. The ability of the Palestinians in the territories to carry out the uprising, with all of its human costs, turned this potential into a reality. The news media played a major role by enlarging the scope of the conflict and granting the Palestinians an important boost in morale. But without the success on the ground there would have been no story at all.

The Gulf war

The Gulf war offers a stark contrast to the *intifada* where the more powerful antagonist was able to control the political environment. The lack of independence afforded the press is already well documented (Bennett and Paletz, 1994; Fialka, 1991; Gannett Foundation, 1991; Smith, 1992). The purpose of this essay is to explain better *why* the news media was unable to achieve any semblance of autonomy in the Gulf war, and to point to some important exceptions where the allied domination over the news media faltered. Such variations offer critical insights about how the role of the news media can change over the course of a conflict.

Initiation and control of events

In direct contrast to the situation that characterized the *intifada*, the United States and its allies had a great deal of control over the Gulf war. It was the Allies who decided when the air war would begin, when the ground war would start, and when the war would end. With the possible exception of the battle of Khafji, the Iraqis spent most of the war buried in their bunkers. The ability to control the battlefield offers antagonists an important advantage in planning information campaigns because all of the press releases and briefings can be prepared in advance. Jack Nelson, the Washington bureau chief of the *Los Angeles Times*, made a similar point in a roundtable discussion about the media held soon after the end of the war.

... I think the priorities about what to cover were clearly laid down in the briefing sessions. One day you had to focus on particular kinds of air-raids, another day you had to focus on polluting the gulf or the burning of Kuwait, another day you had to focus on the prisoners of war. The initiative came from the government itself, or from the military. (Gannett Foundation, 1991, p. 73)

This is a perfect example of how organization and resources allow an antagonist to initiate and control events. The Allies' tremendous military superiority should not be seen as a separate issue: it allowed them to dominate totally the battlefield, a factor which allowed them to dominate the public arena. If the Iraqis had even a small proportion of the military might attributed to them before the start of hostilities, the coverage would have been much less uni-dimensional.

In the case of the Gulf war, it was the Iraqis who were reacting, or more accurately, not reacting to the actions of the Allies. One of the American senior officers who dealt with the news media during the Gulf war was able to plan, months in advance, the types of stories the press would cover during different phases of the campaign. For example, he had his staff prepare personal interest stories about the troops during the buildup stage, and find the proper air force films highlighting the latest technology during the air war. The Allies were rarely surprised by the events in the Gulf war and this ensured that they were also seldom surprised by media coverage of the war.

Regulating the flow of information

The Allies also had an extremely high level of control over the flow of information. Indeed, press restrictions were the major "media story" of the war. The news media complained bitterly and publicly about the constraints being placed on their coverage. This story appeared in *Time* magazine on January 21, 1991, and is typical of the genre:

As soon as the Pentagon rules for dealing with the news media were made final, the presidents of the four major US television news networks sent a letter of protest to Secretary of Defense Dick Cheney. So did editors of the *Washington Post*, the *Chicago Tribune*, the *Philadelphia Inquirer*, *Time* and the Associated Press, while the *New York Times* issued a similar statement. The network presidents charged that the rules "go far beyond what is required to protect troop safety and mission security ... and raise the specter of government censorship of a free press."

The methods of information control were both direct and effective. All contacts with the reporters were centralized through "JIBs": Journalist Information Bureaux. Pools were organized to ensure that the flow of information could be strictly regulated, and all stories had to be submitted to the military censor for approval. Reporters were forced to sign secrecy agreements in which they consented, among other things, not to send any pictures of American casualties without the approval of the censor.[3] The vast majority of the information was provided in briefing sessions in Dhahran and Riyadh, where the military supplied not only all of the information, but also many of the films which would be shown around the world.

The journalists were extremely frustrated by their lack of indepen-

---

[3] Part of the reason for this regulation was concern that relatives might learn about the casualties from the news media before the military could inform them.

dence but there was little they could do about it. There was tremendous demand for information and only one supply source. One journalist said he had never known reporters under such pressure to explain to their editors why they couldn't get to the story. It was impossible to check the accuracy of the facts they were given. The journalists' anger hardly diminished after the war was over, when many discovered how many stories they had gotten wrong. One reporter was asked whether he felt that their stories were influenced by the need to side with the Allies:

No, I really think the information was simply not available. In a lot of the stories I was writing at the last day or two of the ground war and the week afterward, every single one of those stories is wrong with regard to every single fact. I reported, for example that the war stopped because the Americans ran out of targets, and it simply wasn't true. If I was told there were a hundred facts, maybe ninety of them have proven false.

The exact statistics are less important than the sense of frustration which lies behind them. The evidence suggests that conventional wisdom is quite accurate: the Allies in the Gulf war were able to exercise a remarkable amount of informational control. As Lawrence Grossman, former president of NBC News and PBS put it: "the press was held captive" (Gannett Foundation, 1991).

What is often forgotten, however, is that the Allies' ability to control the flow of information in the Gulf was more a matter of geography than brilliant strategy. The briefing sessions given by the military took place in one of the only areas accessible to journalists. They needed military vehicles to get to the battle scenes; a number of reporters who went out on their own got lost, and CBS television correspondent Bob Simon and his crew were captured by the Iraqis. One of the senior press officers compared the situation in the Gulf with his experience in Vietnam: "They realized that this was not Vietnam, the size of California where you could run out and get a quick fire fight, come back to the hotel Rex, file your story and that was the end of it".

There were probably over 1,000 reporters in Saudi Arabia at the height of the war. Nevertheless, their presence could hardly be felt by the troops themselves, especially as the vast majority of correspondents were centered in Dhahran. The geographic size of the war zone also had a detrimental effect on the ability of journalists to cover the conflict, and further increased their dependence on the military bureaucracy. One journalist who covered both the *intifada* and the Gulf war talked about the differences he experienced from a reporter's perspective:

It's a different type of battle and a different kind of battlefield. The *intifada* when it was really going on was a low-grade conflict. I mean Scud missiles weren't flying – it was rocks against rubber bullets. For a journalist that's a very attractive conflict to cover. Its very close and you get terrific pictures ... I mean you can take a cab, you can hitchhike, you can walk; these places are on the map. In Saudi Arabia it was very inhospitable terrain – very few roads. I mean you needed special vehicles, tanks, or helicopters to get around. You couldn't just rent a car and go out there. I tried, and where you could go with a car there was nothing to see.

The difficulty in obtaining information was not just a matter of geography, however, for the situation in Washington was not much better. Transactions between journalists and leaders become very different in times of war. One of the correspondents described the effects of the war on the flow of information in the Pentagon:

This building tightened up like a ship at war. It went to general quarters. You just couldn't talk to people. Nobody returned phone calls. People wouldn't go for walks with you like they sometimes do to give a sense of what was going on, because they just didn't know what was happening, because the information was so tightly controlled and funneled from the Central Command right to the war room, that I don't know what else we could have done ... I think that as long as there is an environment like the one this war occurred in, with the short very rigid chain of command and with a powerful press spokesman, we are just going to have to accept the facts as the Pentagon tells us here at the briefing.

A few cracks in the wall

While the ability of the Allies to regulate the flow of information was extraordinary, there were several points during the war in which the news media did achieve some degree of independence. An examination of these exceptions offers important lessons about how situational variables can alter the role of the press.

One of the most revealing of these examples was the change in the media's ability to collect information as the Allies moved from the air war to the ground war. In any air war the inability of journalists to accompany the military into battle severely limits their independence and enhances the capability of the government to control the informational environment. Knightley (1975) reports a similar set of circumstances during the later stages of the Vietnam war in which the bombing of North Vietnam, Laos, and Cambodia was given much less publicity than the ground war, despite the fact that these air attacks were much more devastating.

The ground war in the Gulf conflict was extremely brief. Nevertheless, all of the journalists and military people who were interviewed agreed that the control over correspondents began to break down when the

army and the marines started to move into Kuwait and Iraq (see also
Fialka, 1991). The military was especially concerned with the increasing
number of "unilaterals" who were breaking away from the pools and
independently collecting information. One of the officers in charge of
dealing with the media talked about this change:

The only breakdown I felt occurred was once the ground war started; you had
unilaterals out there on their own and actually providing some pretty decent
coverage in cases. What we had anticipated that never occurred was that once
the ground war started, the entire country would be a kind of garrison. That is to
say, that there would not be unrestricted travel on the roads of Saudi Arabia, that
news media who were trying to get into the battlefield would essentially be
stopped on the road. Well that didn't happen ... Our great fear was that pool
reporters seeing that would say, why do I have to put up with these pool
restrictions which most of them hated.

The journalists were well aware of the opportunities which the ground
war offered even before it began. Consider the following comments by
one of the television reporters who covered the war:

I was one who did not feel that it was worth all the risks before the ground war
started ... in terms of breaking the pool rules because I thought the time to
break them would be the time when you'd actually get something out of breaking
them, which would be during the ground war. I thought the ground war would
go on for some weeks and this would be the time to go out ... So I felt the time
to break them was when the ground war started and then just say "fuck you" to
the Army and do whatever you wanted to do. And by then things would be too
chaotic to really deal with it.

In the final analysis this had very little impact on the role of the media
because the ground war was so short. It is a critical reminder, however,
that the informational environment is subject to change, and with it the
level of antagonist control and media dependence.

Three other incidents in which the allies lost control over the flow of
information provide important evidence about how quickly the role of
the news media can change. The three events are the bombing of what
the Iraqis claimed was a baby milk factory, the destruction of the
Amiriya bunker in Baghdad, and at the very end of the war, the
"Highway of Death" in which about 1,000 Iraqi army vehicles were
trapped and destroyed by Allied aircraft.

In each of these cases the pictures of destruction and devastation
offered a very different frame of the war than that which was promoted
by the Allies. The Iraqis were providing a certain amount of information
to the press throughout the war, especially through Peter Arnett, the
CNN correspondent in Baghdad. Nevertheless, the images produced by
these three incidents were far more vivid and powerful, and the United

States found itself very much on the defensive in its attempt to discount Iraqi claims about the brutality of the American attack. More than anything else, these exceptions illustrate how quickly the authorities can lose control over the flow of information. As will be discussed later on, such a lack of control can have dramatic consequences on authorities' attempts to dictate media frames, and on the role the news media can play in such conflicts.

Mobilizing elite consensus

It is extremely revealing to examine the *changing* level of political consensus among elites in the United States about the Gulf war and its effects on news coverage. An important key to understanding media coverage of this conflict can be found by examining the varying amount of congressional opposition to the war. The great debate about whether or not to allow the President to go to war was heated, and the news media offered a great deal of coverage of that controversy. The final vote in the Senate took place on January 13 when the President was given the green light, in a vote of 52 to 47, to use military force. After the outbreak of the war, however, the Congress was mostly silent, apart from expressing support for the troops.

This change in political consensus is reflected directly in the way the news media covered the conflict. A report published by ADT Research (Gannett Foundation, 1991) examined television news stories which appeared before and after the outbreak of the war. They found that in the three weeks prior to the war "controversy stories" outnumbered "yellow ribbon" stories (in support of the troops) by 45 to 8, but in the following six weeks "ribbon" stories dominated, 36 to 19.

One of the journalists based in Washington talked about the differences between covering the story during "Desert Shield" (the buildup period) and "Desert Storm." When asked whether or not it was easier to get information before the war broke out, he replied:

Yes, because more people had opinions. There were more critics, critics in the Congress, critics in the think tanks. But once there was a declaration of war basically because Congress voted and the US committed its young men and women to fight, the critics were no longer critical. They immediately turned to support the Commander-in-Chief. In some ways it was a nice thing to see and feel but if the war would have lasted longer, I think people would have raised more questions about what we were doing.

Once again, the ebbs and flows of the political process dictate the role of the news media. The need for the American opposition to close ranks with the Bush administration after the initiation of the fighting left the journalists without any alternative sources. Had those same political forces broken away, the news media would have reflected that debate and found themselves playing a more active role. A short, successful military campaign ensured the Bush administration easy control of the political environment and with it the news media.

Two revealing postscripts

The goal of this chapter has been to show that the authorities' level of control over the political environment can be critical in deciding the competition between the authorities and challengers over the news media. I would like to provide two other illustrations of this idea which show how quickly such control can be lost and gained, and how such changes have dramatic consequences for the access of challengers to the news media. Both examples are conveniently linked to the Gulf war.

The first example brings us back to the conflict between the Palestinians and the Israelis, but this time in the context of the Gulf war. The Israelis took complete control over the political environment during this period, in direct contrast to what happened during the *intifada*. They declared a complete curfew in the West Bank and the Gaza Strip which prevented the Palestinians from initiating any activities in support of Saddam Hussein. Not one single riot or terrorist attack occurred during this period, and the Israeli leadership made it very clear that they would react to any such actions very differently within the context of a war.

The Israelis also managed to achieve a high level of control over the flow of information from the territories, a task which seemed impossible during the *intifada*. There was very little contact between Western journalists and the Palestinians during the war. The Palestinians were a relatively minor story compared with the drama of the Scuds falling on Tel Aviv and Haifa. Even those correspondents who did have a burning desire to return to their old haunting grounds were required to take a military escort with them.

The Israelis were also finally able to enjoy the fruits of national and international consensus. The PLO had declared their unconditional support of Saddam Hussein which placed them squarely in the enemy camp. There was a clear political consensus within Israel and the Western world against the Palestinians. Thus, when the Palestinians were given access to the Israeli and Western media it was a very different type of passage than they had experienced during the *intifada*.

Thus, as the political context changed so did the transactions between journalists, the Israeli authorities, and the Palestinian challengers. The

Palestinians were unable to initiate events, they found it extremely difficult to break through the Israeli domination over the flow of information to the journalists, and the high level of consensus against their position in the war turned them from victims into aggressors.[4]

The second example refers to the Kurd insurrection against Iraq which took place immediately after the ceasefire at the end of the Gulf war. The weaker Kurds were being slaughtered by Iraqi troops and their only hope of survival was Western intervention. The Western press, shackled during the course of the Gulf war, was suddenly free to cover the conflict as they saw fit. The stronger antagonist in this conflict was Iraq. While it was the Iraqis who were initiating the major events in this stage of the confrontation, they had no control over the flow of information, and Western consensus was, once again, against the Iraqi position.

At this point in the strife the Bush administration had no intention of intervening in the conflict. Here, as in the case of the *intifada*, the news media placed a major emphasis on the Kurds as victims, and Bush was being blamed for the Kurdish plight. *Newsweek* (1991), for example, featured a destitute Kurdish child on their cover with the caption "Why won't he help us?" The press was pressuring for American intervention. The tragic pictures sent around the world may very well have led to Bush's change of heart, when he reluctantly decided to intervene in that conflict. Daniel Schoor (1991) is one of those who believe the role of the media was critical:

Score one for the power of the media, especially television, as a policy making force. Coverage of the massacre and exodus of the Kurds generated public pressures that were instrumental in slowing the hasty American military withdrawal from Iraq and forcing a return to help guard and care for the victims of Saddam Hussein's vengeance. (p. 21)

If these assertions are accurate, the media played an important equalizing role in that conflict by serving as a catalyst for the mobilization of the United States and Britain into the conflict. In order to add one more twist to this story it is useful to think back to the Kurdish rebellion in 1988, when even more Kurds were killed. The news media were not there to cover those events and the conflict took its expected course with the Iraqis destroying the Kurdish forces.

Thus, these two last cases once again appear to represent opposite ends of the theoretical continuum. The Israelis were able to take control over the political environment and the Iraqis were not. The news media

[4] On the other hand Saddam Hussein did manage to keep the Palestinian issue on the international agenda by linking an Israeli withdrawal to his own withdrawal from Kuwait. This issue is discussed in the next chapter.

can serve as a lifeline for challengers engaged in insurrections and wars. Those who make it often find themselves lifted into a political world filled with important allies and significant opportunities. Nevertheless, getting to that line is rarely easy and the authorities do everything in their power to pull the rope away and to make the ascent as difficult as possible.

7   The contest over media frames in the *intifada*: David versus Goliath

In constructing such enemies and the narrative plots that define their place in history, people are manifestly defining themselves and their place in history as well; the self-definition lends passion to the whole transaction. To support a war against a foreign aggressor who threatens national sovereignty and moral decencies is to construct oneself as a member of a nation of innocent heros. To define the people one hurts as evil is to define oneself as virtuous. The narrative establishes the identities of enemy and victim–savior by defining the latter as emerging from an innocent past and as destined to help bring about a brighter future world cleansed of the contamination the enemy embodies. (Edelman, 1988, p. 76)

The competition between authorities and challengers over the news media in insurrections and wars cannot be understood by focusing exclusively on the question of access. There is also a very important struggle over frames of the conflict that determines the role of the news media. Terrorists, for example, are often able to use exceptionally horrid acts of violence to achieve access to the news media, but the ensuing media frames are unlikely to bring third-party support.

There are two competing meta-frames that appear regularly in insurgencies and unequal wars. The first is the *law and order* frame, promoted by the authorities or, in unequal wars, by the more powerful antagonist. The major focus of this frame is the need to respond to a *threat* being posed by some upstart and the justification for using force to stop that threat and maintain order. The more powerful antagonist normally has a stake in maintaining the *status quo*: therefore, the need to maintain social, national, or international order is a central enduring interest.

The weaker antagonist, on the other hand, has an inherent interest in change. The *injustice and defiance* frame attempts to promote a particular grievance against a more powerful antagonist and includes a call for the oppressed to confront the more powerful enemy. The injustice may be general in nature (e.g., fight against Western imperialism) or related specifically to the behavior of the powerful during a conflict (e.g., the slaughter of innocent civilians). There are of course many other injustice

141

frames (Gamson, 1992) which do not specifically call for an uprising. This package of ideas contains two elements that distinguish it from other injustice frames:

1. The injustice is believed to be rooted in the inequality in power or resources at the disposal of the two antagonists.
2. There is an implicit or explicit call for rebellion or war as a means of ending the injustice.

Each of these cultural themes is easily recognized in Western culture. The *law and order* frame has an especially long history in American lore. The wagon train filled with innocent women and children that must be saved by the cavalry from rampaging Indians, Eliot Ness and the Untouchables bringing order to Chicago, and the modern action movies with the lone policeman/soldier annihilating hundreds of terrorists and/ or enemy soldiers are all important stories that contribute to the political socialization of Americans.

The American Civil War and World War II are probably the most important historical exemplars for Americans. The story of the Civil War as told in the northern part of the United States has two major themes. The first tells of the North coming to save the Negro slaves from the oppression of their southern masters, while the second emphasizes how the evil rebellion of the South had to be put down by force. The World War II story tells about the need to punish aggression, and again it is the Americans coming to rescue Europe.

The *injustice and defiance* frame also has a rich cultural history although many of these stories have been less popular within the entertainment industry in recent years: the biblical story of the Jews rising up against the evil Pharaoh of Egypt, the French revolution against the monarchy, the story of Robin Hood, the American revolution against Great Britain, the civil rights movement, and more recently the revolutions in Eastern Europe to overthrow communism. In each of these stories a victim rises up and defeats an evil and more powerful oppressor, sometimes with outside help.

The notion of cultural resonance suggests that the popularity of these two narratives within the entertainment industry offers some indication about the political mood of different periods. When Americans are more concerned with law and order than injustice, action movies will make much more money than those concerned with the suffering and injustice of the downtrodden. It should also be remembered, however, that there is no shortage of books or movies that point to the incompetency and brutality of those in power. Indeed, the frame for fictional politicians in the late twentieth century is probably just as contemptuous as that used for journalists.

The cultural contest between these two meta-frames is hardly a new phenomenon. Consider the following example of an *injustice and defiance* frame from a well-known insurrection that took place in the eighteenth century.

when a long train of abuses and usurpations, pursuing invariably the same object evinces a design to reduce them under absolute despotism, it is their right, it is their duty to throw off such government, and to provide new guards for their future security. Such has been the patient sufferance of these Colonies; The history of the present King of Great Britain is a history of repeated injuries and usurpations, all having in direct object the establishment of an absolute tyranny over these States. To prove this let facts be submitted to a candid world.

He has refused to assent to laws, the most wholesome and necessary for the public good.

He has forbidden his Governors to pass law of immediate and pressing importance, unless suspended in the operation till his assent should be obtained; and when so suspended, he has utterly neglected to attend to them ...

He has plundered our seas, ravaged our coasts, burnt our towns and destroyed the lives of our people.

He is at this time transporting large armies of foreign mercenaries to complete the work of death, desolation, and tyranny, already begun with circumstances of cruelty and perfidy scarcely paralleled in the most barbarous ages, and totally unworthy the head of a civilized nation. (American Declaration of Independence, July 4, 1776)

This is a list of grievances that justifies the need for insurrection and calls for defiance against tyranny. One should also note the appeal to third parties for help: "Let facts be submitted to a candid world."

The British naturally had their own frames about the colonial insurrection, and the need for *law and order* played an important role in these frames. In a debate held in the British Parliament on February 20, 1775 about the use of force, Governor Pownall was especially explicit in using this frame.

When I see that the Americans are actually resisting the government which is derived from the crown, and by the authority of parliament; when I see them opposing rights which they always acknowledged ... when I see them arming and arraying themselves, and carrying out this opposition into force by arms; seeing the question brought to an issue, not on a point of right but a trial of power; I cannot but say, that it is become necessary, that this government should oppose force to force; when that force is to be employed only in maintaining the laws and constitution of the empire. (Kallich and MacLeish, 1962, p. 56)

The more powerful antagonist inevitably writes the laws and then relies on them to legitimize the use of force against those who wish to change the rules of the game. The American rebels, however, saw themselves as victims and stories about such incidents as the Boston "massacre" fueled the fires of revolution. It is fascinating nonetheless to read an account of that incident as told by the British army captain in charge.

The mob still increased, and were more outrageous, striking bludgeons against another, and calling out, "Come on, you rascals, you bloody backs, you lobster scoundrels; fire if you dare; G–d damn you, fire and be damned; we know you dare not;" and much more such language was used. They advanced to the points of the bayonets, struck some of them, and even the muzzles of the pieces, and seemed to be endeavouring to close with the soldiers. A soldier having received a severe blow with a stick, instantly fired. On reprimanding him, I was struck with a club on my arm, so violent a blow, that had it fallen on my head, probably it would have destroyed me. A general attack was then made on the men by heaving clubs, and snow balls, by which our lives were in imminent danger; some persons from behind called out, "Damn your bloods, why don't you fire?" Instantly three or four of the soldiers fired, one after another, and directly after, three more in the same confusion and hurry.

The mob then ran away, except for three unhappy men who instantly expired ... The whole of this melancholy affair was transacted in almost 20 minutes. (Kallich and MacLeish, 1962, pp. 35–36)

Threat, like beauty, is in the eyes of the beholder. One can only wonder how much the American press was willing to publicize the idea that the British soldiers acted with restraint (even in the face of snow balls).

The cultural struggle in both the *intifada* and the Persian Gulf conflict centered on this same competition between the two frames. In both conflicts the stronger side called for *law and order* and the weaker side called for defiance to end injustice. I intend to argue that the Palestinians enjoyed a significant amount of success in promoting their frames, while Iraqi attempts ended in failure. While the structural factors detailed in the previous chapter explain an important part of these differences, the cultural analysis provides a critical supplement to that dimension.

This first analysis deals with the battle over media frames of the *intifada*. The investigation begins by examining the frames being promoted by the two sides and then uses the principles developed in Chapter 2 to explain why the Palestinians achieved much greater success in promoting their frames than the Israelis.

Israeli and Palestinian frames of the *intifada*

The discussion up till now may have given the impression that antagonist leaders have no real beliefs about the conflict but rather spend most of their time cynically planning public relations campaigns that will find just the right gimmick to win over the hearts and minds of others. As strange as it may seem, most political leaders have genuine convictions that are culturally born and bred.

As before, the frames of each side are summarized in Table 7.1 using a signature matrix. These details are based on interviews with Israeli and Palestinian leaders, material published by both sides, and detailed knowledge of the conflict. I do not mean to suggest that every Israeli or Palestinian agrees with all these components. One could come up with two or three more variations for each society. There were strong disagreements within the Israeli government about the true aims of the Palestinians, and possible solutions to the problem. While the right-wing members saw Palestinian violence as another attempt to destroy Israel, those from the Labor party considered it a predictable reaction to the occupation. There were similar disagreements among the Palestinian factions about the final goals of the *intifada*. While all agreed, for example, on the need to end the occupation, they disagreed about whether that referred to all of Palestine or just the West Bank and Gaza. Nevertheless, the signature matrix offers a good summary of the frames being promoted by the two antagonists.

The *law and order* frame being advanced by the Israeli government had a great deal of cultural resonance within Israeli society. Israelis felt genuinely threatened by the *intifada*. Until December 1987, Israelis traveled freely through the West Bank and Gaza for both business and pleasure. The occupied territories had, for all intents and purposes, become another part of Israel. Almost overnight that area became a virtual war zone in which Israeli cars were attacked with stones, Molotov cocktails, and (in later stages) automatic weapons. Many Israeli men found themselves doing a month or two months of reserve duty in the territories every year attempting to suppress the *intifada*; many were injured and some were killed.

The Israeli settlers faced especially serious threats as every trip outside the settlement meant crossing into hostile territories. While many Westerners view these settlers as right-wing extremists, they are seen by many Israelis as heroic pioneers reminiscent of the early settlers who were the founders of the Jewish state. Therefore, the pictures of school buses being accompanied by army vehicles were especially frightening.

Israelis viewed the *intifada* within a very different political context than the rest of the world. The Palestinians had been enemies of the state long before the state even existed. Many Israelis firmly believe that the Arab–Israeli conflict is a struggle over the very existence of the state of Israel and that any power which is relinquished to the Arabs brings Israel one step closer to destruction. It would be hard to find an Israeli who does not have friends and/or relatives who were injured or killed in

Table 7.1 *Competing frames of the intifada*

Meta-frame	Law and order	Injustice and defiance
Package	Palestinian violence	*Intifada*
Core frame	The issue is whether Palestinians who break the law and use violence will be stopped.	The issue is whether Israel will end the occupation of Palestine.
Core position	Israel must bring a halt to the violence in the territories and protect the lives and properties of Israelis and Palestinians.	The Palestinians must stand up and fight for their rights against the Israeli oppression. Israel must leave the occupied territories.
Metaphors	Time bomb/Fire	The rock/Zionism as cancer
Historical exemplars	Palestinian terrorism/Arab–Israeli wars	Vietnam/South Africa/Dir Yassin/1936 uprising
Catchphrases	No prizes for violence	With blood and fire we will liberate Palestine/Allah is great
Depictions	PLO as terrorist organization agitating local population into acts of violence against Israelis and Palestinians.	Israel as brutal, imperialist, and racist/Palestinians as victims fighting for their legitimate national rights
Visual images	Masked Palestinians attacking cars with rocks and Molotov cocktails/Armed Palestinians in military march	Soldiers beating Palestinian youth/Palestinian youth throwing rocks/Dome of the Rock mosque
Roots	Arabs attempt to destroy Israel/Outside agitation of local population	Israel's brutal occupation of West Bank and Gaza
Consequences	Increased political violence against Israel/A Palestinian state	The liberation of Palestine/A Palestinian state
Appeals to principle	The need for law and order/Never surrender to violence	Self-determination for the Palestinian people/Justice

the ongoing conflict. The PLO has, throughout the years, carried out hundreds of terrorist activities against Israeli citizens and the *intifada* is often considered by many Israelis to be just a more ingenious way of achieving their goals. The idea of having a Palestinian state on Israel's border, run by either the PLO or Islamic fundamentalists, is a truly frightening proposition for most Israelis.

Israeli frames of the *intifada* should be viewed in this context. Israelis felt threatened by violence and their government was trying to counter that threat. The *law and order* frame was the most natural one for the Israeli leadership to promote and for Israeli citizens to embrace. As an example, consider the following excerpt from an information sheet prepared by the Israel Foreign Ministry to mark the one year "anniversary" of the *intifada*:

Israel's measures are directed against incitement to violence, riots, terrorist attacks, and assaults against the life or property of Jews and Arabs by local radical elements. The unrest has been accompanied by massive stoning of persons and moving vehicles, attacks with slings, iron bars, chains, knives, and home-fashioned lethal weapons of all types. Increasingly, Molotov cocktails have been used, and the lethal effects of this weapon were seen in the October 30 firebomb attack on a public bus in Jericho, in which a mother and her three children were burned to death. It is regrettable that Arab residents have suffered casualties in the course of the rioting. However, it is a little known fact that since the outbreak of the disturbances in December 1987, more than 1100 Israelis – about 700 soldiers and 400 civilians – have been injured, some of them critically.

Israel is empowered, indeed obliged, by international law to maintain order and public safety in the territories, for the benefit of Jews and Arabs alike. The orders under which Israeli security personnel operate are explicit and well-known to every soldier in the field. The principles of restraint and gradual response are applied . . .

Those residents of the territories who are suspected of having committed security offenses are dealt with in accordance with international law and the humanitarian provisions of the Geneva Conventions. Article 43 of the Hague regulations stipulates that the controlling authority "shall take all the measures in his power to restore and ensure, as far as possible public order and safety." (Israel Foreign Ministry, 1988, pp. 2–3)

The script is by now familiar. The demonstration of a threat through the elaboration of the victims of violence followed by the legal basis for responding to that threat. The authorities have an obligation to restore law and order and they will do so. The only variation, which is worth noting, is the fact that Israel felt the need to convince the world that its soldiers were acting with restraint. This is a defensive frame that attempts to answer the many charges of brutality against Israeli soldiers. The need to promote such a frame is an important indicator of the uphill battle facing the Israeli government.

The Palestinian frame of *intifada* focuses on two issues: the evils of Israeli occupation and the need to stand up and fight for Palestinian rights. It is a classic *injustice and defiance* frame. Here too, the anger, the pain, and the mourning for friends and relatives are very real. They believe that the Israelis have driven Palestinians out of their homeland and forced them to live in the squalor and poverty of refugee camps; Zionism is racism; life for the Palestinians under Israeli oppression is considered a form of slavery in which humiliation is an everyday affair.

The term *intifada* is usually translated as "uprising" but a more literal translation of the term is "shaking off," as of a burden. The Palestinians are united in their belief that they have long been victims and they have a right to self-determination and their own independent state. The reaction of the Israelis to the *intifada*, most Palestinians believe, has been brutal and is symptomatic of the oppressive nature of that state. Hundreds of defenseless Palestinians have been killed and thousands injured. Many Palestinians believe that Israeli soldiers have been given a license to kill and that this license includes the murder of Palestinian women and children. The *intifada* has proven to the world that the Palestinian people have legitimate rights to a state of their own and this must be recognized by the Israelis and the world. The best source for these frames is the leaflets printed by the Unified National Command, considered a driving force behind the *intifada* (Schiff and Ya'ari, 1990). The leaflets, printed in Arabic and distributed to the local population, publicize both the political positions of the leadership and directives about which collective actions should be carried out to further the causes of the uprising:[1]

Hail to the revolutionary masses of the occupied homeland. You who have soared to the skies and pushed the nose of the tyrant into the mud, you who have beaten the tyranny machine and the criminal Rabin's clubs, you who patiently bear the blood and the victims who create the dawn of a free future, you who bring on the Tel Aviv rulers the strangling isolation and increasing international condemnation, you whose children and martyrs spit in the hated face of the enemies's generals, the murderers of children, of babies, the killers of women, of pregnant women, you uncovered the hated face for the whole world ... you brought out the truth to light, about the oppressive and racist "Israel." (Mishal and Aharoni, 1989, p. 77)

As with the Israeli message, the leaflet contains a statement of the problem and a solution. The problem is injustice, the solution is defiance. An ideological statement is always a call for action. It is also noteworthy that this and many other leaflets point to the importance of bringing the plight of the Palestinians to the attention of the world. This again illustrates the need for weaker antagonists to use the news media to bring third parties into the conflict. The Palestinian people can only be saved when the "true face" of Israel has been exposed to the world.

The second Palestinian text is an opinion piece written by Edward Said, a Palestinian professor of English at Columbia University who is a member of the Palestinian National Council. The piece appeared in the

---

[1] The leaflets distributed by Hamas are different in tone and use more religious metaphors and historical examples. It should also be noted that these leaflets were designed for internal consumption and not therefore completely comparable to the Israeli publications which were designed for the Israeli and foreign press.

Washington Post on April 26, 1988 and understandably differs from the leaflet in language and tone:

the Palestinians as a whole have now gone into direct mass confrontation with the Israeli military in the occupied territories, and politically they have successfully defied and stalemated what is in effect one of the most redoubtable armies in the world. More important, in showing no fear but acting with great resourcefulness, the Palestinians have reduced the Israeli presence and its schemes on the West Bank and Gaza to reactive measures – cruel, stupid, politically bankrupt . . .

Internationally, there is little sympathy for Israel now as, unconditionally armed and supported politically by the United States, it lurches from refusal and negation to killing and bombing, pretending that the issue is simply one of law and order. Whose law and order?

The uprising is an eruption of history compressed into the daily energies of a long-suffering, often forgotten and routinely abused people. Slowly the great disparity diminishes between Western praise and admiration for Israel as a democracy and pioneering state, on the one hand, and, on the other, the ignorant opprobrium Palestinians have had heaped on them since their world was shattered in 1948 . . .

By sheer force of will, this has been our achievement, symbolized by the uprising. No one, I think, doubts that our march to self-determination is now irreversible.

The US media, for all their fidelity to the uprising's more sensational scenes, still repeat cliche's about recognition and terrorism, even as our people are simultaneously unrecognized as having sovereign rights and are terrorized by Israel.

The frame of *injustice and defiance* is just as clear in this text as in the first despite the large difference in style. Oppression has been met with a revolt and the march towards self-determination is irreversible. Said also raises an interesting question about whether the U.S. media has somehow failed to capture an important part of the message the Palestinians are trying to send. The discussion turns to just this issue: to what extent were Israel and the Palestinians successful in promoting their frame to the news media?

Media frames of the *intifada*

The three major framing questions will again serve as guidelines for the discussion. The first framing question asks: "What do we 'know' about this conflict?" In the case of the Arab–Israeli conflict, the answer is: quite a bit. This analysis will focus on the frames that characterized the American press coverage – one of the most important targets for both the Palestinians and the Israelis.

Gamson (1992) has provided an extremely useful index of the frames used to cover the Arab–Israeli conflict, and it offers important insights as to why the *intifada* was more likely to be interpreted as a problem of *injustice* rather than *law and order*. His research looked at a wide range of American news material covering nine "critical discourse moments," spanning the Israeli declaration of independence to the period of the *intifada*.

Gamson identified four major frames used in media discourse about the Arab–Israeli conflict throughout these years. The *strategic interests* frame "understands the issue in geopolitical terms and views the Middle East as a theater of major power competition, a battleground for the cold war" (pp. 54–55). The *feuding neighbors* frame focuses on "the fanaticism and the nurturing of longstanding grievances" (p. 54) as the core of the problem. As the author points out: "the real victims, in this frame, are the bystanders, not the combatants" (p. 54). The *Arab intransigence* frame states that the roots of the Arab–Israeli conflict lay in the Arabs' unwillingness to recognize Israel's right to exist. Finally, the *Israeli expansionism* frame places the blame on Israel as a Western imperialist state which is attempting to expand its size at the expense of its Arab neighbors.

It should be noted that only two of the four frames – *Arab intransigence* and *Israeli expansionism* – clearly place the blame on one of the sides of the conflict. Gamson charts the four frames through the nine periods. He found that while *feuding neighbors* was the most consistent frame over the entire period, there was a genuine reversal of blame in recent years:

Arab intransigence and *Israeli expansionism* did offer competing targets for moral indignation, but it was a strange sort of competition. At any given moment, their competition was not so much with each other as with those frames that played down injustice claims. It is as if only one injustice frame at a time is allowed into this forum of discourse. Until the 1980s, the injustice slot was filled by *Arab intransigence* that even bested *feuding neighbors* in 1948 to win a majority. But after the Israeli invasion of Lebanon in 1982, this frame surrendered the injustice slot to its rival, *Israeli expansionism*, which currently carries on with the nonpartisan *feuding neighbors*. (p. 56)

The fact that the news media only allow for one injustice frame at a time is in keeping with its need to tell simple stories. It would, after all, be quite confusing to have two sets of victims, although the *feuding neighbors* frame does seem to have two villains.

The Lebanese war in 1982 was a clear turning point for Israel's international image, and the press began to use the ironic portrayal of the Palestinian David being victimized by the Israeli Goliath. Israel had attempted to promote the war as a defense of the Galil (the northern section of the country) and was infuriated at the Western news media when it was cast as the bully of the story. As with the *intifada*, however, the frame adopted by the media was based not only on the best pictures they could find but also on the political climate surrounding the war.

There can be little doubt that existing frames about the Israeli treatment of the Palestinians had a tremendous impact on the coverage of these events. One of the most experienced officers in the army spokesperson's office offered his own understanding about Israel's changing fortunes in the international news media:

The best we can achieve now is damage control. Because the stereotypes of the story have been reversed. Even during the honeymoon between the [Israeli army] and the foreign media up to 1973, the image which was created, which was very flattering, was not an accurate image. It was a stereotype: the supermen, the guys flying to Entebbe to rescue hostages, the impeccable, invincible Israeli army. So those old cows were slaughtered in 1973. So we are dealing with a new reality. That over-inflated image laid the seeds for the role reversal we see today. What is required in both cases, is the lowering of expectations to try to adjust them to realities. But if you don't use stereotypes you don't get a good story. The essence of this story is the color, the drama, the action, the black and white. The news "Dynasty" about Israel. There is still a love affair with the Israel story, not with Israel, not with the [Israeli army], but with the Israeli story because it is a top of the line story which can be projected on the electronic media.

It's an ongoing Dynasty. A mini-series and between chapter 19 and 23 it is going to be the Palestinians who are the heros and the Israelis who are going to be the villains, but between chapter 123 and 150 it may still reverse itself and then the Israelis will be the heros and the Arabs will be the villains again. So I think we will see another cycle of role reversal simply because of the infatuation with the Israeli story. It is a story which will go on until chapter 255 and then we'll have reruns.

It is worth mentioning that his remarks were made almost two years before the role reversal which took place during the Gulf war.

Lederman (1992) offers a similar assessment on the impact of previous story lines on coverage of the *intifada*. Lederman, one of the most veteran correspondents based in Israel, argues that many American journalists were "trapped in a story line" which offered a simplistic frame for the Israeli–Palestinian conflict:

Our problem as analysts is that once a story line does become widely accepted, we rarely question it ... The longer an incorrect story line remains in use, the more people begin to accept it as truth – and the more difficult it is to change the thrust of the theme or to find an acceptable alternate narrative thread ... Television, which has become the prime source of foreign news for most people, is particularly susceptible to the charms of a well-defined story line because, since there is never enough air time on the nightly news to discuss complicated subjects in depth, television reporters need a simple and clear narrative with vivid characters to describe an event . . .

Well-aged story lines feel good. They go down smoothly as fine sour mash. They can lull the most skilled journalistic and political practitioners into a kind of trance in which events are automatically slotted into the frame of the story line without considering that the story line may not be appropriate for the events being described. (pp. 13, 15)

To summarize, the dominant media frame in the United States concerning the Israeli occupation provided important advantages to an *injustice* frame. It was, however, a dormant frame that without Palestinian action would have remained a minor issue with little need for Western intervention.

Follow the journalists

The second framing question is: What is the most newsworthy part of the conflict? To answer this question we begin with the first month of the conflict in December of 1987. Israeli leaders did not take the initial riots too seriously, and the general assumption was that they would die down as they had in the past (Schiff and Ya'ari, 1990).

As the incidents began to grow in scope and duration, two things became clear. Firstly, the violence in the territories was going to be a more important political story than anyone had imagined. Secondly, the most newsworthy part of the story concerned the violent confrontations between Israeli soldiers and Palestinian youth. These scenes provided the major drama of the *intifada*.

It was an exceptionally visual drama that made for wonderful television. As Lederman (1992) put it: "It is doubtful whether any public relations outfit, no matter how experienced and skilled, could have created a media drama as successfully as did the Palestinian youngsters who took to the streets in December 1987" (p. 61). The now-familiar scenes of children throwing stones at armed Israeli soldiers, the black smoke from burning tires, soldiers aiming and firing tear gas or rubber bullets, arrests, and beatings all made for riveting television. There was nothing else in Israel that could compete with these scenes. Journalists follow the action, and the action was in the West Bank and Gaza.[2]

The fact that the street scenes were the most newsworthy part of the

---

[2]   It is rare that journalists get access to this type of action. When journalists attempted to cover the Palestinian rebellion against King Hussein in 1970, they were kept locked in a hotel basement for three weeks and then evacuated out of the country (Lederman, 1992).

story clearly had an important impact on framing. There was no escaping the obvious inequality of these skirmishes – Israel's attempts to place the events within a wider political context were doomed to failure. The Israelis did try to promote their own information and images but they could hardly compete with these scenes of violence. Claims that the Palestinians were a threat to Israel's security or attempts to place this insurrection within the larger historic and institutional context of the Arab–Israeli conflict, were bound to fail.

The confrontations in the streets and alleys of the West Bank and Gaza provided more than just journalistic resonance: they also had a good narrative fit with Palestinian claims concerning Israeli brutality. This became especially clear in January and February 1988, when the news media succeeded in filming Israeli soldiers beating Palestinian prisoners. The information and images which the journalists were processing gave tremendous narrative advantages to the *injustice and defiance* frame and made it difficult for the Israelis to promote a *law and order* frame.

One way to show the impact of the events themselves is to examine how each antagonist related to what was happening in the field. The words of one journalist who covered Israel for both the local and the international press provides a helpful insight in this direction:

The natural thing for Israel to do is to close up, the natural thing for the Palestinians is to be open – for obvious reasons. If anyone is sitting around brainstorming, figuring out how to do PR, it is the Israelis. Israel has to figure out how to be open, first they open an information center, then they close it. Should Rabin talk about the beatings or should he not . . . It's sort of funny when you think about it, because Israel has more control in the field, yet there's more confusion about what it should so.

The fact that one antagonist is constantly attempting to close a particular area from coverage while the other is trying to open it tells us that images and information have a power of their own. The political resonance of these scenes was never in doubt. The greatest hope from the Israeli point of view was that this story would just "go away"; realistically, the most they could hope for was damage control. The story in the territories was ugly. When the major framing question centered on who were victims, the events in the field offered very few advantages to the Israelis.

Many Israelis were unhappy about the way the army spokesperson's office was dealing with the press, and implied that a partial solution might be offered by initiating some type of military activity that would place Israel in a more positive light. A senior officer in that office responded to that idea:

We should never get our priorities mixed up. Whereas the Palestinians' main objective is to attract media attention, our main objective is to *play it down* [said in English] ... We have no interest in getting attention. People come to me all the time and say "why don't you initiate something?" Initiate? What exactly should I initiate? The ideal from my point of view is to be able to say: "Today nothing happened in the field."

One of the three army spokespersons who served during the *intifada* offered what I believe to be an extremely insightful analysis of the problems the Israeli army had to face in attempting to construct an attractive frame around an inherently ugly picture:

This may be the first war that the people of Israel have fought where there will not be any medals of honor given out ... There may not even be any ribbons. This is a completely different war ...

Here we have a war whose characteristics are completely different. If you examine this conflict, it is different from those we've faced in the past. Here we are confronting just the Palestinian people and not regular armies. As a result of all that, the quality of the [Israeli army] is never expressed.

This conflict is also in an area that is totally under our control, you're not crossing some border. That makes it more difficult for us ... we're not striking at some strategic area or striking behind the lines.

And also this conflict has no background. You're isolated. You are across from the Palestinians. You don't know the history, you can't say that it belongs to the perennial Arab–Israeli conflict, because it just doesn't look like that ... And all that has a bad influence on the media, on our image.

The images and the information simply did not have a good fit with the traditional narrative of Israel fighting off a large number of Arab states. The image of the *intifada* which best fit was that of a popular uprising against Israeli occupation. Because that is what it was.[3]

The struggle over legitimacy

From the start then, Israel already had two strikes against it. Television cameras were focused on the ugliest part of the conflict and previous media coverage had already established the Palestinians as victims. Which brings us to the third, and perhaps most important, framing question: "Who are the good guys?"

[3]   Those who still believe that political events have no influence on media frames should consider the complete reversal which occurred during the Gulf war (Wolfsfeld, 1993a). As noted, one of the reasons Israelis found it much easier to take control over the political environment was because of the national and international consensus against the Palestinians. As Iraqi Scuds fell on Israel, news frames centered on the victimization of that country and Arafat's support of Saddam Hussein gained little understanding in the Western press. The Palestinians were portrayed as Hussein sycophants joyously dancing on the roof as each Scud passed over their heads.

As noted, questions about the legitimacy of each side depend, more than anything else, on journalistic perceptions about the goals and methods used by the challenger, and beliefs about whether the response of the authorities was appropriate. Is the challenger suffering from a genuine injustice? Is the challenger using a reasonable amount of force in the insurrection? Are the authorities using a reasonable amount of force to oppose the insurrection?

Decisions among the media about what is a "genuine" injustice and what is a "reasonable" amount of force depend on how the information and images resonate within the political culture of each news medium. The principles of political resonance point to the fact that every news organ has its *own political belief system* that is reflected in the way it frames political conflicts. One way to illustrate the importance of this principle is to compare Israeli news coverage of the *intifada* with coverage from other countries, especially the United States.[4] The trick is not merely to show that there are differences – which should be obvious to even the most trusting of media observers – but to attempt to explain the thematic basis of those differences and how such themes are translated into news copy.

At the most basic level we would expect that the Israeli press would be more likely to employ a *law and order* frame for covering the *intifada*, while the foreign press would be more likely to use an *injustice and defiance* frame. Nevertheless, there were also groups within Israel who were advocating an end to the Israeli occupation, and thus one would also expect to find these stories within Israeli coverage of the uprising. An excellent example of this phenomenon can be seen by comparing the headlines published during the first month of the *intifada* in the *New York Times* with those published in two Israeli newspapers, *Yediot Ahronot* and *Ha'aretz*.[5] The headlines were divided into eleven categories, five of which were considered good news for the Palestinians,

---

4   The Palestinian press is not included in this analysis because it cannot be considered a "free press" in any meaningful sense. Firstly, it is considered by its editors to be a mobilized press which serves, as in most liberation movements, as a tool of the movement. Secondly, its content is heavily censored by the Israeli army and this also has an important effect on the content of the newspapers (Wolfsfeld and Rabihiya, 1988). I am not suggesting, however, that these news organs do not play a significant role in the mobilization of Palestinians.

5   The cases which are presented rely solely on news coverage as opposed to editorials which is in keeping with much research carried out in the field of communication. There is no reason, however, to treat editorials and cartoons as missing cases in such an analysis. While it is true that one format is supposed to be opinion and the other is not, and that it is more interesting to study the ways in which political opinions find their way into the news, editorials may have as much (or even more) impact on the political process as news reports. Thus the editorial section can be studied as both an independent variable (explaining news content) or a dependent variable where it serves

four that were considered good news for the Israelis, and two categories that could be considered ambiguous.[6] The analysis is presented in Table 7.2.

The distinction whether a category should be considered good news for the Palestinians or for the Israelis was based on which types of stories tended to represent best the respective frames. The distinction is not always as clear as one might assume. When Israeli leaders are quoted, for example, they are often attempting to defend themselves from attack, rather than promoting their own frames against Palestinian violence.[7] In general, however, the analysis does provide a reasonably accurate picture of how each newspaper covered the initial weeks of the uprising.

As expected, the Israeli government had much more success in promoting its *law and order* frame to the Israeli press than to the foreign media. While about 40 percent of the Israeli stories provided the government's approach to the issue, only 20 percent of the *New York Times* stories did so. The *New York Times* was more likely to emphasize Palestinian suffering and injuries and Palestinian anger and defiance both of which provide important advantages to the *injustice and defiance* frame.

Nevertheless, the Israeli papers did produce quite a few stories about Palestinian suffering and about international condemnation of Israel's actions in the territories. The Israeli news media provided a more complex view of the *intifada* that allowed for a more equal competition among the two frames. This does not mean that the Israeli press was offering a more "accurate" view of the *intifada*, but that each news medium was constructing frames according to its own cultural base.

The Israeli newspapers were trying to tell their readers "what is happening to us" while the American papers are trying to answer "what is happening to them?" There are other, more subtle differences, in the coverage that reflect these cultural differences. The word "Palestinian," which often appears in American headlines never appears in the Israeli papers. One can think of several reasons for this difference (e.g., geographic frames of reference) but the use of the word Palestinian provides legitimacy to that people's struggle for recognition.

as an indicator of how successful antagonists have been in getting their frames adopted by the editorial staff of the news media.

[6]   The categorization was based on a coding sheet which is presented in the methodological appendix. The coding sheet was given to two independent coders and the final instrument produced a 93 percent rate of agreement.

[7]   It was decided to classify arrests, trials, and deportations in the "mixed news" category because such stories could easily give advantages to either side in the contest. An Israeli might see the arrests and trials as part of a *law and order* story while a Palestinian could see it as further evidence of Israeli oppression.

Table 7.2 Intifada *headlines in three newspapers (December 10–31, 1987)*

	Yediot	Ha'aretz	New York Times
Good news for Palestinians			
Topic			
Palestinian suffering/injuries	7 (7%)	10 (12%)	8 (17%)
Palestinian anger/defiance	3 (3%)	3 (3%)	7 (15%)
Outside condemnation of Israel	19 (19%)	7 (8%)	6 (13%)
Internal opposition to government[a]	9 (9%)	4 (5%)	3 (6%)
Palestinian society	1 (1%)	4 (5%)	4 (9%)
Total	39 (39%)	28 (33%)	28 (60%)
Good news for Israel			
Topic			
Israeli leaders quoted	15 (15%)	16 (18%)	3 (6%)
Palestinian violence	16 (16%)	4 (5%)	1 (2%)
Israeli government policy	8 (8%)	14 (16%)	4 (9%)
Group/country defends Israel	1 (1%)	3 (3%)	1 (2%)
Total	40 (40%)	37 (43%)	9 (19%)
Mixed news			
Topic			
Arrests/trials of Palestinians	11 (11%)	13 (15%)	4 (9%)
Uncodable headlines	9 (9%)	8 (9%)	6 (13%)
Total	20 (20%)	21 (24%)	10 (21%)
Grand total	99 (99%)[b]	86 (100%)	47 (100%)

Notes: [a] Refers only to *leftist* opposition to government
[b] Totals are less than 100% due to rounding

Another significant difference between the two sets of headlines, also reflected in the full news stories, was whether to refer to Palestinian actions as "disorders" or "protests." Israeli officials and the Israeli press are much more likely to talk about "disorder in the territories" which justifies the use of force to restore order. The American press, on the other hand, is more likely to talk of "protests" which makes any armed response appear extreme. This topology is extremely important for it sets the stage for all of the other information that is given in the reports.

Yet another variable has to do with how the two news cultures report Palestinian injuries and deaths. The American press generally talks about "Israelis killing Palestinians" while the Israeli press is much more likely to report that "A Palestinian was killed." Use of the passive sentence structure lessens Israeli culpability. A more extensive review of Israeli news coverage carried out by Roeh and Nir (1993) found that Israeli newspapers were more likely to use an active sentence structure when an Arab attacked a Jew ("Terrorists kill store owner"), and to use a passive structure when Jews attacked Arabs ("Woman is killed during riots").[8]

Differences in the way the news media construct frames of death are an important cultural difference. When Israelis were killed, the coverage in Israel often includes biographies of the victims, interviews with friends and relatives, and television coverage of the funerals. The news media serve as a forum for national mourning. Palestinian deaths were more likely to be reported statistically, especially in the later parts of the *intifada*. The American press reports about deaths of American soldiers in a similar fashion especially in the local news. Media constructions of death in any country both reflect and reinforce the more general cultural beliefs about which deaths are important.[9]

A second look at Table 7.2 shows why professional influences are just as important in the construction of media frames as political ones. One reason why the Israeli papers offer a more complex view of the *intifada* is that they devote much more room to the story. There are twice as many stories about the uprising in the Israeli press and what is not shown on the table is that the stories are longer and much more likely to be placed on page 1. If the Israeli press were only interested in serving the needs of the state, they would downplay the story. The journalistic considerations of proximity and impact, however, are much more important than any political considerations.

Professional differences are also apparent when one compares the coverage of the more popular newspaper *Yediot* with the more elitist *Ha'aretz*. Consider, for example, the differences within the "Good News for Israel" topics. While both papers are much more likely than the *New York Times* to center their stories around quotes from Israeli leaders, *Yediot* is much more likely than *Ha'aretz* to focus on acts of Palestinian violence. This emphasis on the more sensational aspects of the Palestinian threat is in keeping with the more popular tone of the newspaper. *Ha'aretz*, on the other hand, emphasizes what the government plans to do about the threat of violence, which reflects that paper's more analytical approach to the news. While both types of coverage are consistent with a *law and order* frame, professional differences lead to important variations in tone.

Another example of the differences between Israeli and foreign media

---

[8] The difference in language is frequently noted by Israeli columnists, but this has not led to any changes in editorial policy.

[9] This phenomenon goes beyond the subject of political conflicts. A soldier killed in war is treated differently than one killed in a traffic accident; news of a murder in a violence-ridden neighborhood is much less likely to be covered than when a middle- or upper-class person is murdered, and the ultimate mourning is reserved for celebrities. The size of one's obituary is one of the best indicators of social status.

frames of the *intifada* comes from television newscasts that were broadcast in three countries on December 17, 1987 when the uprising was only about a week old.[10] It is an interesting day to look at because it was a much "quieter" day in the field and thus journalists were able (or perhaps forced) to step back and offer a deeper analysis about the events they had been covering. The first excerpt comes from the NBC broadcast:

ANNOUNCER: Also in the Middle East. Once again today, Palestinians carried their rage into the streets of Israeli-occupied territories; however, their battles with Israeli troops today were less intense. In the Gaza Strip a young Palestinian died of gunshot wounds, bringing to at least fourteen the number of deaths since the violence began there last week. Tonight, NBC's Martin Fletcher reports how young Palestinians are leading the struggle.

FLETCHER: They call themselves shabab – street boys. A new Palestinian youth league dedicated to revolution on the West Bank and Gaza Strip, occupied by Israel twenty years ago. As the rioting of the past week subsides, the street boys try to keep alive the flame of revolt. Israel has increased its forces in Gaza by 50 percent this week. Elite fighting troops keep a high profile and force older Palestinians to clean up after young Palestinians rioted. There's only one reasons for all this – the occupation. It breeds hatred even Israelis say sometimes has to boil over. The Palestinians say they live a life without hope.

MARY HART: I don't see many chances for our children. They grow up angry. How do you expect them to feel for God's sake?

FLETCHER: Mary Hart has worked with the children of Gaza for seven years.

HART: It's enough for them to have been through what has been going on for the last week here. Seeing shooting, killing, blood, demonstrations, raids of their homes. That should be enough. That's how they live; what do you expect of them? . . .

FLETCHER: In a room in a refugee camp, a family describes how soldiers shot a relative in a demonstration protesting the occupation. They're proud of him and ask: if you lived here, what would you do? One thing is clear – the longer the occupation lasts, the tougher it has to be. And the more the hatred grows.

There is nothing very subtle about this story; it is perhaps best labeled an "Evils of occupation" story. Such stories have several variations – the wealth of the Israeli settlers in comparison to the poverty of the refugees, the daily humiliations suffered by Palestinians as they deal with the Israeli army, and the number of Palestinians in prison – but they all tell of the injustice associated with occupation. It is surprising to see

---

[10] I want to thank Akiba Cohen for providing me with the transcripts of these broadcasts which were collected for his own research on the topic (Cohen, Adoni, and Bantz 1990).

Fletcher offer such a clear-cut causal explanation for the uprising ("There's only one reason for this – the occupation") but it offers a useful summary of the story line: the uprising is fully justified because of the evils of occupation.

The point of this is not to rant and rave about media "bias" against Israel, but to point out that media frames of political conflicts – especially unequal foreign conflicts – usually contain a political position on the issue of legitimacy. This was true in the Soviet invasion of Hungary and Czechoslovakia, in Afghanistan, in the Kurdish rebellion against Iraq, in Bosnia, in Somalia, in Chechnya, and in the *intifada*. There are many alternative frames that could have been adopted in the *intifada*. Right-wing Israelis would argue that this uprising is merely one more attempt at the destruction of the Jewish presence in the Middle East, a goal that has remained unchanged for over 100 years. Hamas, the Islamic fundamentalists who played a major role in the uprising, would emphasize that the violence was part of a more general plan for building an Islamic state in all of Palestine. The communist faction in the Palestinian camp often framed the *intifada* not only as a fight against Israeli imperialism but also against the bourgeois elements in Palestinian society (see Schiff and Ya'ari, 1990). Fletcher, however, is forced to choose only one frame – the one that dominates the political culture of American television news.

The second broadcast comes from the ITN network in the UK on the same day. It is a much shorter piece, but it reveals the other major theme of most *intifada* coverage: Israeli brutality.

ANNOUNCER: A United Nations official has warned Israel that its tough reaction to Palestinian protests in the occupied West Bank and the Gaza Strip would spark off more violence. The Israelis have begun a top-level investigation after a secret service agent was filmed firing on Palestinian demonstrators.

SADLER: Although they say the heated atmosphere has been cooled down, the debate about the army's lethal use of force is raging. Israel television has showed pictures of an incident that's been heavily criticized. A young Palestinian tries to light a barricade on a main road. Troops then approached a small group of youths, and one of them is seen hurling a rock. A man wearing civilian clothes is then seen to take steady aim and fire in their direction. The army took the unusual step of identifying him as a government agent. The military's behavior has divided Israeli society. A left-wing group of Israelis tried to pay their respects to bereaved Palestinians but their condolences turned to turmoil, the army preventing another riot. And though the wreaths go through, the Palestinians were crying, more in defiance of Israeli rule – than sorrow for their dead.

This short piece combines all the elements of the *injustice and defiance* frame. Even the mourning for the dead is seen as symbolizing both victimization and defiance at the same time. This genre of *intifada* coverage is best considered investigative reporting in which the journalists (here Israeli journalists) uncover brutal behavior by the authorities. Investigative reports uncover shocking truths and demand justice. This genre of news reporting has a specific type of format – *Sixty Minutes* is the best-known American example – in which pieces of evidence are placed together to build a case against an individual or an institution in an effort to rectify the alleged injustice.

Many of the most famous *intifada* stories both in the Israeli and international press used the investigative format to demonstrate Israeli brutality. The "Rodney King" story of the *intifada* was a film on CBS that aired on February 26, 1988 with footage of three Israeli soldiers continuously beating a Palestinian youth as he lay helplessly on the ground. The constant showing of this film is probably better attributed to journalistic than political resonance. As pointed out by Lederman (1992), on the other hand, many *intifada* stories used particularly vivid archive files of Israeli beatings – without labeling them as such – to illustrate the standard story line.[11]

The third example comes from Israel Broadcasting Authority's coverage of the *intifada* on the same day. As with newspapers, Israeli television stories about the *intifada* are always much longer than those broadcast from abroad, offering a more complex story. There were two major stories that day. The first was a status report on the confrontation between Israeli troops and the Palestinians:

ELIEZER YA'ARI: And in the territories – in Judaea and Samaria, as in Gaza and East Jerusalem, there was a calming [Regiah] in the scope of the disorders today. The Israeli police are this moment releasing nine of the ten Arab students who were arrested last night in front of the Prime Minister's house. A curfew was placed on the refugee camp of Balata this afternoon following a protest by women and the throwing of stones at the security forces. In the Kasba of Nablus, our reporter Victor Nachmias reports,

---

[11] The filming of these beatings offers a rather worrisome lesson about the political ramifications of televised imagery. The so-called "beating policy" was introduced by then Minister of Defense Rabin as a means of offering Israeli soldiers an alternative to using live ammunition against Palestinian protesters/rioters. The number of deaths among Palestinians did in fact go down during this period. However, it was much easier to film these incidents as compared to the shootings because shootings were much less frequent and more dangerous to cover. The imagery of the beatings was much more powerful than any dry reading of statistics about the number of Palestinians killed. The most serious round of international condemnation of Israel, and George Shultz's decision to come and deal with the uprising, took place immediately after the beating pictures were shown around the world. Just as the Rodney King pictures had much more political impact than un-filmed stories of blacks being beaten (sometimes to death) by police, images proved to be much more powerful than words.

there were incidents of disorder and the security forces responded with rubber bullets that slightly injured one youngster. In Rafiach there were more disorders in the last hour. In Jerusalem, the strike continues in its third day and about that we have a report from our police reporter, Uri Cohen-Aharonof.

The police reporter then interviewed the Israeli police commissioner about what had been going on and emphasized that things seemed a little calmer. He closed his report: "The police are getting ready for the Friday [Muslim] prayers tomorrow on the Temple Mount, in the hope that the calm which characterized today will continue tomorrow." Threats and reassurance, threats and reassurance: this is a clear police story from the beginning to the end that has *law and order* written all over it.

There are a few linguistic points that are worthy of note. Words such as disorder, calm, police, arrests, and security forces all help place this story in the familiar context. Indeed the whole issue of how to deal with Palestinian violence is considered in Israel to be a *security* issue and thus directly related to all other security issues such as the defense of the northern border. Although Rabin's position in the government was referred to by the foreign press as the "Minister of Defense," the literal translation of his position is "Minister of Security."

In addition, use of the terms Judaea and Samaria, the biblical names for the West Bank, also makes a political statement about Israel's claims over those lands. When Menachem Begin became Prime Minister in 1977, he insisted that the government news media (radio and television) use these terms; when the Labor party again took power in 1992, the broadcast authorities went back to using the more neutral term of "the territories." The foreign press consistently refers to these lands as "occupied territories." Each of these terms offers a different perspective on the legitimacy of the Palestinian uprising.

The second *intifada* story broadcast on Israeli television that day told about the damage being done to Israel. The Israeli news media was much more likely than the foreign press to focus on such damage, especially when Israelis were being injured or killed. In this early stage of the conflict, however, the damage was more economic in nature. Apart from any political differences, it is unlikely that this kind of story would be used outside Israel due to the strict criteria of "newsworthiness" which is applied to foreign news.

SARI RAZ: The riots in the Gaza strip are causing damage to Jewish settlements in the area. In the Gush Katif area the vacation sites are empty, and the agriculture has been hurt because the workers are not coming to work these days. The problem of traveling on the roads is causing disruptions of the transfer of mail and goods to the settlements. Our correspondent for settlements, Menachem Hadar, visited the Gush Katif settlements and here is his report.

MENACHEM HADAR: The Gaza Strip does not look inviting to the visitor. You need a lot of courage to travel on the main roads, because every hundred meters there is a barricade of burning tires. The [Israeli army] takes care of putting out the fire in one place and then it immediately breaks out somewhere else. The settlement of Netzarim is the closest to Gaza. The youngsters from B'nai Akiva are trying to keep a high morale, they work as usual, but the feeling is one of being under siege [matzor].

ANAT (FROM NETZARIM): The dealers are not willing to come in and take our produce. They're scared. Sometimes the mail never gets here, the mailman is scared of the noise and all the confusion [balagan]. We try to get along.

MENACHEM HADAR: Is mom worried in Jerusalem?

ANAT: Mom is very worried.

Here we have a very Israeli perspective on the *intifada*. There is an Israeli reporter who covers the settlement "beat" and can tell the Israeli public how the settlers feel about what is going on. The viewer senses the fear that Israelis have living under siege, of being scared to travel the roads, and mothers being frightened for their daughters. The spreading fire serves not only as a description of the events but also as a convenient metaphor for the dangers posed by the *intifada*. The feeling of threat and the disruption of the normal order is clearly conveyed in the article – all of this is well in keeping with a *law and order* perspective. The Israeli press also carried many stories that looked at the conflict from the soldiers' perspective, including not only his fears of being wounded, but the personal conflicts about having to confront and arrest children rather than fighting a "real" war as he had been trained to do.

Bringing it all together

Constructing media frames is a complex affair in which images and information serve as the stimuli that are then evaluated in terms of journalistic needs and political fit. The last example of news coverage will be used to show how important it is to take both factors into consideration in explaining the construction of media frames.

I have chosen two cases, which on the surface seem almost identical. Both incidents involve an attack on an Israeli bus by Palestinians in which many passengers were killed. The first event occurred on March 11, 1978 and the second on July 6, 1989. The two stories presented below are both taken from the *Washington Post*. A relatively large portion of the news stories is presented in order to provide the reader with a reliable version of the two texts.

> Arab terrorist raid in Israel kills 30; leaves scores
> hurt; Fatah says its force staged attack

Palestinian terrorists aboard rafts landed on the northern coast of Israel yesterday, hijacked a tour bus, and went on a shooting rampage that climaxed in a deadly gun battle at a police roadblock just outside Tel Aviv.

At least 30 persons were killed and scores wounded, by official Israeli count, in what appears to be the worst terrorist attack in Israel's history.

A communique issued in Beirut by the largest Palestinian guerrilla organization, Al Fatah, claimed responsibility for the operation, and said it was launched as part of the Palestinians' determination to step up "revolutionary armed violence against Zionist occupation."

The communique said the attack was code-named "The Operation of the Martyr Kamal Adman," after a Palestinian leader killed in an Israeli commando raid on the center of Beirut in April 1973 ...

A youth who passed by the scene just after the first bus was attacked said, "We saw wreckage and a lot of blood. At first we thought it was a road accident and we wanted to help. Then we heard policeman shouting: 'Terrorists! Terrorists!' A car went by full of bloodied people. I don't know if they were dead or alive" ...

By the time the main incident ended at a roadblock just north of Tel Aviv, the tourist bus was a smoking skeleton and hundreds of Israeli army and police forces were scouring beaches and farms in the area for members of the terrorist gang who apparently escaped during the gun battle.

Reports from eyewitnesses broadcast on Israel radio said that the Palestinians sang patriotic songs, cursed both Egyptian President Anwar Sadat and Prime Minister Begin and killed several passengers who begged for their lives. [The text was accompanied by a photograph of the gutted remains of the tourist bus on a roadside outside Tel Aviv after it exploded during the gun battle.]

This is a classic terrorist story. The attackers are called "terrorists" in both the headlines and throughout the text – although the term "guerilla" is also used – and it is very much a police story. The major part of the story that is not included contains more direct quotes and descriptions by the victims of the incident. No other comments are made by Palestinian spokespeople.

The year was 1978, six years after the attack in which Israeli athletes were killed during the Munich Olympics. The Palestinians were framed as terrorists and, while they had gained a good deal of standing in the international media, very little of it granted any legitimacy to their struggle.

The second attack, while similar in nature, occurred on July 6, 1989 after the Lebanese War and the *intifada*. The differences in coverage are striking.

> 14 die as Arab steers Israeli bus off road; dozens injured in fiery wreck

A Palestinian shouting "God is great!" grabbed the steering wheel of an Israeli passenger bus today and plunged it into a deep ravine where it burst into flames, killing at least 14 people and injuring 27 others.

Israeli police said bus number 405 was about eight miles west of [Jerusalem] on its regular run from Tel Aviv to Jerusalem at noon when an Arab passenger jumped on the driver and jerked the wheel sharply to the right. The bus sheared through a metal fence and plummeted down a steep, 100 foot incline, rolling over several times before it exploded in flames.

Several of the victims were burned to death, while others were crushed by the bus chassis. When a crane pulled aside the charred wreck, three more bodies were found beneath the vehicle.

It was the deadliest single incident of violence since the Palestinian uprising began more than 18 months ago, and it resulted in one of the highest death tolls of civilians in peacetime Israel. There were reports of reprisals against Arabs and renewed calls here tonight from politicians of both major parties to impose the death penalty.

The alleged assailant, whom witnesses described as a bearded man in his mid-twenties, survived the crash and was captured by police. He was treated for two broken legs while under heavy police guard at Hadassah Hospital here.

Although police did not immediately release his identity, security sources said the man is a resident of the occupied Gaza Strip. He reportedly told interrogators that he acted to avenge his brother, who was wounded by Israeli army gunfire in the uprising. Police said the man claimed to have acted on his own.

"It looks as if it was an insane act of terrorism by a terrorist full of crazy hatred who decided to kill as many Jews as possible," said Prime Minister Yitzhak Shamir. "It is frightening that one man can cause so many losses. But that is apparently the result of the environment, the hatred of Israel with which certain people are raised and educated."

But PLO spokesman Bassam Abu Sharif, while not endorsing the action, was quoted by Radio Monte Carlo as saying he understood the motive for the attack.

"It is a natural human reaction for someone who sees members of his family and his children killed before his eyes," said Abu Sharif. "It is not terrorism, but opposition to the Israeli occupation. The only terrorists are Israeli soldiers, and at their head is Yitzhak Shamir, whose words we heard last night." Abu Sharif was referring to Shamir's decision Wednesday to bow to the demands of right wing rivals within his Likud political party and endorse tough new restrictions designed to limit severely his recent peace initiative.

One of the injured, Netanai Shamri, told Army Radio: "The bus started to swerve, and I knew that it would turn over because it was swerving so much. I bent over a little and protected my head with my arms. After doing this, the bus began to break apart. I was thrown within the bus and then I don't know how I found myself outside."

Two small army helicopters swooped down into the ravine and ferried victims up to a larger helicopter and ambulances on the highway. Most of the injured were rushed to Hadassah and Shaare Tzedek hospitals in Jerusalem. The corpses were wrapped inside white plastic shrouds and taken away from the scene in burial society vans.

"I can't describe it ... You see something black that just a few minutes ago was a human being," said Rami Yaffe, head of the fire brigade that helped in rescue operations.

There were reports tonight of two revenge attacks on Arabs in Jerusalem. In one instance, police arrested two Jews who allegedly attacked two Arabs at the open-air Mahane Yehuda market. In another incident, supporters of ultrarightist Rabbi Meir Kahane reportedly assaulted three Arabs on a bus. Israel Radio reported police were increasing their forces in Jerusalem to prevent further outbreaks of violence.

The incident increased to at least 37 the number of Israelis killed since the uprising began in December 1987. Some 550 Palestinians have died in the violence.

It was the worst such incident since March 11, 1978, when Palestinian gunmen infiltrated Israel and hijacked a bus north of Tel Aviv. Thirty three people were killed. [The text was accompanied by a photograph of rescue workers searching the wreckage of the burned bus.]

In this story the two frames are competing on a much more equal basis. One still finds elements of the terrorist story, especially when Israelis – including the Prime Minister of Israel – offer their frames of the incident. But now the Palestinians are allowed to offer an alternative *injustice and defiance* frame which states that the attack was justified. The newspaper account attempts to be balanced. The word terrorist is clearly missing from the headline and most of the story and intriguingly even those who carried out the attack in 1978 are now called "gunmen."[12] The question of whether this act should be considered an act of terrorism has moved from an uncontested assumption to a contest between two points of view.

There is also a clear attempt to place this act within the broader context of the *intifada*, especially when the newspaper points to the fact that so many more Palestinians were killed than Israelis since the uprising began. Yet the photo that is used to depict this incident is almost identical to that used in 1978: a burned bus.

How can we best explain the similarities and the differences in these two stories? Why is the first attack on the bus seen as clear act of terrorism and the second, if not legitimate, at least debatable? The best explanation is provided by considering the two types of resonance.

Journalistic resonance helps explain the similarities between the two stories due to the ways in which professional norms dictate how such events are to be covered and turned into news. Both events are considered newsworthy due to the inherent drama of a bus full of passengers being attacked. In both cases the eyewitness descriptions of horror and death add to this drama and are part of the standard routines for covering both natural and less natural disasters. The differences

[12] It is also worth noting that the newer headline uses the passive sentence structure ("14 die as Arab steers . . . ") while the older one uses an active formulation ("Arab terrorist raid in Israel kills 30"). This is the same pattern found in the Israeli news coverage of Jewish and Arab violence which was discussed earlier.

between the two news stories are best explained by considering the changing political culture within the American news media. The contrast between the tone of the two stories serves as a useful reminder that political resonance varies over time and also among cultures. The Palestinian movement had gained a good deal of international legitimacy between the dates of the two attacks and this is clearly reflected in the *Washington Post* coverage. As discussed, Palestinian claims of injustice resonated much better with the Western news media after the Lebanese war in 1982 and especially after the initial year and a half of the *intifada*. The *political context* of the story had changed and with it the way it was framed. This was considered an *intifada* story and Palestinians were given the chance to tell their side of the story.

The story about the second bus attack helps make the point that events matter. In direct contrast to most *intifada* stories, it is the Israelis who are the most obvious victims. It is true that the *Washington Post* is much more likely to place this event within the context of the *intifada*, but the story could hardly be considered good news for the Palestinians. The Palestinian spokesperson is careful not endorse the action, and although he offers his own claims of victimization as a justification for the violence, it is reasonable to assume that it is he, rather than the Israelis, who would prefer to have this story fade into oblivion.

Thus, although the incidents seem on the surface very similar, the transactions occurred within a very different news environment and it is this interaction between the stimuli and the news processors that produced the final stories. News stories are never completely "information driven" nor "frame driven": they are a combination of the two.

Summary

The Palestinians were the clear winners in the cultural contest over the *intifada*. The information and images collected by American journalists resonated both professionally and politically with an *injustice and defiance* frame. Israeli claims about the threat posed by the rebellion appeared to be distant and abstract while the victimization of the Palestinian people was vivid. The *law and order* frame resonated better within the political culture of the Israeli press, but competing frames emerged even within Israel.

There were three major reasons why the Israelis were unable to translate their political power into power over the news media during the *intifada*. First, as described in the previous chapter, they were unable to take control over the political environment. Second, the *intifada* quickly became an international conflict and the power differences between

Israel and the Palestinians become less significant on this level. Finally, the professional and political resonance of the available information and images gave clear advantages to the Palestinian's *injustice and defiance* frame over the *law and order* frame being promoted by the Israelis.

The degree of success achieved by the Palestinians may be unusual when compared with other challengers. Nevertheless, the case offers important evidence that challengers can compete and even win the cultural war when they have the ability to carry out actions that are considered not only newsworthy but legitimate, when the news media are politically receptive to their claims of injustice, and when the reactions of the authorities serve to reinforce their role as victims. Politics is a central element in every one of these processes.

8 The cultural struggle over the Gulf war: Iraqi aggression or American imperialism?

It was a time of great and exalting excitement,
the country was up in arms,
the war was on,
in every breast
burned the holy fire of patriotism;
the drums were beating,
the bands playing,
the toy pistols popping,
the bunched firecrackers
hissing and spluttering ...
It was indeed a glad and gracious time,
and the half-dozen rash spirits
that ventured to disapprove of the war
and cast a doubt upon its righteousness
straightway got such a stern,
and angry warning,
that for their personal safety's sake
they quickly ran out of sight
and offended no more in that way ...

When you have prayed for victory,
you have prayed for,
many unmentioned results,
which follow victory – *must* follow it,
cannot help but follow it. Upon the listening spirit,
of God the Father fell also,
the unspoken part of the prayer. He commandeth me,
to put it into words,
Listen! ...
O Lord our God,
help us,
to tear their soldiers to bloody shreds,
with our shells,
help us to cover their smiling fields,
with the pale forms,
of their patriot dead,

help us,
to drown the thunder,
of the guns,
with the shrieks,
of their wounded,
writhing in pain,
help us,
to lay waste,
to their humble homes,
with a hurricane of fire,
help us,
to wring the hearts of their unoffending widows,
with unavailing grief,
help us,
to turn them out roofless,
with their little children,
to wander unfriended,
the wastes,
of their desolated land,
in rags and hunger,
and thirst . . .
We ask it, in the spirit of love, of Him Who is the Source of Love,
. . . Amen.   (Mark Twain, 1970, pp. 1–14)

The Gulf conflict represents an excellent example in which the news media enthusiastically adopted the authorities' *law and order* frame and virtually ignored the *injustice and defiance* frame being promoted by the challenger. The promotion of this frame was an important element in US President George Bush's effort to mobilize domestic and international support for military action against Iraq. In hindsight this victory seems almost inevitable, especially as Saddam Hussein seemed so willing to play the role of villain. Nevertheless, a closer analysis reveals that even here there were some important exceptions to this rule offering valuable lessons about how the role of the news media can change.

It is worth recalling the first unequal conflict between Iraq and Kuwait. The news media played an important role in mobilizing international sympathy for Kuwait though, here, the message was one of *injustice* with very little *defiance*. The Kuwaiti authorities in exile found it relatively easy to promote their frame to the Western news media. As detailed in Manheim (1994), the Kuwaitis used their money to hire the public relations firm of Hill and Knowlton, already experienced in the field of "public diplomacy." The carefully prepared stories of Iraqi atrocities (at least some of which proved to be untrue) were broadcast around the world to ensure international intervention.

In any case, the more significant conflict between the United States and Iraq quickly became the focus of world attention. The Bush administration became the main promoter of Kuwaiti victimization that served as the linchpin for the *law and order* frame, while Iraq was promoting its own version of the *injustice and defiance* frame. The discussion turns then to a specification of the two competing frames.

Iraqi aggression versus American imperialism

The signature matrix that summarizes the two frames is presented in Table 8.1. The matrix was constructed from speeches made by President Bush and Saddam Hussein. As always, the summary should be seen as an attempt to capture the general tone of each frame rather than a detailed description of each component.

The Bush administration's frame of the conflict was straightforward from very early in the conflict. The Iraqi invasion of Kuwait was seen as a clear act of international aggression to which the world must respond, if necessary by force. The decisions of the United Nations Security Council offered an important legal framework for military action and the frequent uses of the historical exemplar of "Hitler" and the catch-phrase "New World Order" offered a clear *law and order* frame.

An example of the Bush rhetoric can be found in a speech to American troops stationed in Saudi Arabia on November 22, 1990, about two months before the outbreak of war:

Why are we here? It's not that complicated. There are three key reasons why we are here with our UN allies making a stand in defense of freedom. We're here to protect freedom, we're here to protect our future, and we're here to protect innocent life ... Turns your stomach when you listen to the tales of those that have escaped the brutality of Saddam, the invader. Mass hangings. Babies pulled from incubators and scattered like firewood across the floor. Kids shot for failing to display the photos of Saddam Hussein. And he has unleashed a horror on the people of Kuwait ...

As in World War II, the threat to American lives from a seemingly distant enemy must be measured against the nature of the aggression itself. A dictator who has gassed his own people, innocent women and children, unleashing chemical weapons of mass destruction, weapons that were considered unthinkable in the civilized world for over 70 years ... What we're confronting is a classic bully who thinks he can get away with kicking sand in the face of the world. (*New York Times*, 1990b)

As always, the establishment of a *law and order* frame depends on defining the nature of the threat. The United States will save innocent lives just as it did in World War II. These images of brutality that resonate so well with the public and the press can often serve as a boomerang at the end of the conflict when the dictators refuse to

Table 8.1 *Competing frames of the Gulf war*

Meta-frame	Law and order	Injustice and defiance
Package	Iraqi aggression	American imperialism
Core frame	The issue is whether the Iraqi aggression against Kuwait will go unchallenged.	The issue is whether the weaker nations of the world will stand up to Zionism and US aggression
Core position	Iraq must either pull out of Kuwait or be forced out of Kuwait.	"Kuwait" is an integral part of Iraq which will not be taken away from the motherland.
Metaphors	Bully	Jihad/The Mother of All Wars/Pro-Western Arab leaders as camels
Historical exemplars	World War II	Vietnam/Zionist occupation of Palestine
Catchphrases	This will not stand/New World Order/Must stand up to bullies	God is great/The noble Iraqi nation
Depictions	Saddam Hussein as Hitler carrying out mass murder and destruction/Brave American troops rescuing Kuwait from occupation	Bush as Hitler/Cowardly Allies murdering Iraqi civilians/Iraq as noble defender of Muslim honor/American–Zionist conspiracy
Visual images	Smart bombs/American pilots/Scuds falling on Israel and Saudi Arabia	Pictures of Saddam Hussein with troops/Civilian casualties
Roots	Hussein's desire to take over Kuwait and Saudi Arabia	US and Israel plot to destroy Iraq and control the Middle East
Consequences	International chaos/Loss of oil supplies/A new World Order	The destruction of Iraq/US domination of the world
Appeals to principle	Need for law and order/Standing up to aggression	Struggle against imperialism/Injustice and oppression by the rich and powerful

complete the script by committing suicide in the bunker. President Bill Clinton had a similar problem in Haiti when he signed an accord with the military leaders on that island when only days earlier he had portrayed them as butchers on national television.

An illustration of the Iraqi frame of the Gulf conflict comes from a major speech given by Saddam Hussein on February 20, 1991. While it is true that the address was given over a month after the war began, it contains a good summary of the major themes of argument developed by Hussein throughout the confrontation with the US.

The *injustice and defiance* frame promoted by Iraq ran along similar lines as those put forth by other challengers who have had to face the United States. While the ideas have been adapted to resonate with the Arab culture, the underlying claims center on the tyranny of the powerful and the need to resist oppression:

O great people; O stalwart men in our valiant armed forces; O faithful, honest Muslims, wherever you may be; O people wherever faith in God has found its way to your hearts, and wherever it found what embodies it in the sincerity of your intentions and deeds; O lovers of humanity, virtue, and fairness, who reject aggressiveness, injustice, and unfairness. In difficult circumstances and their events, some people – more often than not – lose the connection with the beginning and preoccupy themselves with the results – or forget, when there are resemblances – the connection between any result and the reasons that gave rise to those events, and on whose basis those results were based ... Many facts between causes and effects, or between the prelude to and the results of the circumstances and events that preceded 2 August and what took place on 2 August and afterward, have been missed.

This description was in most cases applicable to some Arabs and to many foreigners so that some of them could not remember what Zionism and US imperialism have done against Iraq, beginning with the Irangate plot or the Iran–Contra scandal in 1986 until the first months of 1990, when the plot against Iraq reached its dangerous phases when US and Western media began to prepare for the Israeli aggression against us, but which we confronted in the statement of 8 April 1990; when the Americans cut off bread from Iraq and canceled the grain deal concluded with US companies in the third month of the same year, that is 1990; and when they raised the slogan of an economic, technologic [sic], and scientific boycott of Iraq and worked to make Europe and Japan do the same.

We have faced serious difficulties in making them understand that what happened on 2 August, despite the clarity of the entirely just historic dimension, is basically not a cause within the course of the conflict between Iraq – as a bastion of faith and honorable aspiration – and Zionism and US imperialism. The events of that day are one aspect of the results of the battle or the conflict that preceded 2 August. The measure taken on the glorious day of the call is a means of self-defense, and one aimed at defending all honorable principles and values of Iraq. Although [inaudible] an offensive form, and account of the events of this day should not be taken out from the general context of developments. A correct account of this requires that it be placed within its comprehensive framework. (*New York Times*, 1991b)

One of the more interesting components of this speech is the demand to place the events of August 2 in a larger historic context. Antagonists are perennially thwarted by the inability of the press to provide a longer time frame in news reports although which side is disadvantaged by this practice varies. It will be remembered that in the battle over world opinion during the *intifada* it was the more powerful Israelis who were demanding that the news media place those events within a wider historical context. Those who believed that the Persian Gulf story only began on August 2, 1990 could conveniently ignore the drilling disputes between Iraq and Kuwait before this time, but also the earlier financial and military support given to Hussein by the United States.

It is also noteworthy that Hussein placed quite a bit of emphasis in this speech on the role of the news media in the conflict:

This flood of media campaigns officially conducted against us by 30 countries further complicated the prospect of establishing a link between causes and effects, and between what happened to the Arabs and to the Iraqis prior to 2 August, what happened on the day of the call to glory, and what happened after 2 August. All the accumulated extensions and influences of these countries accompany these campaigns, and are affected by them. Nevertheless, the noble person has remained noble, and is guided by the facts – not merely through what he sees and hears, but through that which his heart and his faithful empathy with jihad and his destiny with the Iraqi stance lead him . . .

Faced with this state of affairs, we found that the enemy media and the enemy policy dropped a heavy screen on every event, stand, or cause that preceded 2 August 1990 that could shed some light on these incidents and explain their true nature. Palestine – whose just cause dates back more than 40 years – as well as its future and the positions on it has been one of the most important pillars of the conspiracy in which the oil rulers have participated as conspirators against Iraq, led by the agent sheiks of Kuwait and the Saudi rulers.

Biased people have even tried to neglect the fate of Palestine as being one of the causes of these events. The tendentious media, which have widespread influence and impact, and the suspect politicians and those who seek personal objectives – backed by Zionism everywhere – began to focus on the 2 August events to depict them as having taken place without any basis or background and as though our attention were being devoted only to these events. They even issued orders to silence voices and prevent them from mentioning any historical background that would explain to the foreigner or the Arab what he does not know about the reality of the relationship that exists between Kuwait and Iraq, and that Kuwait is part of Iraq, but was annexed following the partitioning conspiracy to weaken the Arab nation, harm its status and role, and weaken every Arab country that has some kind of leverage. (*New York Times*, 1991b)

The importance that Hussein attributes to media coverage is understandable when one considers how central the press was to his strategy after the invasion of Kuwait. The news media were supposed to undermine the willingness of the United States and her allies to go to war, to convince the Arab countries to join him in a battle against Western imperialists, and to pull the Third World to his side. If the conflict with the Western world could somehow be placed within the context of American imperialism and Zionist aggression, his battle for world opinion just might stand a chance.

Hussein's backup plan focused on the civilian casualties brought on by the Allied attack. As with other challengers, the use of a victims strategy carries with it one major disadvantage. It is very difficult to be framed as a defiant victim. One can either be a weak victim or a defiant challenger, but an over-emphasis on either image undermines the other. Saddam Hussein's earlier speeches spoke proudly of the Iraqi armed forces and the damage they would do to any who dared oppose him. By the end of the war, when the Iraqi army had been decimated, only the *injustice* part of the frame could be promoted; the notion of *defiance* seemed almost comical.

This, then, was the essence of the two frames being promoted by the antagonists. The United States stressed the need for *law and order* and the need to respond to Iraqi aggression. Iraq's frame focused on the historical injustice of Western imperialism and Zionist aggression, defiantly challenging the West to the "mother of all wars." The news media had the potential to play an important part in this contest. In the end, however, the war over media frames proved to be as one-sided as the real war.

Media frames of the Gulf conflict

The cultural war was clearly won by the Allies, especially where it mattered most. While Hussein may have found a more sympathetic response within some Third World countries, and with those who considered themselves enemies of the US, the Iraqi leader had very little success in promoting his frame to the Western press (Mowlana, Gerbner, and Schiller, 1991). The reasons for the Allied success, and for some partial failures, can be best understood by returning to the three framing questions that have served us in the past.

What do we know about this conflict?

A factor that enabled the Bush administration to successfully promote the *law and order* frame to the American news media was the lack of existing frames for the Gulf conflict. In contrast to the ongoing Arab–Israeli conflict, the lack of knowledge among leaders, journalists, and citizens about Iraq provided a fertile soil for planting new seeds. It is always much easier to *create* frames than to *change* them.

Lang and Lang (1994) carried out a review of the way the press covered Iraq in the decade before the invasion of Kuwait. They came to the same conclusion:

Not until August 2, 1990 when Iraq invaded Kuwait did the news media depict either Saddam Hussein or the regime he had headed since 1979 as a major player on the world stage or as a potential disturber of world peace. Public opinion, according to what little polling data was available, had been equally oblivious to the threat. Nor, so it appears, had the foreign policy establishment been much concerned with gauging the likely public response in case of a confrontation with Iraq. The crisis, when it came, was a near-total surprise. People, even habitual followers of foreign affairs, had no ready-made framework from which to derive a reaction. To fill this void and so guide the debate, the political leadership resurrected the memory of two events: the improvised analogy of Saddam Hussein with Hitler and the haunting specter of yet another Vietnam. (p. 43)

Journalists, like generals, are often fighting the last war. The major cultural debate within the United States during this time centered on whether the approaching war would prove to be Word War II or Vietnam, a noble act of liberation or a quagmire. An extremely comprehensive content analysis carried out by the Gannett Foundation (1991) found that the term "Vietnam" was used more often than any other word in the coverage of the Gulf conflict. Bush himself used Vietnam as a reverse analogy to show how important it was for the United States to overcome the earlier trauma of defeat. This was a particularly American debate in which the symbols and rhetoric could only be understood within the context of the American political culture. The American news media were very much a part of that culture and thus it should come as no surprise that the coverage ran along similar lines as the political debate.

What is the most newsworthy part of the conflict?

The Gulf story was not only the story of the war itself. One cannot fully understand the plot if one skips to the exciting bits near the end. Dorman and Livingston (1994) and Entman and Page (1994) propose dividing the Gulf story into three chronological phases:
1. the *establishment phase* (August 2 to November 8, 1990) lasting from the invasion until President Bush's announcement to send 150,000 additional troops to the Gulf;
2. the *nominal debate phase* (November 9, 1990 to January 15, 1991) centering on the congressional debate about whether to use force; and
3. the *war phase* (January 16 to February 28, 1991).

The only change I intend to make for the present discussion is to drop the word "nominal" from the second stage.

While other classifications are conceivable, this categorization offers a useful summary of the major story lines for covering the Gulf conflict. It also offers an excellent illustration of how control over media frames varies with control over the political environment. The Bush administration took political control during the establishment phase, competed for it in the debate phase, and regained it during the war. By following the political action we can better understand both the successes and failures of the Bush administration in promoting its frames of the conflict to the news media.

As pointed out by Dorman and Livingston (1994) the establishment phase of Persian Gulf policy was critical to all that followed. In this initial phase of the story, the American news media faithfully followed the narrative offered by Bush, establishing Saddam Hussein as a genuine threat to world order. The most newsworthy part of the story was the Iraqi invasion and occupation of Kuwait and the immediate threat to Saudi Arabia. The Bush administration and others were extremely successful in using the news media to establish this threat by producing a variety of stories:

1. Stories of victimization of Kuwait, especially the baby incubator story (Manheim, 1994).
2. Stories about Saddam Hussein as another Hitler (Dorman and Livingston, 1994; Gannett Foundation, 1991).
3. Stories about Iraq's intention to invade Saudi Arabia (Kellner, 1991).
4. Stories of Iraq maintaining the fourth largest army in the world equipped with a large cache of nuclear, chemical, and biological weapons (Jowett, 1992).
5. Stories linking Saddam Hussein to international terrorism (Kellner, 1991).
6. Stories about Hussein's taking of hostages and using them as human shields (Gannett Foundation, 1991).

The Hitler analogy was especially effective during the establishment phase of the confrontation. A poll published by the *New York Times* during the first two weeks of the conflict showed that 60 percent of the American public "accepted Bush's comparison of Saddam Hussein to Hitler" (cited in Dorman and Livingston, 1994). The use of Hitler, the Nazis, and World War II has become the standard historical exemplar for almost every political conflict; the specter of Hitler resonates in cultures around the world.

The American news media also contributed to the establishment of a threat by declaring the Gulf conflict a *crisis*. It was the Bush administration that decided that the Iraqi invasion "would not stand," and the news media immediately went into a crisis mode of reporting. The use of the term "crisis" establishes that there is a genuine threat to the prevailing order and something must be done (Raboy and Dagenais,

1992). It is the political leadership that often decides which challenges constitute a crisis. Carter, perhaps regretfully, declared the taking of hostages in Iran a crisis, while the subsequent taking of hostages in Lebanon was never defined by Reagan as a crisis. One reason the invasion and occupation of Kuwait became so newsworthy was precisely because the Bush administration defined it as a crisis, and the potential for war was real. While some would argue that it is the news media that create such crises, it makes more sense to see the role of the press as a catalyst which is set in motion by political leaders.

While the size and importance of the Iraqi threat were soon taken for granted it is important to bear in mind that there was nothing inevitable about this process. The much larger invasion of Iran was not framed in this manner, nor was attention given to Iraq's earlier repression of the Kurds. An alternative frame might have put greater emphasis on the risk to the United States' oil supply, a claim many opponents cited as the real reason for confronting Saddam Hussein. Indeed the Bush administration initially emphasized this line when the story first broke (Jowett, 1992). Such an approach, however, would have been less consistent with a *law and order* frame; innocent victims provide a more convincing reason for war than oil does.

In the debate phase of the story the action moved to Washington and most coverage centered on the controversy about whether the United States should use force to remove Iraqi forces from Kuwait. Critics in Congress were now providing alternative frames of the conflict suggesting that the Bush administration might be over-reacting. The change in the political environment led to an important and dramatic change in media frames. Entman and Page (1994) studied media coverage in the *New York Times*, the *Washington Post* and ABC news programs during this period. They pointed out that the debate preceding the Gulf war offered an almost ideal environment for the news media to develop independent frames about the conflict.[1]

Their study of the media coverage found a substantial amount of criticism of the Bush administration. Of all the assertions coded during this time, 55 percent were critical of the administration and 45 percent were supportive. The editorial pages of the newspapers were especially critical of the Bush policy during this period. The *Times* editorials and opinion pieces outnumbered supportive ones by almost four to one. Hegemony indeed!

It is true, as Entman and Page (1994) point out, that the supportive news coverage was given more prominence than critical coverage. This

[1]   An even more ideal environment, I would argue, would be one in which the vast majority of the Congress opposed the President on a particular issue.

is consistent with a central theme in this work about the relationship between political power and preferential access to the news media. As Entman and Page put it: "The prominence of media attention was calibrated according to the degree of power over war policy they exerted" (p. 85). While critics would suggest that such a pattern shows a lack of independence, many journalists would argue that good reporting demands allocating space in proportion to political impact.

Entman and Page also found that a good deal of the criticism dealt with issues of procedure (e.g., Bush asking for congressional approval) rather than substance (e.g., whether the United States should go to war). But their data show that the amount of substantive criticism varied considerably along with the political process. The vast majority of criticism was substantive when Congress held hearings on the issue. I would argue that there was nothing nominal about either the debate in Congress or the coverage of that conflict. It was a genuine debate about whether the United States should go to war, in which the public was presented with alternative frames on this issue. The Bush administration enjoyed inherent advantages that come with the position – especially in the area of foreign policy – but the political opposition was given many opportunities to express its views.

What *is* true is that the debate in Congress did nothing to undermine Bush's attempts at promoting the *law and order* frame. The debate in Congress centered on the best way to achieve law and order: through sanctions or through war. Nevertheless, if the public debate that took place in the news media was too "narrow," it was merely a reflection of the range of political opinions within the US Congress. While there were also probably some groups within America that supported Iraq's claims against American imperialism, one would be hard-pressed to blame their lack of impact on the media.

Meanwhile, back in Iraq, Hussein was attempting to change the story line. In the months before the actual war, Hussein was trying to shift the focus of attention from Kuwait to the Palestinians. The issue of how to frame the Gulf conflict became an integral part of an international debate that centered on the question of "linkage." Iraq demanded an international conference that would deal with all of the problems in the area and argued that the oppression of the Palestinians was the primary cause for all of the problems in the Middle East. The Bush administration rejected the notion of linkage, arguing that Hussein's true purpose was to delay international intervention and to break up the Allied coalition with the other Arab states.

It is extremely revealing to look at the history of the linkage debate as it appeared in the *New York Times* in the months leading up to the war.

A Nexis search was conducted to locate all articles (including editorials) which dealt with the issue of linkage before the actual war.[2] Seventy-six articles were found and coded by topic. The topics were then placed into three general categories as to whether they should be considered "Good news for Iraq," "Neutral/mixed news for Iraq," or "Bad news for Iraq." The results are presented in Table 8.2.

The findings reveal that Iraq did much better at getting this frame across than might be generally assumed by hegemonists. The fact that 47 percent of the articles and editorials tended to give some credence to the notion of linkage, and that only 17 percent completely rejected it, shows again that challengers can have an effect on the news media, even when they suffer from very serious disadvantages. Even some "neutral" news put the Bush administration in an uncomfortable political position, especially articles suggesting that Bush was backtracking on his opposition to linkage.

The history of this debate also serves as a further reminder how political events can change the tilt of the cultural playing field. One of the most important events in this process was an incident that occurred in October 1990, in which eighteen Palestinians were killed on the Temple Mount in Jerusalem. As the action was in Jerusalem, so was the news story. Israel's actions precipitated an enormous amount of international condemnation, and the US became understandably concerned that the event would be a great boon to those calling for linkage. Events do matter. Consider, for example, an article that appeared in the *New York Times* on October 9, 1990:

Administration officials said that the clash on Monday between the Israeli police and Palestinian rock-throwers was bound to complicate their efforts to keep world, and particularly Arab, attention focused on the seizure and occupation of Kuwait by the forces of President Saddam Hussein of Iraq.

Since the Gulf crisis began, President Hussein has been trying – largely without success – to link a resolution of his invasion of Kuwait with Israel's occupation of the West Bank and the Gaza Strip. The same is true of the Palestine Liberation Organization leader, Yasar Arafat, who has been trying to use the Kuwait issue to refocus attention on the Israeli occupation. His efforts include seeking a resolution by the United Nations Security Council condemning Israel for its continued occupation of Arab lands . . .

Finally, such a link would give the Iraqi President more of an opportunity to pose not as the occupier of Kuwait but as the potential liberator of Palestine, while making it increasingly difficult for Washington's Arab allies – particularly

[2] The search looked for any articles which appeared after August 2, 1990 which contained the key words "linkage," "Palestinian," and "Iraq." The analysis discusses all of those articles which appeared before the outbreak of the war. For details see the methodological appendix.

Table 8.2 New York Times *coverage of the linkage issue (September 1, 1990 to March 1, 1991)*

	Articles	Percentage
Good news for Iraq		
1. Iraq favors linkage	7	10%
2. Others favor linkage	13	17%
3. Editorials favor linkage	3	4%
4. Bush/UN giving mixed messages on linkage	9	12%
5. Temple Mount incident linked to Gulf conflict	7	10%
Total	39	53%
Mixed news for Iraq		
6. US disagrees with Iraq or others about linkage	9	12%
7. There is an internal debate going on within certain countries/organizations about linkage	3	4%
Total	12	16%
Bad news for Iraq		
8. The US Opposes Linkage	7	10%
9. Others Oppose Linkage	3	4%
10. Editorials Against Linkage	11	15%
Total	21	29%

Egypt and Saudi Arabia – to justify their pro-American stances. (*New York Times*, 1990a, p. A10)

The very publication of this type of article served to reinforce the notion of linkage, but it was the events on the Temple Mount that altered media frames about the idea. The notion of linkage also did much better than some of Iraq's other frames because it had more political resonance around the world. The Soviet Union and France had an ongoing dispute with the United States over this issue. They believed that offering some type of linkage to the Palestinian problem would allow Saddam Hussein a diplomatic fig leaf for pulling out of Iraq. This idea was also put forth in several opinion pieces by some Arab commentators and by some more liberal columnists in the *New York Times*. The following is an editorial by Leslie Gelb that appeared on January 13, 1991, three days before the outbreak of war:

With Congress now backing force to oust Iraq from Kuwait, President Bush has a decent chance to win without fighting. Here is what he has to do: First, pause and let the message of American resolve sink into Saddam Hussein's head.

Second, help fashion an Arab fig leaf to cover Iraqi withdrawal. Third, provide a moment for Israel to consider doing now what it surely will do later – present its own plan for Mideast peace talks, to be discussed and implemented only after Iraq leaves Kuwait. This is not diplomatic linkage, but diplomatic imagination. Its aim is not to appease Iraq, but to invigorate Israel in its own longstanding interests to deal creatively with the Palestinian uprising . . .

Mr. Shamir owes Israel this chance to carve its own path to negotiations and to insure that should war come with Iraq, the blame would fall where it belongs – on Baghdad. (*New York Times*, 1991a, p. A19)

The linkage issue was not, of course, the major news story of this period. It was, however, an important part of the international debate between the United States and Iraq and the fact that Iraq had so much success within the *New York Times* suggests that the administration's control over the American news media in the months leading up to the war was not as complete as has been assumed.[3]

The final stage of the Gulf story was the war itself. This was the end of the story that had begun in August of the previous year and the frame for the actual fighting can only be understood in light of what came before. The center of the news story in the establishment phase had been the Iraqi threat to world order; in the debate phase it was the dispute over what to do about that threat; and in the final stage it was what was being done. The major news question focused on whether the Allied forces could "get the job done." The center of the action was no longer in Washington, it was at the scene of the battle, or at least as close as the press could get to the battle.

It is hard to exaggerate the importance of this change to a war mode of reporting. Claims and counter-claims about the justification for military intervention became secondary as attention turned to questions concerning the actual combat. Who's winning? What does the battle look like? What does it feel like? How many of our people are getting wounded and killed? What's the strategy? What weapons are being used? When will the ground war start? Will there be a cease fire? Are the Americans going to go after Saddam Hussein?

Hallin and Gitlin's (1994) analysis of war news on American television points to two major themes that dominated coverage. The first was the notion of American prowess: "a story of the firmness of American leaders, the potency of American technology, and the bravery, determi-

---

[3] The linkage frame also did fairly well during the actual war although the proportion of good news for Iraq did decline slightly. There were fifteen articles which dealt with the linkage issue during this period and the proportion which could be considered good news for Iraq was 40 percent as opposed to 47 percent before the war. The percentage of neutral and mixed news remained about the same while the proportion of bad news rose from 17 percent before the war to 25 percent during the war.

nation and skill of American soldiers. It was the story of a job well done" (p. 153). The final episode of the Gulf story was, in many ways, a particularly violent sports story with statistics, interviews with the coaches and the players, briefings that described strategies (complete with the perennial black board filled with lines and arrows) and many replays. One could argue that sports imitate war, but the story lines are the same: a dramatic physical contest between two sides in which the only truly important question is who will win.

The second major theme identified by Hallin and Gitlin was that of *community*. The Gulf war was not just any contest: it was a contest between our team and theirs. The theme of community was especially strong in local news that produced a tremendous amount of "home front" stories. As one journalist who was interviewed by the researchers put it: "The most basic question of the war as far as I was concerned, was whether my son or my dad or whoever is going to come home alive ... Not the politics. Families don't care about the politics" (Hallin and Gitlin, 1994, p. 159).

When the community theme is combined with the prowess theme, it brings us back yet again to the notion of threat and reassurance. The threat is no longer just an abstract threat to world order but also a very real threat to "our" troops, and the public demands reassurance from their government that "we" will win.

This theme of rallying around the flag and the troops was a very important part of news coverage and made it virtually impossible for the Iraqis to promote any alternative themes during the war. In an analysis carried out by the Gannett Foundation (1991) the investigators compared the predominance of "yellow ribbon" stories to those concerned with the political controversy over the war. While political controversy stories outnumber yellow ribbon stories before the outbreak of the fighting, the balance was completely reversed after the actual war began. This was the story that concerned most Americans, and even those groups that opposed the war made a point of stressing their support for the troops. The cultural resonance of this theme can be further demonstrated by noting that in George Bush's State of the Union speech in January 1991 it was his call to support the troops that received the most resounding applause (Jowett, 1992).

The film known as the Gulf war was now complete. The threat had been defined in the establishment phase by the Iraqi invasion and the American response. The middle of the story was dominated by the national and international controversy over what to do about that threat. The end of the story was the US cavalry coming to save Kuwait. As the action moved from scene to scene the journalists moved with it. As Bush was the major mover and shaker in the Gulf conflict, he could produce and direct the production pretty much from beginning to end. He almost lost control of the film in the middle of production when Congress threatened to take over, but regained in time to direct the happy ending.[4]

When seen from the American perspective, the Gulf conflict proved to be a classic *law and order* story.[5] Two editorials will serve as the final illustrations of how firmly the American news media adopted this frame. As noted, the editorials of the *New York Times* and the *Washington Post* were mostly critical of the Bush policy in the early stages of the conflict. While supportive of the need to respond to the Iraqi threat, questions were often raised about the administration's rush towards war. Once the fighting commenced, however, the basic rationale for going to war was clear to the editorial staffs in both New York and Washington:

It is a powerful message on behalf of honorable goals ... They are to liberate Kuwait and restore its legitimate rulers, as President Bush said gravely last night, to insure stability in the region; to keep Saddam Hussein from seizing a chokehold on the world's energy lifeline, and to emerge from the crisis in a way that establishes a resolute, decent precedent for guaranteeing collective security in the post cold-war. (*New York Times*, January 17, 1991, p. A22)

Mr. Bush, to us, made a compelling case. There can be no question of the threat Saddam Hussein has posed to the American interest in an orderly world. Not only did he invade a sovereign state, rape it and remove it from the map – an act of total aggression though perhaps not in itself enough to distinguish him from all other tyrants. What made that threat so distinctive was the combination of his strategic location, his grandiose ambition and his ruthlessness and hatred of the West, taken together with the wealth and weaponry to fulfill his purposes. Saddam Hussein hoped and had the capacity to go on from Kuwait to destabilize and dominate a region crucial to world equilibrium. (*Washington Post*, January 17, 1991, p. A20).

Who are the good guys?

The final framing question attempts to evaluate the question of relative legitimacy. As noted, media frames about legitimacy have the potential to shift during a conflict because incoming images and information

---

[4]   In fact Bush did lose quite a bit of control near the end of the film when Saddam Hussein remained in power. He lost even more control in the epilogue which included the Kurdish rebellion. This loss of political control was directly reflected in the loss of control over media frames.

[5]   It is interesting to note that in an article on the effects of framing on the public, Iyenger and Simon (1994) take it for granted that the Gulf conflict is a law and order story (p. 181). The research question is whether the television audience will react to this as they have to other law and order stories such as terrorism and crime.

change. The key questions in this area center on whether the challenger is suffering from a genuine injustice, whether the challenger is using reasonable means to press its demands, and whether the authorities are using a reasonable amount of force in their response to the challenge.

The answers to the first two questions gave important cultural advantages to the Allies. The Iraqi claim of victimization rang hollow in the context of their invasion of Kuwait. Questions about drilling rights, Iraqi sovereignty, and American imperialism paled in comparison to the act of invading and occupying another country.

Once the war broke out, the only genuine frame competition concerned whether the United States and its allies were using excessive force against Iraq. Again the major question for analysis is whether the challenger becomes framed as a victim. The success of the *law and order* frame depends on the ability of the authorities to keep the moral spotlight squarely focused on the challenger. An alternative story line about the brutality of the powerful is always available from the news shelf and can be quickly taken down and applied when circumstances warrant. This is an extremely important wild card that can change the course of any conflict.

The Allied success must be understood not only in terms of their ability to promote successfully the *law and order* frame but also in their skill at avoiding, for the most part, the *injustice* frame. This accomplishment is especially impressive when one considers the enormous differences in the power of the two antagonists and in the number of casualties suffered by each side. Apart from a few important exceptions that will be discussed below, the legitimacy of the American campaign was rarely questioned by most of the international news media (Mowlana, Gerbner, and Schiller, 1991).

The cultural contest over legitimacy was also won by the Allies because they were, for the most part, sending their messages "home." Quite apart from all of the other advantages that they enjoyed, the fact that there were so many countries joining the American campaign against Iraq ensured a more unified reception by the world media. This is yet another example in which the political process has a critical influence on the role of the news media in conflicts. The ability of the United States to mobilize so many countries into the coalition meant that the news media of each country could also be mobilized. A less united political front would have inevitably led to a less consistent media front. The deafening resonance of patriotism could be heard around the world and this led to an almost seamless transmission of political boosterism from the leaders, through an extremely cooperative press, to an eagerly waiting public. The combined effects of the political power of the sources and the fact that all the sources were telling the same story proved overwhelming.

The differences in political power between the two sides were also reflected in the knowledge and resources available for dealing with the news media. The Allies were in a position to maximize the journalistic and political resonance of the information being given to the news media. The Pentagon employs thousands of professionals who have the knowledge and the experience to promote successfully military frames to the news media. A good deal of the American officer corps takes special seminars that teach them how to deal with the news media.[6] The American military also has the most sophisticated communications technology in the world, providing an exceptionally advanced system for the collection and dissemination of information and news. The ability of the Pentagon to supply the news networks with self-serving images provided the military with tremendous advantages in the production of media frames. There was a huge informational vacuum during the war, and only the Pentagon had the skill and resources to fill it.

Over the years the American military has come to appreciate the importance of the news media and evidently considerations about the role of the news media have become an integral part of military planning. Iraq's production assets, on the other hand, were pitifully small, especially when one considers the enormous task of trying to influence the world media. These differences in the resources of the two sides were reflected not only on the battlefield but also in the contest over world opinion. The fact that the Allies made a point of destroying the communications infrastructure at the very beginning of the war only made things worse for Iraq. While the Allies' production staff were creating a movie fit for Hollywood, the Iraqis were reduced to broadcasting static-filled radio broadcasts of Hussein's speeches.

Evidence also suggests that Iraq did not have a clear policy for dealing with the foreign media. Thus, despite the need for the press to tell their side of the story, the Iraqis began the war by expelling almost all of the foreign journalists, only to try to coax them back a few weeks later (Henderson, 1992). While much has been said about the "advantages" which dictatorships supposedly enjoy when they decide to go to war, they suffer from many disadvantages in selling their message to the Western world. While it is true that having a closed society facilitates informational control, this privilege is overshadowed by the lack of knowledge and experience such leaders have in dealing with an independent press. When one is used merely to dictating media frames,

[6]   A description of some of these courses was given to me during my interviews with the Public Information Officers at the Pentagon.

it takes considerable time and practice to learn the art of public relations.

Consider, for example, the amateurism of the drama in which Saddam Hussein is talking to his "guests" (hostages) about the reasons why he must keep them in Iraq until the Allies come to their senses. It is remarkable to think that the Iraqi information services actually planned this event in an attempt to counter American claims about Iraqi brutality.[7] The now famous scene of Hussein patting Stuart (the young British hostage) on the head was typical of the crude type of propaganda that is regularly broadcast on Iraqi television. It certainly could not be considered a very useful form of public relations in Iraq's attempt to achieve international legitimacy. If anything, the scene probably helped reinforce Hussein's image as an international terrorist and offered an important boon to American attempts to mobilize world opinion against him.[8]

Thus, the tremendous gap in the resources and skills of the two sides magnified the already significant political advantages enjoyed by the Allies. All of this led to tremendous differences in the journalistic and political resonance of the two story lines. The *Iraqi aggression* story being put out by the Allies met all three criteria for journalistic resonance: it was dramatic, simple, and familiar. The Allies were rescuing Kuwait from an evil and powerful dictator who had taken the country prisoner. The *American imperialism* frame being promoted by Iraq, on the other hand, was a complicated narrative that demanded a basic understanding of the ongoing conflict between the rich and poorer nations of the world. Imperialism just does not play very well in the West.

Hussein's message did find political resonance within some countries. The *Times of India* serves as a useful example, for it is a relatively independent newspaper and India remained unaligned during the Gulf conflict. Reading the *Times*' coverage of the war offers some fascinating insights into some alternative sources and frames that were available for dealing with this conflict.

While the Allies' frames of the war are represented in the Indian paper one also has no trouble finding elements of the *injustice and defiance* frame favored by Iraq. Even at the very beginning of the war when the Allies were proclaiming an unqualified victory over Iraq, the *Times of India* was offering a more balanced picture of the conflict. Consider, for

[7] It is not entirely clear who was meant to be the audience for this message. It was shown on Iraqi television and picked up by CNN (Gannett Foundation, 1991).

[8] On the other hand even the most professional handling of this affair could hardly have helped Hussein's image. Thus, Hussein's decision eventually to release the hostages did not garner him any extensive sympathy within the Western news media. The reality of taking of hostages can simply not be "explained away" with good PR.

example, a piece written by the editorial staff of the newspaper, on January 23:

Six days after it was launched, Operation Desert Storm has not been able to bend, let alone break, President Saddam Hussein. Iraq may be battered and bruised but even its most hostile adversaries are not prepared to admit that it is about to capitulate. Indeed every evidence suggests the contrary. President Saddam seems more determined than ever before to widen the conflict and prolong the war . . .

Inexorably the world at large is bound to ask whether the bloody conflict in the desert is meant to uphold the new order dear to President Bush to ensure the respect for international law as has been claimed by the partners of the alliance or even to promote their legitimate interests. What in fact seems to have happened in the course of the past six days is that the American led action has radically altered the image of the Iraqi President, given a strong fillip to fundamentalist forces in the Islamic world and thus dangerously widened the gap between the rulers and the ruled in Arab countries. The image of a tyrant who annexed a small neighbor is swiftly being replaced by the image of a leader who incarnates in his person Arab and Muslim pride and dignity. (*Times of India*, January 23, 1991, p. 1)

In this piece the element of *defiance* is especially strong.[9] Nevertheless, one also finds strong elements of the *injustice* part of the frame. The next example is taken from an opinion piece that appeared on the same day in which among other things the author attempts to explain the basic causes of the war:

More than anything else, the war in West Asia is a media and propaganda conflict. This is not to undermine by any means the enormity of the devastation caused by the hundreds of thousands of tons of explosives unleashed by an alliance of 28 powers against a single country. Nor for that matter should one gloss over the basic as well as immediate causes of the conflict: the intolerance by the West of any regional autonomous power, the economic, political and cultural arrogance of the US-led alliance vis-a-vis a world lacking Soviet countervailing power, the emasculation of the UN through the US repeatedly vetoing and nullifying its resolutions on Palestine or simply ignoring them at the behest of the powerful Jewish lobby and, last but by no means least, the unacceptable annexation of Kuwait by Iraq. (Jansen, 1991, p. 2).

Despite the author's disclaimer, the invasion of Kuwait seems to pale in comparison to all of the sins committed by the West. As expected then, India's neutrality in the war offers a more advantageous playing field for Iraq. Unfortunately for Iraq however, countries such as India had no impact at all on the course of this conflict and thus whatever

---

[9]   The editorial also makes some Iraqi-type predictions which turned out to be wrong. It predicts that Israel will enter the war and that demonstrations which were taking place in Arab capitals will eventually lead to popular uprisings against the Arab leaders.

sympathy Hussein acquired within these news media offered him, at best, a sense of psychological gratification. In the final analysis, the fact that the news media in countries such as India were more sympathetic to Iraq was less important than the fact that such countries had very little political clout in the international community.

The exceptions that prove the rule

The discussion returns to those incidents in which the Allies lost control over the events and the information and images turned against them. The analysis will focus on the way the destruction of the bunker in Amiriya resonated in the news media. The information and images that were being processed during these incidents produced an extremely discordant set of notes in the otherwise euphonious symphony being conducted by the Bush administration and its allies. The scenes of civilians being killed resonated much better with an *injustice* frame than with the *law and order* frame.

The illustrations for this point will be taken from television coverage from two different countries: Jordan and the United States. Jordan offered political and logistical support to Iraq during the Gulf conflict and exhibited a good deal of hostility toward the United States over the war. An article by Laurie Garrett offers a valuable portrait of the atmosphere in the Jordanian television newsroom the day after the bombing:

When Jordan TV news anchor Robah Rousan showed up for work on February 13, she had not yet heard the news of the bombing of the Baghdad air-raid shelter ...

"I walked into the news room and everyone was standing. There were tears in their eyes, people were shaking, some sobbing, and I said, 'What's wrong?'" Rosan recalls.

What had upset the JTV news staff was their viewing of more than half an hour of videotape, most of which the world's public – including Jordanian viewers – has never seen. (JTV did air far more graphic clips of the bombing's impact, obtained from both unedited CNN feeds and Baghdad's WTN, than those shown in the US) ... JTV news director Mohamad Amin was so overwhelmed by the video images that he ordered the worst of the footage withheld from broadcast.

"We felt it deeply," he says. "We were – we are now – all overwhelmed. But, of course, we must remain objective. And we don't want to show the ugliest images of the war." Rousan adds that her colleagues felt that broadcasting the grisliest images would fly in the face of Islamic teachings, which dictate that "the humanity of the individual, the dignity, cannot be defiled" ...

News director Amin recalls cursing the American bombers in a rage that night while his staff wept. "We all felt it," he says, "as if it were Jordanians under those bombs, our people. Because we are one people, we are all Arabs, we could see those children as our children, and it hurt our hearts like I cannot tell you."

On the air, Rousan visibly struggled to keep her emotions under control. She could not keep from sounding sarcastic, however, when she introduced a clip of US Brigadier General Richard Neal's explanation of why US-led forces bombed the site. "I didn't intend to do that, of course," Rousan says. "It was very unprofessional. I just couldn't help it, though." Another of Rousan's colleagues while delivering a news update earlier in the evening, had cracked on the air, tears welling in her eyes and her voice breaking. (Garrett, 1991, p. 32)

This piece offers a perfect example of the complex interplay between professional, political, and personal pressures that go into constructing this type of news story. Professional norms can set important *limits* to political bias. The Jordanian journalists were all struggling to be "objective" and "professional" and the fact that many of the worst pictures were left out of the broadcast can also be attributed to the constraints established by their professional culture. The complete picture can only be understood by considering the nature of the images that were being processed, the political beliefs and emotions of those who were preparing the story, and the training they had received about the "proper" way to present the news.[10]

In the American news media the images were also too powerful to ignore. The tone of the coverage, however, is much more cautious and suggests that there is more than one side to the argument. The following example comes from the television broadcast of ABC news:

PETER JENNINGS: We begin tonight with what all agree is a tragic loss of civilian life in the war and the great debate over who is to blame: the US or Saddam Hussein? An American attack on Baghdad before dawn this morning has left a large number of people dead and for the first time since the war began almost a month ago, other people in other parts of the world have been able to see the death and destruction which can be caused when the US strikes from the air. The US describes the target as an air raid shelter in a civilian neighborhood which had been converted to a command and control center, a legitimate military target, they argue, essential to Saddam Hussein's ability to make war. But they did not know civilians were sleeping inside. General Thomas Kelly said if the Pentagon had understood there were civilians there, there would not have been a raid. But many of the dead are women and children. ABC's Bill Blakemore filed this report which was cleared by the Iraqis.

BILL BLAKEMORE: [rescue] By the end of the day, about 200 bodies had been

---

[10] Garrett also discusses how this newscast resonated within the Jordanian public: "An elderly sheik went berserk minutes after the broadcast. Setting out in search of a target of his rage, he stabbed a German student whom he mistook for an American. For two days, hundreds of enraged Jordanians surrounded the Egyptian and American embassies and the United Nations building in Amman, shouting pro-Saddam slogans, throwing stones, and attacking Western journalists" (p. 32).

brought out of the Amiriya shelter. [mourners] Hundreds more are
expected according to neighborhood officials familiar with the shelter's
use, but no one knows exactly how many. [man] We found this man still
waiting for final proof of the death of his two daughters. [bodies] We could
see plainly as the bodies kept coming out that they are children and
women. [men] The man said to us: "This is the product of your
democracy." [aerial view of shelter] This air-raid shelter is in the center of
the Amiriya residential district. None of the houses were hit. Many of the
men waiting outside here have told us their wives and children have been
sleeping in the shelter every night since the war began. [Janabi] Community leader and shelter supervisor Abdul Janabi told us there are absolutely
no military personnel or military activities connected with the shelter,
which is next to the neighborhood supermarket and school. He told us this
will only increase the determination of the Iraqi people to fight to the end
... [Yousef] One of the survivors, 12-year-old Mohammed Yousef, who
was sleeping near the door, told us the shelter filled up last night as usual
with mothers and grandmothers, including his own who are missing and
with many children. [injured girl] Hospital director Dr. Bogos Bogoseyan.
DR. BOGOS BOGOSEYAN: [pointing to bodies] Is this in conformity with the
   international regulation? Just have a look, please. Would you call this
   mercy and justice? This is the most horrible, the most cruel thing I have
   ever witnessed. (ABC Television Network, 1991b)

These events are pure drama and it is the drama that drives the story.
The narrative gives enormous advantages to the *injustice and defiance*
frame by offering a graphic picture of innocent victims determined to
continue the fight against the United States. The second part of the
story, and a good part of the *Nightline* show that followed, employed
more traditional military sources that promoted the American frame of
this incident:

PETER JENNINGS: Ever since the war began the emphasis of the US military
   spokesmen have been that their attacks are precise and that enormous
   pains have been taken to avoid civilian casualties. The video of the
   bombing attacks that we've all seen has reflected that precision and last
   night in Baghdad they hit exactly what they were aiming for. In
   Washington they say they didn't see the people go inside. Here's our
   Pentagon correspondent Bob Zelnick.
BOB ZELNICK: [reporters in briefing room] US military officials in Saudi Arabia
   delayed the start of their daily briefing as they conferred with Washington
   over how best to explain the event.
BRIGADIER-GENERAL RICHARD NEAL: I'm here to tell you that it was a
   military bunker. It was a command and control facility. It's one of many
   that has been used by the Iraqi government throughout this operation. We
   have been systematically attacking these bunkers since the beginning of the
   campaign.
BOB ZELNICK: Neal said the US had evidence from satellite photos and
   electronic intercepts to prove the facility was military. [building graphics]

He said the roof had been reinforced and camouflaged and the building surrounded by fencing and military guards.

REPORTER: Was it not possible to tell that civilians were using it?

BRIGADIER-GENERAL RICHARD NEAL: Well obviously it must not have been possible or we wouldn't have struck it. We're not going after civilian targets and it was an active command and control structure. (ABC Television Network, 1991a)

This is a story that could only be partially controlled by the US military; it was one that got away. The President's "spin patrol" (McDaniel and Fireman, 1992) was dealing with damage control, and while they seem to have done an admirable job, important limits were being set by the images and information of civilian victims. This was the center of the storm and the government's attempts to set up windbreakers could only offer a partial and temporary protection. Fortunately for the American government the storm quickly died.

Thus, even in most favorable circumstances governments can lose control over a news story. Despite the cultural differences in interpretation, the images of victims that were broadcast around the world clearly put the United States and its allies on the defensive. While there were important differences in the way these images resonated within the political culture of Jordan and in the United States, they had a much better narrative fit in both places with the *injustice and defiance* frame than the *law and order* frame. The fact that so many civilians had been killed established the range of possible frames that could be applied. However few and brief, these windows of opportunities did provide Iraq with some moments of international sympathy for their claims against their powerful enemies.

Summary

The Gulf war stands out as one of the best examples of a war in which the victory of the more powerful side over the news media was as complete as its domination on the battlefield. The Allied forces enjoyed a multitude of advantages in the structural and cultural field that allowed them to control a good deal of the media discourse about the war. Saddam Hussein was defined early by the news media as the aggressor and the international consensus around the *law and order* frame made it extremely difficult for Iraq to promote its particular version of the *injustice and defiance* frame.

This part of the story is well known and accepted. The discussion, however, has also made other points that were missing from previous research on this topic. The first is that a good part of the success over the news media is best seen as a *political* success rather than a success in public relations. The fact that the Bush administration could convince Congress to enlist so many countries to join the Allies ensured that news media would also come along for the ride. This point is also demonstrated by the evidence presented about the second phase of the conflict when the inability of the Bush administration to achieve a broad consensus within Congress in support of the military option was clearly reflected in media coverage of the conflict. The news media can only publicize alternative frames when the political process provides them.

A second amendment to the conventional wisdom about the media and the Gulf war concerns the ability of the Iraqis to promote some of their frames to the American press. One learns important lessons by examining the exceptions to the general rule of American dominance. Incidents such as the riot on the Temple Mount, the destruction of the Amiriya bunker, and the attack on Highway Six provided major headaches for the Allies. The Allies were fairly successful at minimizing the political damage of these events – at least in the American press – but the story line was altered for a time because it was impossible to press the information and images into the usual mold. Political power, political consensus, and even political mistakes all have critical influences on how the news media cover conflicts.

Part 3

Conclusion

9 The multi-purpose arena

This last chapter brings the argument full circle. The central axiom of this work is that the best approach for understanding the role of the press in political conflicts is to look at the competition over the news media as part of a more general contest for political control. The previous five chapters have employed this approach to analyze the structural and cultural competition over the news media that characterized the struggle over the Oslo Accords, the *intifada*, and the Gulf war. The final step is to show how all of this leads to a better understanding of how the role of the news media varies over time and political circumstance.

The three cases were each meant to represent a different point on the "continuum of influence" described in Chapter 3. The role of the news media in the Gulf war was that of a faithful servant dutifully providing services to their Allied masters. The role of the media in the *intifada* was just the opposite; they were advocates of the underdog who played a critical role in focusing international attention on Palestinian claims of injustice. Finally, the role of the news media in the struggle over Oslo, I argue, falls somewhere between these two extremes. In that conflict the media played the part of semi-honest brokers who, despite the many advantages given to the Rabin government, offered a significant forum for public debate.

The goal of this chapter is to present the reader with as much evidence as possible to support these distinctions. While a "smoking gun" is pretty much out of the question, one learns quite a bit about the flow of influence by talking to leaders and journalists about their relationships during the conflicts. This approach is a useful method for discovering just "who was chasing whom": whether it was the authorities who were chasing after the news media or the news media chasing after the authorities.

The analysis will also focus on some *differences* among the news media in each conflict. The flow of influence between antagonists and the news media can only be understood by considering the *relative* power of each side. Thus, while I shall continue to talk mostly about "the" news media, it is also important to talk about differences among the news media. The ideas presented in Chapter 3 pointed to the fact that some news media are more powerful than others and that this has important implications for the extent of accommodation exhibited by journalists and leaders. As with the antagonists, these variations can be better understood by examining the value of the services being provided by each news medium, and the dependence each news medium has on the various actors.

The media as public servant: the Gulf war

The role of the news media in a given conflict, it was argued, should be evaluated by looking at three major issues: the extent to which the news media can break away from the authorities and become independent, the extent to which the antagonists are adapting to promote themselves better to the news media, and the extent to which the balance of power between authorities and challengers appears to have changed due to news coverage of the conflict. The Gulf war offers one of the clearest examples in recent history in which the authorities were able completely to dominate the press. All of the evidence suggests that the flow of influence was almost entirely in one direction: from the authorities to the news media.

The high level of control over the journalists covering the Gulf war would have been less significant if there had not been such an enormous demand for information about the conflict. The authorities' power over the news media was a question of supply *and* demand. There were tremendous news holes and only the military could fill them. One reason cited by television journalists for filming so many briefing sessions was that they provided a convenient vehicle for filling a great deal of air time. A reporter stationed at the Pentagon was asked whether he felt he had to broadcast almost everything the Pentagon gave him:

You had to because you're on the air so often or your newspaper had special sections devoted to the war, anything they'd give you, you had to go with. So basically we became a mouth piece of them and resented it, and at the same time, we didn't like it but you had no choice.

This need to get the story and the massive number of journalists assigned to the war led to tremendous competition among the reporters. There were 1,000 representatives from the news media stationed in Dhahran and less then 200 were able to get into the pools. Just as the competition among challengers increases the power of the news media, so the competition among journalists increases the power of antagonists. The American public affairs officers felt the pressure of this competition more than anybody. One told a story about how many of his men preferred to stay in the desert rather than come back to the Dhahran International Hotel where they had rooms. Whatever the difference in physical comforts, the officers preferred the peace of the desert to the pressures of trying to ward off the hordes of journalists beating their door down at all hours of the night. Another officer told of having a note passed to him under a bathroom stall asking for a "unilateral opportunity" to go out and cover something.

While all of the news media found it difficult to collect information independently, some news organs were in worse shape than others. As in all conflicts, the authorities gave priority to those news media who could provide the best services. While there is some debate about whether the television crews received preference over the print journalists, there is no question that each country was most concerned about the large media outlets from home. As one of the officers put it:

Frankly, the impact of the *Washington Post* and the *New York Times* and the four major networks is so much greater than for instance, the newspaper in Topeka, Kansas or some local news media outlet, that we just tend to go with something that is going to provide wider coverage, unless there is some specific reason to focus on local media, for instance covering their troops from their hometown.

The news media with less organization and resources found it especially difficult to cover the war. Correspondents were often given seventy-two-hour visas that could sometimes expire before they could even contact the troops from home. A more general problem had to do with the lack of knowledge the various news media had about military affairs. Many smaller outlets could not afford to keep a military correspondent on staff, and these media were especially dependent on military sources.

A more senior public affairs officer in the Pentagon was very proud of the fact that he could use the war to "educate" a new generation of journalists. He described the course he gave:

So I get a lady who is the cooking editor or I get the movie review editor from the same outlet sitting here. Well, after about three weeks in December, I realized that it is going to be a long education process. So what did we do? I started what I call Army 101 ... Twenty of them would show up every Friday morning for two hours and they would sit there and I started off with a primer and I said: That's a soldier. Ten of those make a squad ... That's a tank. That's a Bradley. They loved it because they had to have an understanding of what they were reporting.

Knowledge is one of the most important weapons journalists have in their struggle for independence. The lack of knowledge was just one more factor that reinforced the dominance of the military over the press. One should also bear in mind that ignorance was mostly one-sided: almost all of the public affairs officers working for the US military had graduate degrees in journalism. The military knew much more about how to influence the journalists than the journalists knew about how to obtain and process information about the military.

Evidence about the flow of influence also comes from interviews with the officers, who expressed a good deal of satisfaction over the coverage of the conflict. The use of pools and advance planning gave the authorities a fairly accurate notion of what was going to be publicized in the media. As might be expected from what has been said before the greatest satisfaction came during the actual war:

First of all I think the general public was pleased with the coverage. They had a lot. They had actually more than anybody ever dreamed of. It was more timely than they had ever experienced before and that was evidently a good thing for most of the American public. They loved it. The military, I think, you will find a variety of opinions on that. I think, in general, there is an agreement that most of the coverage was the kind of coverage that they were looking for, particularly during the war itself. The time building up to it, the Desert Shield period, I think you will find people who would be very critical about the kind of coverage that they got.

Again, we find a distinction between coverage during the buildup and during the actual war that illustrates how the political environment influences the construction of media frames. Besides the change in the level of political consensus that characterized the two periods, the military also had much less to "feed" the journalists during Desert Shield. When journalists get hungry, they often look elsewhere for information and angles.

The journalists who were interviewed also confirmed the fact that the military had little trouble getting its message through. One who was stationed at the Pentagon responded to the charges of being co-opted by the military:

I think it is only natural. I mean the press are individuals who are human as well and I think it is very easy to get swept up into the moment and the fact you are not getting any other information. I think the press coverage was colored just the way the Pentagon wanted it colored. By the very nature of us carrying the briefings here in this briefing room live, all that was, was a stage for them to get their message out. Our questions were really irrelevant because they would answer the question however they wanted and at times didn't answer the question and just said: "Well, let me talk about something else" and talked about the bravery of American troops and how well they are doing and that was going right out to the American people.

When antagonists are important enough to be covered live, it gives them tremendous advantages over less important speakers who are vulnerable to the editing process. The power to edit is the power to construct frames.

The military had good reason to be pleased with the coverage of the Gulf war. A content analysis carried out by Lichter and Lichter (1991) revealed that the Allied military campaign tended to dominate the news: the top three topics covered during the war were the air war, the ground war, and the military's strategy and tactics. The US military received an incredible amount of favorable coverage: over 95 percent of news sources praised the performance of the US military.

In the Gulf war, then, it was the press chasing after the military. The military had a great product to sell and they were pretty much the only store in town.

Behavioral and political outcomes

There is very little evidence of a reverse flow of influence in the Gulf war. The Allies, after all, had no real need to change their behavior when they were getting such supportive coverage in the Western press. There is also no real reason to believe that the news coverage greatly affected the balance of power between the Allies and Iraq. Although the Arab press may have been much less enthusiastic about the war, none of the Arab coalition partners abandoned the cause, and no new antagonists joined the battle after it had begun.[1]

What is surprising, however, is that the news media did play such a central part in American military planning. The public information officers working for General Schwarzkopf all attested to his tremendous involvement in media policy. Schwarzkopf was consulted on a variety of day-to-day decisions including the planning of briefing sessions, choosing footage for media release, and deciding which correspondents would be granted personal interviews. One of his chief assistants talked about the rationale for this approach:

Early on, I think, there was a recognition on the part of the leadership that in order for the deployment to work well, there would have to be public support and in order to achieve public support, there would have to be information

---

[1]   There were protests in several Arab capitals which may have been accelerated through extensive coverage of Iraqi casualties in some of the Arab press. Even here, however, there is no reason to believe that any of these events had any effect on the course of the war itself.

provided to the public. My personal experience, of course, was with General Schwarzkopf and I can tell you for a fact that he was interested in not only what the news media were doing but in how we were going to set up an apparatus that would enable them to cover what the troops were doing.

One journalist went as far as to suggest that the military leadership stationed in Riyadh were obsessed with the news media. Another possible explanation for this may have been the question of who was going to get credit for the victory. Several journalists suggested that the competition among the officers and the various armed forces for publicity was a primary motivation for media coverage. Officers complained about the excessive amount of media attention the Marines received during the war, which they felt may have affected the appropriations given to each branch.[2]

Thus, it would be inaccurate to say that the American authorities had no need to adapt themselves to the needs of the news media. The press was still the central arena and the authorities depended on the news media as a tool for rallying public opinion and for improving the military's public image. Such adaptations, however, all centered in the area of public relations, on how to best "sell" the story. There was virtually no evidence that any military operations were modified because of the news media.

There is only one major exception to this rule that is important to note. *Newsweek* (1992) carried out an investigative report that offers convincing evidence that the images being shown from the "Highway of Death" affected the final stage of the war. Media frames focused on the cruelty of killing Iraqi soldiers who were trapped and defenseless. According to the report, Chief of Staff Colin Powell and President Bush were both concerned that more pictures like that could turn public opinion against them. One of the reporters I interviewed offered a similar assessment when he talked about the combined effect of the Amiriya bunker, and the attack on Highway Six:

I think the military and the administration realized right away that they couldn't stand to make more of these. That the public was so gung-ho on the war that they'd overlook the first couple, but it became clear that if there were many images of civilians killed, that wasn't going to work. I think they were hypersensitive about that. I think it may have affected what Bush did when he ended the war, brought it to a close and saved the Iraqi army from a massacre. He knew the media images of a massacre wouldn't be helpful.

---

[2]   One of the reasons for the Marines' media success was that their commanding officer, General Boomer, was the former chief of information for the Marine Corps. He made a special effort to have as many reporters as possible covering the Marines and their contribution to the war.

Even in the Gulf war then, there may have been instances where the news media played an independent role. There was also strong evidence that the number of such incidents would have risen if the war had continued.

Nevertheless, the bulk of evidence all points in the same direction. The role of the news media in the Gulf war was that of a passive tool, another weapon in the Allies' vast arsenal to defeat Iraq.

The news media as advocates for the weak: the *intifada*

The role of the news media in the *intifada*, I argue, falls on the opposite end of the continuum. They played an independent, active role with an unusual amount of influence on the behavior of the participants and on the balance of power between the two antagonists. There were, however, some important differences among the news media and the concepts of value and independence help explain these variations.

The news media's ability to gain a higher level of independence in this conflict can be understood by considering the three factors raised in chapter 3. The Israeli attempts at official control were largely unsuccessful; the press' need for official information was low; and almost all of the national and international news media had sufficient organization and resources to cover the conflict.

The reasons for the lack of official control were discussed in chapter 6. The legal, ethical, and practical difficulties of sealing the occupied territories ensured a steady flow of information and images about the *intifada*. Israel, however, had some control over its own broadcast media and thus it comes as no surprise that almost all of the truly controversial footage was taken by foreign television crews. One reason for this was that the foreign media often had *more* film crews traveling though the territories than Israeli television. Whether this was for political or economic reasons is unclear, but it clearly increased their ability to collect information independently about the *intifada*.

The Israeli press was also much more dependent on official information than the foreign press. There was a much larger demand in Israel for information about the *intifada*, especially for official information. The public wanted to know what their side was going "to do" about the violence. The foreign news teams, on the other hand, had little need for Israeli government sources – the reporters often knew what was happening long before the officials. The limited amount of space that would be devoted to the *intifada* in the foreign media would be dedicated almost exclusively to the action taking place in the territories. Here too, one finds an overlap between cultural and structural considerations: Israeli journalists are more dependent on government sources because it is "their" government and their conflict.

Unlike the Gulf war, the foreign press had little trouble finding sufficient organization and resources to cover the *intifada*. As noted, the terrain and the distances were much more conducive to reporters and the small scope of the conflict also made it a much easier type of news story. Equally important, Israel had become the media capital of the Middle East long before the outbreak of the *intifada* (Lederman, 1992). The journalists stationed there often had years of experience in which they had developed hundreds of contacts and considerable knowledge about the conflict. As Lederman (1992) points out, this was in direct contrast to the situation in the late 1960s when most of the reporters were stringers who tended to spend most of their time in the press room of the Government Press Office. This also illustrates the relationship between resources and independence.

It should also be remembered that there was nothing complicated about covering the *intifada*. It was a story of Israeli soldiers attempting to disperse defiant Palestinian protesters. The television crews would roam the territories looking for the best shots of the day and correspondents could then add a short voice over to summarize the day's events. There was no sophisticated weapons technology to learn about, no grandiose strategic maneuvers to grasp, and almost all of the action was limited to one small area. Journalists could cover the *intifada* without ever having attended a single class in "Army 101." The final piece of evidence about the independence of the news media comes from what might be best termed "the frustration quotient." Whereas it was the journalists who were the most frustrated in the Gulf war, it was the Israeli authorities who were stymied in the *intifada*. While Israeli officials had some success getting their message through to the Israeli public, their inability to influence the foreign press was blatantly obvious. Politicians screamed and yelled about media bias against Israel, and those who were supposed to be "dealing" with the news media quickly became political scapegoats. The journalists did complain from time to time about government censorship and the repeated attempts to deny them access, but none would argue that they had become a "mouthpiece" for the Israeli government. Attacks by officials on the media are an important indicator that journalists have broken away from their minders.

Establishing independence, however, is only the first stage in placing the conflict on the continuum of influence.

Behavioral and political outcomes

The struggle known as the *intifada* was above all a struggle over world opinion. The news media are especially likely to play a central role in just these types of conflicts. The Palestinians were hoping to use their protests to mobilize the international community against the Israeli occupation. The relative military power of the two sides was irrelevant. If anything, the superior power of the Israelis probably worked against them, at least in the cultural realm. A senior member of the army spokespersons' office put it this way:

The battle for the media and the battle on the ground during the *intifada* are closely integrated. In this type of war, where it is not the amount of force which determines the outcome of battle, but rather the extent to which you can gain more external support for your case, clearly the media plays a very important role ... In limited wars where you have limited goals the media are likely to play an increasingly important role in affecting decision makers about whether or not to intervene in conflicts and on public opinion.

A similar point was made by one of the journalists who covered the Palestinian *intifada* for a major Israeli paper:

These demonstrations are not a war. The demonstrators do not expect to "beat" the soldiers, not even really to hurt them. The entire struggle over the territories is symbolic. It is a struggle over symbols, expressed in flags, in slogans, in calls and even in curses. Even the rocks are in a sense a symbol, it is also a weapon that could kill someone, but its primary use is as a symbol of protest.

They must send these symbols to the outside and not just to their enemy. And they are very aware of the need for the media to send these messages to the world. They are very aware of the political aspects of the struggle and do not see it as a war against the army or the settlers.

The interviews with journalists and leaders from both sides point to the centrality of the news media in this conflict. The power of the press was reflected in the willingness of each side to adapt its behavior in order more effectively to send its message. As pointed out in Chapter 3, such adaptation should be seen not as a mindless reflex, but as a calculated attempt to use the news media to achieve political goals. These calculations set important limits on just how far each antagonist will go to achieve better coverage.

Israeli authorities were especially concerned with the damage the *intifada* was doing to their image in the United States. Here too, the role of the news media cannot be separated from the political context of the conflict. Israel's economic dependence on the United States leads to a dependence on the American news media. It is not surprising therefore that the Israelis spent a considerable amount of time and effort attempting to control the damage from the news reports coming out of the territories. One of the people who participated in many general planning sessions of the Israeli army was asked how often the subject of the news media came up:

Very often, very often. People talk about what is being said in the media, and everyone talks about what happened before and after what was shown. And whenever there is a decision to carry out some type of operation there is a decision whether or not to close it to the media or not. The major reason for closing the area is that the media causes a great deal of problems.

As in the Gulf war, the Israeli military was very cognizant of the differences in the power of the various news media and worked especially hard to promote their frames to the American press, especially television. The television images were a driving force in the *intifada*, and thus these journalists were give top priority in the military's public relations strategy. The comments of an officer who worked in the army spokesperson's office are typical.

Well there's no doubt that when someone comes with a big set up like *Nightline* with Ted Koppel or *Sixty Minutes*, we have a pre-production meeting where we list all the requests. We find out where we can accommodate and where we can't. Clearly just the scale of the operation, requires from us, to give more resources ... Yes, there is an awareness of the impact of the program. We make an analysis of the impact of the media, or that particular media channel, before we go into any great effort to accommodate them.

One of the clearest examples of Israeli adaptation to the news media occurred in the field. The presence of the news media had a direct influence on restraining soldiers' behavior: soldiers were understandably less likely to beat Palestinians or to open fire when the cameras were filming. The officers and the enlisted men were all very aware of the international implications when "beating scenes" were broadcast around the world. Indeed, the influence of the news media on Israeli behavior is perhaps best illustrated by the fact that many training sessions for soldiers going into the territories included clips of these news broadcasts as a vivid reminder of the risks of such behavior.

The Palestinians also reacted to the presence of the news media during these confrontations, by becoming more militant. While there is some controversy over this point among those who were interviewed, most journalists admit that television cameras were especially likely to have an inflammatory influence on protests. Part of the reason for this may be related to the fact that the protesters had less to fear from the soldiers when the press was there.[3] What is clear is that public confrontations between Israeli soldiers and Palestinians protesters took on a very different dynamic than those that took place without the press.

There is an important lesson here for those who ask about the relationship between the presence of the news media and political violence. While most assume that the media increase the level of violence, the direction of influence depends on the antagonists' political goals (Wolfsfeld, 1991). The Israelis wanted to send the world a message of restraint while the Palestinians were sending a message of defiance. The ways in which each side reacted to the presence of the news media varied accordingly.

There is also quite a bit of evidence that the international publicity offered an important sense of accomplishment to the Palestinians. This too should be considered a political outcome, as such accomplishments increase the level of group solidarity among challengers which is an essential element for continued mobilization. Lederman (1992) came to a similar conclusion in his own study of the *intifada*:

The arrival of fax machines not only enabled the Palestinians with access to the machines to receive orders from abroad, they enabled Palestinian leaders to find out in real time the impact the rioting was having on others around the world. A newspaper page could be faxed from abroad showing the exact front-page headlines and the pictures being displayed ... It is impossible to underestimate the effect this feedback mechanism had on local Palestinians. They translated the enormous publicity they were receiving into a perception that they were winning their struggle for the first time. Within hours, rather than days, of an event taking place, they could tell how much impact their actions were having on others around the world. They could receive positive reinforcement that they were influencing international perceptions by their actions–and this helped fuel the intifada and strengthen the resolve of the demonstrators and their leaders. (p. 135)

One particularly interesting manifestation of this phenomenon was the competition among the Palestinians for public recognition. Many Palestinians monitored the radio broadcasts coming out of Syria and Monte Carlo that honored those towns and villages that had the courage to stand up to the Israeli forces. Political competition leads to competition over media space. This can be seen in the competition

---

[3] It is ironic that many of those who minimize the role of the news media in the *intifada* point to the fact that some of the most "violent" protests occurred away from the cameras' eyes. Violence, however, is often "measured" by the number of Palestinian injuries and deaths. The same evidence could also be used to bolster the more convincing argument that the presence of the news media tends to limit the use of force by soldiers.

among the armed forces in Gulf war and in the competition among Palestinian villages and factions in the *intifada*.

Many Palestinians saw the news media as their only hope for ending Israeli occupation. The term "advocate" also describes the personal relationships that developed between the reporters and the local residents in the early stages of the *intifada*. When journalists would arrive, they would be surrounded by people trying to tell them of their suffering.[4] In some ways the contacts with the news media were almost a form of therapy because the reporters were the only sympathetic channels available. A journalist who spent considerable time in the territories put it this way:

Well, its sort of a very natural thing. I mean the media serves as their only recourse for this great injustice which is being done to them by a powerful Israel. They have to appeal to people's consciences, appeal to world opinion. The way to do it is through the media. They don't see the media in the classic Western notion of objective reporting of the facts. They tend to see the journalists who come to see them as a way of getting out their problems, getting out their story.

The centrality of the news media to the Palestinian struggle was felt throughout the territories. Another journalist offered a particularly telling story that further illustrates this point.

I was in a very remote village not so long ago and I can't even remember the name. According to what the villagers say, it seems that the soldiers carried out a bit of vandalism there. There was one house where they had been conducting a search and had wrecked the place pretty badly. Anyway, we came to the place about two days after this happened, and they hadn't touched anything – the house was totally upside down and there must be at least twenty people living in that house. People live there and it is clear that the mess really bothered them – even the refrigerator in the kitchen was upside down. We asked them: "Why didn't you straighten things up after it happened?" They said: "We were waiting for the televisions to come, we were waiting for somebody to take a picture of it."

The news media not only had an important influence on the behavior of the antagonists in the *intifada*, they also changed the balance of power between Israel and the Palestinians. This is one point that the Israelis and the Palestinians agree on: the news media placed the Palestinians on a more equal footing with Israel. Consider, for example, the words of one of the more skeptical of the Palestinian interviewees:

---

[4]   In later stages there was more antagonism to the press, especially towards the Israeli media. There were two major reasons for this change. One was that Israeli intelligence agents apparently went undercover disguised as journalists. The second was that the pictures which were taken by the television cameras were sometimes used as evidence against Palestinians in subsequent trials.

What it [the press] mainly did was to expose Israel. Something that Israel is not used to. Israel got used to getting away with everything here. Now, even the Israeli reporters cover what is happening in those towns ... You expose them. The mass media is an advantage to you; the important thing is that you are equal to them [the Israelis]. And secondly when we talk about public opinion, do you know that it took us twenty-one years to convince the world that we are under occupation. And after twenty-one years Mr. Shultz comes here to speak of improving the plight of the occupation.

Another Palestinian talked about the feeling among the leadership after the first year of the *intifada*:

They [the Palestinians] feel they have gained what they deserve, this is the normal way of thinking. At least the world is willing to listen to what the Palestinians have to say and not only to what the Israelis have to say. So now the balance is more even. In this respect, of course, we have succeeded.

There are some statistics that shed some light on this issue. I carried out a Nexis search of what percentage of stories about Israel mentioned the Palestinian issue. The search was carried out for the months January to March for the years 1984 to 1993. One finds that the lowest proportion was in the beginning of 1987, before the outbreak of the *intifada*, when only 26 percent of the stories about Israel mentioned the Palestinians. In 1988, which was the most important year for such publicity, 60 percent of the stories dealt with the Palestinians. While the percentage dropped to an average of 44 percent of all stories in the subsequent years, it never again went below 40 percent.

There is also good reason to suspect that the news media's focus on the *intifada* had at least something to do with mobilizing several third parties into the conflict. This is again a difficult point to prove because it is never easy to separate the effects of the incidents themselves – say Israeli soldiers beating Palestinian protesters – from the effects that can be attributed to the way the incidents were covered. US officials who were interviewed about these issues by Makovsky (1989) do suggest that media coverage of the *intifada* played a "key contributing factor" to Secretary of State Shultz's decision to intervene in the dispute. It is virtually impossible for political leaders to ignore any political conflict that is being placed so high on the public agenda.

The bulk of evidence then points in the same direction. The news media played an independent and central role in the *intifada*. The press served as a critical catalyst for turning the Palestinians' initial success on the ground into a genuine political achievement, whose ramifications continued for years to come. The international status achieved by the Palestinians during the *intifada* was an important element in the political standing they were given during the Madrid peace conference, the subsequent negotiations in Washington, and the Oslo Accords. This returns us to the final case.

The news media as semi-honest brokers: the struggle over the Oslo Accords

The role the news media played in the Oslo Accords is probably more typical than that which characterized the Gulf war and the *intifada*. While the Rabin government was granted important advantages over those who opposed the Accords, a significant amount of time and space was also devoted to challengers. When the news media play the role of semi-honest brokers they resemble many other enterprises. They depend on their "preferred customers" for most of their business, but are open to offers from any challengers who can come up with a reasonable bid.

It is much easier to place a given conflict on the continuum of influence when one can compare it to other more radical situations that define the end points. The extremely high level of dependence that characterized the Gulf war was attributed to three factors: a high level of official control, a tremendously high need for official information, and the difficulties the press faced in mobilizing sufficient organization and resources to cover the war. The lack of dependence that characterized the *intifada* was attributed to those same three factors: the attempts at official control failed, the need for official sources of information was restricted to gaining reactions, and the news media's level of organization and resources were quite sufficient, due to the smaller scale of the conflict.

The level of media dependence in the conflict over the Oslo Accords, on the other hand, tended to rise and fall along a single axis: the need for official information. There were no serious political controls and all of the news media had sufficient organization and resources to cover the conflict. In addition, this need for official information was much more likely to vary during the conflict over Oslo than in the other two conflicts. When the government could keep events moving in the preferred direction the need for authoritative information went up, but when other actors were calling the shots, the need tended to drop. This illustrates again why the level of political control plays such a critical part in defining the role of the news media in political conflicts.

These differences in the level of dependence also emerge in the interviews conducted with leaders and journalists in each conflict. The journalists were completely frustrated during the Gulf war, the Israeli authorities felt that way during most of the *intifada* and neither side was particularly frustrated during the conflict over the Oslo Accords. The Oslo conflict was an internal debate over government policy and the press covers such conflict by bringing information from both sides. As discussed, this was also true in the congressional debate that preceded the Gulf war.

Here too, however, one finds variations over time and circumstances. While officials were extremely pleased with the coverage accorded to the peace process during the first breakthrough, they were much less satisfied with the coverage in subsequent weeks. In the middle of January 1990, for example, Rabin chastised then Minister of Communication Shulamit Aloni who, he said, had failed in her job by allowing the television to "incessantly film and broadcast the protests against the agreement with the PLO." Rabin complained that Israeli television was allowing right-wing spokespeople to appear much more often than government representatives (Shiffer, 1990).[5]

Evidence on this point also comes from the interviews with the settlers. While the leaders of the Settlers' Council expressed the usual anger at what they saw as the leftist bias of the press, many also admitted that they were managing to get their message across:

In these important months after the Oslo Accords, I can't complain that we don't have any place to express ourselves. I can complain about other things, that the vast majority of the media, or at least those who make the decisions in the media are still very much against us. And that certainly has an influence on coverage ... But paradoxically, one can say that since Oslo we get to talk much more, we get to express ourselves much more, and the media is much more open to us. We are the subject. It is clear that we find it relatively easy when we want to say something. The public is interested and the media believes the public is interested in hearing.

The dependence of the news media on the authorities falls in the middle of the continuum in these types of conflicts because such stories call for information from a variety of sources.

Behavioral and political outcomes

The pecking order during the conflict over the Oslo Accords was fairly clear to all of the participants: the press was running after the authorities, the challengers were running after the press, and the weakest challengers had to run much harder and longer to catch up. In other words, it was pretty much business as usual.

[5] Aloni countered that she had no intention of "shutting people's mouths." She suggested that Rabin appoint an official spokesperson for the government in order to compete better with the oppositional spokespeople.

The Rabin government's strongest position was during the initial weeks following the breakthrough at Oslo, the time known as the "peace festival." The national and international press were forced to adapt itself by pulling dozens of reporters off other beats to cover the new story. The competition for any scrap of information was at its highest, and those reporters who broke the news first were the envy of all of their colleagues. The journalists were chasing the leaders around the world trying to keep up with every new development.

It is hardly a coincidence that the largest newspaper in Israel, *Yediot Ahronot* was given the first major scoop about the Gaza–Jericho agreement. *Yediot* is read by a majority of the Israeli population and has never been accused of understatement. Several journalists who were interviewed felt that giving *Yediot* the first leak also served to commit that paper to the subsequent parts of the story.

The power of the Rabin government over the press returned to a more standard mode as the months progressed. The political reporters in Israel spend every Sunday waiting outside the Prime Minister's office for the results of the weekly cabinet meeting. They then spend most of the rest of the week talking to officials and the spokespeople about the most recent political developments.

The Rabin government had no reason to alter any policies or actions because of the news media. In contrast to the *intifada*, where the major issue was damage control, here the question was how to gain as much mileage as possible from the success associated with the peace process. The only adaptation that did occur was in the area of public relations, which apparently was left in the hands of the professionals. Unlike Schwarzkopf, it seems that Rabin himself had very little to do with planning media strategy.

There is one possible exception to this rule and that has to do with the terrorist attacks. There is no doubt that these attacks placed Rabin's government on the defensive, and some would argue that the media's sensational treatment of these attacks was one factor that inhibited progress in the peace process. The problem, as always, is to decide whether any changes in policy should be attributed to the events themselves or to the ways in which the news media reported those events.

While there is no easy answer to this question, it is important to note that Rabin's own advisors believe that the political realities were far more significant here than any journalistic propensities towards sensationalism. While they criticize the news media for over-dramatizing these events, they viewed terrorist attacks as genuine failures that must be addressed. Terrorism, they say, will always be given sensational coverage; the important question is how to stop the killings.

The influences of the news media on the movements that opposed the Oslo Accords were much more apparent. The interactions with the news media brought changes in movement tactics, strategy, and behavior, internal changes within the movement itself, and changes in political standing.

The centrality of news considerations in the planning of collective action has already been discussed in Chapter 4. This was especially true for the weaker groups whose very existence depended on staying in the news media. The words of a leader of the Professors Circle illustrate that point:

Almost every action of ours is planned with the thought that we have to get to the media. The general idea is that without the press it's as if we haven't done anything.

As in the other two conflicts one finds differences in the amount of influence attributed to the various news media. Even the Settlers' Council found it difficult to break into the evening television news. One of their spokespeople talked about this hierarchy of influence:

When twenty people come and yell "boo" to Rabin during a Mimuna festival [holiday after Passover] that has a big influence on him. So I'm in favor of interpersonal communication. But that's one level of influence. If that event appears in *Ha'aretz* on the next day, that's a bigger influence. When it appears in *Yediot*, it will be even bigger. And if it will be carried by *Mabat* [evening television news] that will really be a big story.

To analyze the flow of influence one must consider the services being offered by each news medium. The very fact that antagonists believe in these differences has an effect on who is running after whom.

As discussed, "media gimmicks" were the most common forms of behavioral adaptation during the conflict over Oslo. The major difference between the settlers' movement and the weaker challengers was the centrality of gimmicks in their general strategy. The weaker the group, the greater the need for these gimmicks.

One also finds, however, that even the weakest groups set limits on what they are willing to do to achieve publicity. Decisions about the form and extent of adaptation go beyond simple calculations of value and dependence. Political ideology has a critical impact on such decisions. The Professors Circle was one of the weakest groups but they were moderates and thus unable to compete with Kach for media attention. Kach itself had limits on what it was willing to do to achieve publicity as noted by one of its leaders.

The media usually helps us and therefore we have certain things that we will do, as long as it doesn't make it more difficult to achieve our goals. I'm not going to break the Sabbath because there's an important reporter who wants to interview me. Why? Because the Sabbath is more important to me than the media.

The news media was seen by all these groups as a means to achieve political goals, not an end. There were disagreements in almost every group about the role media considerations should play in planning. While the "purists" emphasized the need for greater efforts in the field, the "pragmatists" were much more willing to adapt their strategies to achieve more attention in the media. While such debates were rarely bitter, they sometimes led to tensions, especially between the various groups. These tensions over media issues tended to reduce the overall level of solidarity among those attempting to defeat the Oslo agreement.

There was another important political outcome that can be partially attributed to the news media. The Settlers' Council had become the major representative of the right-wing movement in Israel. Until Oslo, the Settlers' Council was one of many oppositional voices. The massive amount of publicity they achieved separated them from the rest of the pack. Media status both reflects and creates political status. The fact that Council leaders are near the top of every important journalist's phone list means that their views are always part of the Israeli political agenda. The interviews also suggest that the national and international publicity generated by the Settlers' Council gave an important boost to their efforts at mobilization and fund-raising.

There is also good evidence that the Settlers' Council used the news media to modify their image. They were very careful to avoid being associated with any radical actions. Thus, they were careful not to be involved in too many physical confrontations with the army or the police, and were careful to maintain their distance from groups such as Kach. As a newspaper editor put it, the Settlers' Council had become part of the "consensus."

It is important to bear in mind that these outcomes are often the result of a cycle of influence. Antagonists carry out an act, the news media respond by covering that action, which can result in political outcomes for the antagonists. Transactions between antagonists and the news media often lead to outcomes for both sides. Differences in power are reflected in how significant the changes are for each side. While dealing with the news media is one of many things that the government does, and one of several things the Settlers' Council does, it is the most important thing that weak groups do. Many of the weak groups that opposed Oslo, without publicity, simply disappeared. Similarly, the news media spend a good deal of time adapting to the demands of the government, they invest less time and resources to cover the Settlers' Council, and virtually no time at all covering the weaker groups.

When the news media play the role of government servant they magnify political power by glorifying the authorities and marginalizing the opposition. The playing field in the arena is not only tilted against challengers, it is insurmountable. When the press takes on the role of advocate of the weak, it undermines political power by raising the political standing of challengers. In these cases the field is tilted against the authorities, and they are the ones that have to fight an uphill battle.

Usually, however, the news media play the role of semi-honest brokers, as they did in Oslo. Here the press is much more likely to mirror differences in political power than to alter them. The field is tilted against the challengers but still surmountable. The challengers have to fight much harder to remain contestants and many are destroyed in the process. The more resourceful, however, often become empowered by the experience. They make a name for themselves and those that put up a good fight are always welcome to return and fight again.

Summary

For several years I had a recurring problem when I was interviewing authorities and group leaders about their relations with the news media. I would always be asking them about the media and they would always be talking to me about politics. I would keep trying to get them back on "the track" and they would keep veering off to talk about political ideologies and strategies. It took me a while, but eventually I got the point: you cannot understand the role of the news media in politics without looking at it within the more general contest for political control.

The goal of this work was to promote a more dynamic approach for studying the role of the news media in political conflicts. The political contest model rests on five major arguments. These final pages will be used to review those claims in light of the three case studies analyzed.

Argument number 1: the centrality of the political process

The first argument was that the political process is more likely to have an influence on the news media than the news media are on the political process. Despite the colossal power attributed to the press in recent years one finds that journalists spend most of their time reacting, not initiating. They respond to political power, they reflect the political values and norms of their society in which they operate and they react to events produced by political actors.

The advantages given by the media to President Bush in the Gulf war, Prime Minister Rabin in the Oslo peace process, and the Palestinians in the *intifada* are all the result of political processes that go far beyond any particular set of news stories. The large amount of national and international political support given to Bush during the Gulf war, the massive amounts of international political backing given to the Palestinians during the *intifada*, and the genuine divisions in Israel over the Oslo Accords offer critical insights into how each of these conflicts was covered.

Politics was also shown to have other important influences on the role of the news media. The range of political ideologies in a given social system helps shape the range of legitimate viewpoints that appear in the news media. The differences between Republicans and Democrats during the debate over the Gulf conflict, for example, centered on the issue of whether sanctions or military force was the best response to Iraqi aggression. Both parties supported the *law and order* frame and thus this was the only frame represented in the American news media.

The political process was also shown to have an important influence on the relationship between challengers and the news media. When the right-wing Likud party was voted out of government in 1992, it had a dramatic impact on the settlers' dependence on the news media. The Palestinians' desperate need for the news media can also be attributed to their lack of alternative channels of influence. Finally, the political goals and ideologies of the various challengers had an important influence on their willingness to adapt to the demands of the news media. While some groups such as Kach were willing to play the role of radicals for the news media, other groups were much more restrained in their reactions.

Argument number 2: control over the political environment

The second argument was that the authorities' level of control over the political environment is one of the key variables that determine the role of the news media in political conflicts. Nothing succeeds like success. When the authorities take control of the political world, they have no trouble at all taking control of the news media. President Bush's success in maintaining the initiative in the Gulf war, in regulating the flow of information about that conflict, and in generating a broad level of national and international consensus all contributed to his ability to exploit the press.

In reviewing the three cases, however, one finds that the authorities are rarely able to take full control over the environment and this provides important opportunities for a greater level of independence for the media. While the *intifada* may have been an extreme case of this phenomenon, Rabin's difficulties in keeping the peace process on track are probably more typical. The continuing acts of terrorism were one of the most important indicators that the process was failing. One even found such lapses during the Gulf war concerning the Amiriya bunker and the Highway of Death. Both incidents illustrated how quickly a loss of political control can lead to a changing role for the news media.

Argument number 3: the role of the news media varies

Which brings us to the third argument: the role of the news media in political conflicts varies over time and circumstance. It is hoped this is one claim that will receive a good deal of support among readers. While many may disagree with the specific classification I have made concerning the three roles the news media play, static models of media influence do not make any sense. The role the news media play in conflicts varies primarily because politics is in a constant state of flux. The ability of the authorities and challengers to create newsworthy events, the willingness and the ability of the news media to become independent of the authorities, and editorial decisions about how to frame political conflicts all vary – and with them, so does the role of the press.

These changes can also take place during a conflict. The American news media became much more of a government servant after the critical congressional vote on the Gulf war. A reverse change was noted regarding the Oslo peace process. After the initial euphoria during the "peace festival" in which Israeli government sources tended to dominate media discourse, the news media returned to a more standard mode of reporting about the debate.

Argument number 4: the structural and cultural dimensions

The fourth argument says that those who hope to understand variations in the role of the news media must look at the competition among antagonists along two dimensions: one structural and the other cultural. The major reason for making the distinction between these two dimensions of analysis is that the competition over access to the news media follows different rules than the contest over frames. While the contest over access can be understood by looking at more mechanical factors such as organization and resources, the battle over media frames is a cultural struggle over meaning. Although there is a clear overlap between the two dimensions, wearing two sets of glasses brings different parts of the picture into focus.

One lesson that emerges from these analyses is that gaining access to the news media should not be confused with success. This is especially true for back-door challengers such as Iraq and Kach. It is also true, however, for the authorities. While the peace process remained firmly planted on the top of the Israeli news media for the entire period, a good many stories raised serious doubts about the wisdom and the viability of the peace process.

One reason it is important to use both dimensions is because the actors themselves use both types of considerations in their interactions with the news media. The officials at the Pentagon talk about the fierce competition among the journalists, but they also talk about the "spin" of the various news stories. The Palestinians talk about the relative impact of the various news media and they also think about how different stories will influence their international image. The settlers are always trying to find new ways to gain access to the news media, but they fully realize that there are some stories they could easily live without. One cannot seriously talk about news coverage of conflicts without evaluating its quantity and its quality.

Argument number 5: challengers can compete

The fifth and final argument is that while authorities have tremendous advantages over challengers in the quantity and quality of media coverage they receive, many challengers can overcome these obstacles and use the news media as a tool for political influence. There are far too many studies in the field of political communication that ignore this side of the coin.

The Palestinians are a perfect example of a group that was able to overcome a multitude of disadvantages to exploit the news media. The Israelis had a much greater level of organization and resources. But the willingness of the Palestinians to mobilize on a massive scale, their high level of previous media status, and the international sympathy for their plight all led to a successful political campaign in which the international news media played a major role.

There were other challengers who were also able to promote their political frames to the news media. The Settlers' Council was able to give the Rabin government a genuine battle and to use the media for increasing their political standing. The Kach movement could use the Hebron massacre to become a major player, and Hamas achieved a similar status with terrorism. Even Iraq had some partial successes as challengers. The issue of linkage received some serious consideration by the American news media, especially after the killings on the Temple Mount.

In the introduction to this work I was impertinent enough to suggest that this model might be useful for those who are interested in building a more comprehensive model of political communication. I believe that each of these five points can be used to understand better the role of the news media in other types of political processes, such as elections. Here too, one finds incumbents and challengers with different levels of access to the news media, transactions based on power and dependence, a competition among antagonists to promote their frames to the news media, and a genuine struggle for control over the political environment. But that story will have to wait.

Impertinence is one thing, delusions of grandeur quite another. The role of the news media in politics is far too broad and complicated an issue to be captured by any one model. I hope, however, this work can provide enthusiasts with an understanding of a few of the rules that govern contests in the central arena.

Methodological appendix

This appendix includes a list of the interview schedules and coding sheets which were used in conjunction with the three case studies. All schedules and coding sheets are presented in their entirety, but not all of the results were discussed within the framework of this work.

All interviews were carried out using a semi-structured type of format. While a core set of questions was used to guide every interview, new questions and ideas emerged within the course of the session. It was also sometimes necessary to skip some questions because of a lack of time. Interviews usually lasted between an hour and an hour and a half and all were taped and then transcribed. All interviewees were promised anonymity.

THE CONFLICT OVER THE OSLO ACCORDS (CHAPTERS 4, 5, AND 9)

INTERVIEWS WITH EXPERT WITNESSES

In-depth interviews were carried out with a total of thirty-five individuals including movement leaders, journalists covering the story, and several government spokespeople responsible for promoting official frames of the conflict.

QUESTIONS FOR MOVEMENT LEADERS

Organization and resources
1. Tell me something about how the group became organized.
2. How many active members does the group have?
3. Is there a clear division of labor within the leadership? Is there anyone who is specifically responsible for dealing with the news media?
4. Where do most of your funds for activities come from?
5. What other resources do you have at your disposal (office, secretaries, fax, etc.)?

Group goals and messages

6. What are the group's goals? What would you say is the central message you are trying to get out?

7. What are your specific goals with regard to the present peace process?

8. How would you compare your goals to those of some of the other protest groups?

9. Have there been any changes in the group's goals since the first period when the agreement was first announced?

The centrality of the media for the group

10. To what extent would you say the media is central with regard to the actions and goals of the group?

11. Why is the media central (or not central) for the group?

12. To what extent do people argue about the role of the news media within the group?

13. Have there been any changes with regard to the centrality of the media since the first period when the agreement was first announced?

The coverage of the group in the media

14. What is your opinion about the coverage the group is getting in the news media?

   (a) Would you say that the group is getting as *much* coverage as it deserves? Does it reflect the amount of activity the group carries out?

   (b) What about the *kind* of coverage given to the group? Is the coverage fair? Does it reflect the positions and actions of the group? Would you say that the coverage is either sympathetic or antagonistic?

   (c) Have there been any changes in the coverage the group has received since the first period when the agreement was announced?

15. Are there important differences between the various news media in terms of the quantity and quality of coverage given to the group?

Influences of the news media on the group

16. To what extent did the media have an influence on the group and its activities?

17. To what extent did the *presence* of the reporters and/or the cameras have an influence on what happened during your protests?

18. To what extent did the media have an influence on any decisions

made by the group or on any of your positions (changing policies because of media influence, taking actions in order to carry get more media attention, group manipulation of the media)?

19. To what extent would you say the media had an influence on the level of group solidarity?

Concluding questions

20. What are your major lessons you learned about dealing with the news media? What succeeds and what doesn't succeed when you are working with the news media?

21. To what extent would you say you succeeded in your efforts to influence the news media?

22. Is there anything else you'd like to add to what you've already said?

QUESTIONS FOR OFFICIAL SPOKESPEOPLE

Overall strategy and evaluation of success

1. How would you describe your overall strategy for promoting Israel's position on the peace process?

2. Where do you think you've had more success and where less? Would you say your message is getting through? In what ways are the journalists (domestic and foreign) publishing a different story from what you want to send?

3. What parts of the story are they most interested in?

4. Would you say the peace story pretty much "sells itself" or that how you package and sell it makes a difference? How would you compare it to the other stories (including negative ones)?

5. How successful would you say the opposition has been in getting their message across to the news media?

6. Were there any news stories that you were especially angry or disappointed about?

Control over news stories

7. Were there any stories that you found especially difficult to control?

8. How much coordination is there between the various offices? Is there any discussion about the way the news media should/should not be dealt with?

9. What types of stories are leaked to the press? Are leaks sometimes used as *trial balloons*?

10. Have you used any new technological innovations that have improved your ability to get your message across?

Differences among the news media

11. Would you say the Israeli press has been very enthusiastic about the story?
12. How would you describe the attitude of the foreign press? Are there differences between the American and European press? Have there been any attempts to work with the Arab/Palestinian press?
13. Which type of correspondents seem the most dependent on you for information?
14. Is it easier for the more powerful news media (*New York Times* and the like) to get access to the bigger sources?
15. How do you relate to the *wire services* in terms of power (AP, UPI)?
16. How informed are the correspondents who cover the story? Does this effect their coverage?

Centrality/influence of news media

17. How much do the various offices *monitor* what is published in the Israeli and foreign press? How systematic is it? How are the people higher up kept informed about what is happening?
18. Does media coverage of the peace process have any influence on what happens in terms of policy? Can you give examples?
19. Does media coverage have any influence on how you deal with the news media?
20. Do the news media serve as an important *source of information* about what is happening with the other side? Is this information used in subsequent planning?
21. To which types of stories do you feel most compelled to react?
22. Does publicity sometimes lead to tension among the staff? Among the different offices? Do people discuss it when one person gets more publicity than another?
23. How sensitive are the political leaders in your office to what appears in the press?

The news media and negotiations

24. To what extent (and on what occasions) did the media *interfere* with the negotiation process? Describe.
    (a) Do the sides tend to get angry about things that are published in the media?
    (b) Is it difficult to control the leaks to the media?
    (c) Why is it important to keep the reporters physically away (why can't the negotiators simply ignore them)?
    (d) Was there less media influence as the talks dragged on and became less newsworthy?

25. What steps were taken in order to *prevent* the news media from having an influence on the talks?
26. Were there any incidents in which media coverage actually *accelerated* the peace negotiations?
    (a) Any times when the pressure to bring something out to the press forced the sides to make compromises?
    (b) Any times when what appeared in the press *improved* the atmosphere of the talks?
27. To what extent has the news media served as a useful tool for signaling the other side?

Concluding questions
28. Based on your experience, what would you say are the most important lessons you have learned regarding how to use the news media?
29. Is there anything else you would like to add to what you've said?

QUESTIONS FOR JOURNALISTS

Organization
1. What is your specific set of responsibilities within your organization?
2. What is the division of responsibilities among reporters for covering the conflict between the settlers and the government over the Oslo Accords?
3. Who usually initiates the coverage of the protest events: you, or the groups themselves?

The coverage
4. What do you think about the extent of coverage (amount and salience) which has been given by the media to the right's protest against the agreement? Do you think it offered an accurate reflection of the amount of activity?
5. What is your opinion about the type of coverage the protest received? Do you think it provided an accurate picture of what was happening? Would you say the coverage was generally supportive or antagonistic?
6. What kind of image do you think the protesters had in the media?
7. Did you notice any differences in the coverage over different periods? What kinds of differences did you see after the terrorist attacks? What about after what happened in Hebron?

Differences among the media

8. What kinds of differences did you notice in the ways in which the various news media covered the protest?
9. Were there any specific differences you noticed between the coverage in *Ha'aretz* and *Yediot*? Would you say that this has to do with the fact that one is a more popular paper than the other?
10. Do you think the political position of the news media had an influence on their coverage?

Differences among the groups

11. What differences do you find in the relationships you have with the various protest groups?
12. What differences do you find in the coverage the various protest groups receive?
13. What differences do you find between groups like Moetzet Yesha and some of the smaller groups such as the Professors Circle, the Women in Green, the Blue Group, and This is Our Land? Which of these groups were more successful? Why?

Influence of press on groups (follow-up questions on specifics of each group)

14. How much would you say the various groups carry out acts specifically to get into the media? Can you give some examples?
15. How important would you say the news media are to these groups? How sensitive are they to what gets published about them in the press?
16. Do you think the coverage has had any influence on group solidarity? On their sense of accomplishment?

CONTENT ANALYSIS OF CONFLICT OVER OSLO

A content analysis was carried out on fifty days of news articles that appeared during the period under study: August 27, 1993 to May 5, 1994. The fifty days were selected at random and the analysis looked at all news articles about the peace process that appeared in the first three pages of each newspaper. Editorials and personal columns were excluded from the analysis.

Two separate coders were trained and given a sample of seventy-five articles in order to test the reliability of the coding sheet. Questions which received less then an 85 percent rate of agreement were dropped from the final version. Any subsequent discrepancies were resolved by the principal researcher.

CODING SHEET

1. Article comes from which newspaper?
   (1) *Yediot*
   (2) *Ha'aretz*
   (3) *Jerusalem Post*
2. Day number in list of days (1–50).
3. Article publication date (example: January 9, 1994 – 090194).
4. Article page number.
5. Does the article include a picture?
   (1) No
   (2) Yes
6. Height of article (highest point in centimeters, including picture).
7. Width of the article (widest point, including picture).
8. Is there a direct quote within the article from a government official?
   (1) No (go to question 10)
   (2) Yes
9. Is the name of the official cited?
   (1) No
   (2) Yes
10. Is there a reaction of the opposition in the article (the Shas party is not considered opposition).
    (1) No
    (2) Yes
11. Does the headline include declarations of officials from the Israeli government?
    (1) There is no declaration in the headline (go to question 13)
    (2) Yes
    (3) No
12. Whose declaration is mentioned in the headline (if there is more than one, list the first)?
    (1) Prime Minister
    (2) Foreign Minister
    (3) Other ministers
    (4) Other members of coalition
    (5) Chief Of Staff
    (6) Other army/police officers
    (7) Head of opposition
    (8) Other members of Likud
    (9) Other members of opposition
    (10) Extra-parliamentary opposition
    (11) Palestinians

    (12) American government officials
    (13) Syrian officials
    (14) Others
13. Which personalities appear in headline?
    (1)   Prime Minister
    (2)   Foreign Minister
    (3)   Other ministers
    (4)   Other members of coalition
    (5)   Chief Of Staff
    (6)   Other army/police officers
    (7)   Head of opposition
    (8)   Other members of Likud
    (9)   Other members of opposition
    (10) Extra-parliamentary opposition
    (11) Palestinians
    (12) American government officials
    (13) Syrian officials
    (14) Others
14. The general topic of the headline is?
    (1)   The peace process (go to question 15)
    (2)   Terrorism (go to question 16)
    (3)   Opposition (go to question 15)
    (4)   Hebron massacre (go to question 16)
15. The context of the headline is?
    (1)   Political developments and progress
    (2)   Reports on the negotiations
    (3)   Standstill or difficulties in negotiations
    (4)   Ceremony – preparation or reports
    (5)   Economic benefits related to agreement
    (6)   Non-economic benefits related to agreement
    (7)   International support for agreement
    (8)   Negotiations with Syria
    (9)   Relations with Gulf states or other Muslim countries
    (10) Dangers associated with agreement
    (11) Events or developments among the Palestinians
    (12) Negotiations with Jordan
    (13) Parliamentary opposition to agreement
    (14) Extra-parliamentary opposition to agreement
    (15) Discussions in the Knesset
    (16) General optimistic statements in favor of peace process
16. The main headline (for terrorist attacks) deals with?
    (1)   The actual attack

    (2)   Injured and funerals
    (3)   Terrorists who carry out attacks
    (4)   Fear of terror and concerns for personal safety
    (5)   How the security forces are dealing with terrorism
    (6)   The reaction of the opposition (including protest groups) to
           terrorist attacks
    (7)   Coalition reactions to terrorist attacks
17. Name of reporter _____

**Questions 18–30 refer specifically to articles having to do with protest
groups**
18. Headline deals with which topic?
    (1)   Terrorist attack
    (2)   Official statement or action related to protest
    (3)   Statement or action by parliamentary opposition related to
           protest
    (4)   Statements by protest leaders
    (5)   Legal protest actions
    (6)   Illegal/violent protest actions
    (7)   Other (e.g., statements by experts on protest)
19. Name of first group mentioned in article (see list of groups).
20. Name of second group mentioned in article.
21. Name of third group mentioned in article.
22. Name of fourth group mentioned in article.
23. Name of fifth group mentioned in article.
24. Name of sixth group mentioned in article.
25. Name of seventh group mentioned in article.
26. Type of activity described in article.
    (1)   Article does not describe actual protest (go to question 18)
    (2)   Expression of protest (e.g., condemnation, statement of
           opposition)
    (3)   Report, declaration, or threat of future activity
    (4)   Meeting or convention
    (5)   Demonstration
    (6)   Blocking streets
    (7)   Creation of settlements
    (8)   Religious act of protest (use of Torah or mass praying)
    (9)   Damage Arab property
    (10)   Injuring Arabs
    (11)   Illegal possession of weapons
    (12)   Creation of self-defence group
    (13)   Initiation of publicity campaign

27. Level of violence of actions.
    (1) No signs of violence
    (2) Suspicion of illegal acts (e.g., illegal storage of weapons)
    (3) Illegal act (e.g., illegal demonstrations, setting up of illegal settlements, blocking roads, calling on soldiers to disobey orders)
    (4) Protest which includes physical clash with police or army
    (5) Property damage to Arabs
    (6) Injuring Arabs
    (7) Other
28. Context of protest.
    (1) No specific context is noted
    (2) Terrorist attack
    (3) General security situation
    (4) Government statement or political development
    (5) Hebron incident
    (6) Other
29. Is there a direct quote from protesters?
    (1) No
    (2) Yes
30. Is the name of the protester quoted?
    (1) No
    (2) Yes

THE *INTIFADA* (CHAPTERS 6, 7, AND 9)

INTERVIEWS WITH EXPERT WITNESSES

Twenty interviews were carried out with informants about their experiences in the *intifada*. Interviews were conducted with reporters from a variety of newspapers and television stations (both foreign and local), with the first and second army spokesmen to deal with the *intifada* and representatives of their office, with the political advisor to the Minister of Defense, and with a number of Palestinian leaders who had ongoing contacts with the press.

Most of these interviews were carried out during the first year of violence (1988), although some were carried out in the following years. The word "intifada" was not used in the early interviews, because it was not yet an accepted way to refer to the conflict.

INTERVIEWS WITH JOURNALISTS

Structure of interactions
1. What is your specific set of responsibilities within your organization?
2. How would you describe your relations with the Palestinians? Have these relations changed over time?
3. Where do you get most of your information about what is happening in the territories?
4. Are there Palestinians who are specifically "in charge" of dealing with the press?
5. Would you say the Palestinians have developed a sophisticated public relations strategy?
6. Would you say the Palestinian Press Service helped reporters find stories?
7. How would you describe your relations with the IDF [Israeli army]?
8. Do you find the information you get from the IDF spokesperson's office about what is happening in the territories reliable?
9. Would you say there is much competition among the reporters? Does the spokesperson's office try to exploit the competition among the reporters?
10. How dependent are you are on the information from the army spokesperson's office?
11. Are there reporters who are given better information because they print more positive stories?
12. How would you describe your relations with the settlers?

Success of two sides
13. Would you say that the spokesperson's office has been successful in having an influence on coverage?
14. How successful would you say the Palestinians have been in getting their message across?

Influence of the news media
15. Do you believe that the presence of the news media in the territories is having an effect on what is happening there?
    (a)   On the Palestinians?
    (b)   On the Israeli soldiers?
16. Are there times when the media become participants in the events they are covering?
17. Are there any differences in the amount of influence of the various news media?

18. How central would you say the news media are to the Palestinian struggle against Israel?
19. Do you think the Palestinians have received a lot of encouragement from the press coverage they received?

Nature of coverage

20. There are a lot of complaints in Israel about the coverage of what is happening in the territories. What do you think about it?
21. What differences do you find in the way the Israeli and foreign press cover what is happening in the territories?

INTERVIEWS WITH OFFICIAL SPOKESPEOPLE

Structure of interactions

1. What is your specific set of responsibilities within your organization?

Relations with the press

2. How would you characterize your relationship with the journalists covering the *intifada*? Would you say the relations are mostly positive or negative?
3. How dependent would you say the reporters are on your office? What differences do you find between the Israeli and foreign journalists?
4. Would you say you were able to initiate stories or just react to stories which were initiated by others?
5. There were several attempts to close certain areas to journalists. Why was this done? Did it also have an influence on the coverage?
6. Some journalists have complained that they were misled or fed false information by the army spokesperson's office. What do you think?
7. How would you describe the Palestinians' relationship with the press?
8. Would you say the Palestinians are developing a sophisticated public relations strategy?
9. Why was the Palestinian Press Service office closed?

Influence of the press

10. How central do you think the role of the press has been in the *intifada*?
11. Do you believe that the presence of the news media in the territories is having an effect on what is happening there?
    (a) On the Palestinians?
    (b) On the Israeli soldiers?

12. Are there times when the media become participants in the events they are covering?
13. Are there any differences in the amount of influence of the various news media?
14. Do you think the Palestinians have received a lot of encouragement from the press coverage they received?

Nature of coverage
15. There are a lot of complaints in Israel about the coverage of what is happening in the territories. What do you think about it?
16. What differences do you find in the way the Israeli and foreign press cover what is happening in the territories?

Success of two sides
17. Would you say that the army has been successful in getting its message through to the news media? Are there important differences between the Israeli and foreign press?
18. What are the most important factors that determine how well you do with the news media?
19. Do you think there is anything else you could have done to improve Israel's image?
20. How successful would you say the Palestinians have been in getting their message across?

General conclusions
21. What are the most important lessons you have learned in your dealings with the press?

INTERVIEWS WITH PALESTINIANS

Relations with the press
1. How would you describe your relations with the journalists covering the *intifada*? Would you say your relations are mostly positive or negative?
2. What differences are there in your relations with local and foreign journalists?
3. Would you say you mostly initiate contacts with the journalists or they mostly come looking for you?
4. Have the Israeli attempts to restrict coverage of the *intifada* had much of an effect on your ability to contact journalists?
5. Would you say the Palestinians are developing a more sophisticated public relations strategy?

6. Why was the Palestinian Press Service office closed? Did it have much effect on your efforts to get your message out?

Influence of the mass media
7. How central do you think the role of the press has been in the *intifada*? Have there been any important changes over time?
8. How often would you say does the subject of the news media come up when you and your friends/colleagues are talking about the *intifada*?
9. Do you believe that the presence of the news media in the territories is having an effect on what is happening there?
   (a) On the Palestinians?
   (b) On the Israeli soldiers?
10. Are there times when the media become participants in the events themselves?
11. Are there any differences in the amount of influence of the various news media?
12. Do you think the Palestinians have received a lot of encouragement from the press coverage they received?

Nature of coverage
13. Would you say that the coverage of the *intifada* has been mostly positive or negative?
14. Do you think the coverage provides a fairly accurate picture of what is going on in the territories?
15. How successful do you feel you've been in getting your message across to the world? What about to Israel?
16. What differences do you find between the Israeli and foreign press?
17. Why do you think the Israelis are so angry about the coverage of the *intifada*?
18. What differences do you find in the way the Israeli and foreign press cover what is happening in the territories?

General conclusions
19. What are the most important lessons you have learned in your dealings with the press?

CONTENT ANALYSIS OF HEADLINES IN THREE PAPERS

The content analysis was carried out on all headlines having to do with the *intifada* which appeared in the *New York Times*, *Yediot Ahronot*, and *Ha'aretz* between the dates December 10, 1987 to December 31, 1987. Each newspaper was coded in the original language. After an initial training (based on headlines from another period) two independent coders achieved a 93 percent rate of agreement. In those few cases where multiple categories were used, I attempted to determine which category was more central to the headline. If this was not possible, the case was given the code 99.

Instructions for coders
You will be reading over a list of headlines which appeared in various newspapers about the Palestinian *intifada* during the first month of December. You will then attempt to see the extent to which each coding category applies to the headline. Please note: (1) The codes should be easy to apply. If you are having any difficulty simply record 99 (other) which means it cannot be coded. (2) Sometimes a headline may fit into more than one category. You can use up to two codes for a given headline.

Here are the codes and the explanation for each one. Any headline which:

1. Talks of arrests, trials and deportations of Palestinians.
2. Talks of Palestinians as victims of repression, suffering in some way, being wounded, or being killed.
3. Talks of Palestinians being angry, defiant, or frustrated.
4. Talks about some aspect of Palestinian society (education, welfare, etc.) or political processes (negotiations, taking stands, etc.).
5. Talks of group, country or organization condemning Israel or carrying out a protest or strike or other sanction against Israel. Note that this does *not* include the *intifada* itself but rather groups inside and outside of Israel voicing the opposition to Israeli actions in the territories.
6. Quotes or mentions Israeli political or military leaders.
7. Refers to a group or organization which defends Israel's position or policy.
8. Reports of violence by Palestinians. Talks of possible escalation in level of violence in territories.
9. Talks about Israelis being hurt or injured.
10. Talks about how government or military is "dealing" with situation. Headline talks specifically about government or military policy for handling the territories (e.g., assigning more troops and the like).
11. Internal (leftist) opposition to government policy.
12. Internal (rightist) opposition to government policy.
99. Other (cannot be clearly coded into one of these categories).

THE GULF WAR (CHAPTERS 6, 8, AND 9)

INTERVIEWS WITH EXPERT WITNESSES

Fifteen interviews were conducted with military press officers and journalists about their role in the Gulf war. Interviews were carried out with American print and television journalists who were based in Saudi Arabia during the war as well as several who covered the war from the Pentagon. Most of the public information officers who were interviewed also served in Saudi Arabia during the war, although one was based in Washington. The officers represented the Army, Navy, and Marines and two held senior positions on General Schwartzkopf's staff.

INTERVIEWS WITH JOURNALISTS

Responsibilities and experience
1. Could you describe your experience as a journalist?
2. Where were you stationed during the different parts of the Gulf conflict?

Relations with military
3. How would you describe your relationship with the military during the Gulf war?
4. There was a great deal of discussion about the restrictions which the Allies put on correspondents covering the war. What was your experience?
5. What technical factors were used to make sure the press would report the war in ways which were favorable for the Allies?
6. Did you feel you had to publish almost everything the army had to tell you?
7. Were you able to collect any independent information about the war? Were there any changes during different stages of the conflict?
8. Were there any attempts to reward or punish reporters for what they were sending back?
9. How accurate was the information you were given by the military?
10. How would you compare your experience in covering this war with some of the other conflicts you've covered?
11. Were certain news media given advantages over others in terms of access to information and the like?

The coverage
12. A number of critics have argued that the coverage was too "gung-ho" for the Allies. What do you think?

13. To what extent do you feel that the growing consensus in the US about the war had an effect on the way you covered it? What about your own feelings about the war?
14. To what extent would you say that the "Iraqis as victims" theme was neglected by the Western media? Why?
15. Can you give examples of *adversarial reporting* of the war? Can you think of incidents where the army was dissatisfied with what was being publicized?
16. What kinds of directions/pressure were you receiving from your editor?
17. To what extent do you think the media tended to reinforce certain myths and stereotypes about the war (the elite Republican guard, the Iraqis only have to survive to win)?
18. What differences can you point to in either the coverage or effects of the print and electronic media?
19. Would you say you are generally satisfied or dissatisfied with the way the news media covered this war?

Influence of the news media
20. Can you think of any example where the media coverage had any effect on the course of the war? Did either Iraq or the Allies change any tactics or behavior because of something that was emphasized in the media coverage?
21. How important do you think the news media was to the Allies during the war?
22. To what extent, in your opinion, were the top army officials involved in setting media policy?

INTERVIEWS WITH AMERICAN PUBLIC AFFAIRS OFFICERS

Responsibilities
1. What were your responsibilities during the different stages of the Gulf conflict?

Relations with journalists
2. How would you describe your relationship with the journalists during the Gulf war?
3. There was a great deal of discussion about the restrictions which the Allies put on correspondents covering the war. What was your experience?
4. Was there much hostility from the journalists about how they were dealt with during the war?

5. Was there any way for the journalists to cover the Gulf war in an independent fashion?
6. Some journalists talked about the military being concerned that this not be "another Vietnam." Was this the feeling among the military?
7. Would you say that the journalists were very dependent on you for information about what was happening?
8. How open were the officers in the field to the prospect of having contact with journalists?
9. Were there any attempts to reward or punish reporters for what they were sending back?
10. There were some complaints from reporters that some news media received preferential treatment. What would you say?

Coverage
11. Was the military satisfied with the coverage they received during the conflict? Were there any differences over time?
12. Were there any differences among the various news media?
13. Were there any stories that really angered the people at the top?
14. Do you think you were pretty much able to get your message across during the war?
15. Many critics complained that the press was willing to publish almost anything the military gave them. What was your experience?
16. It was also said that there were very few pictures of Iraqi victims. What do you think?

Influence of the news media
17. Can you think of any example where the media coverage had any effect on the course of the war? Did either Iraq or the Allies change any tactics or behavior because of something that was emphasized in the media coverage?
18. How important do you think the news media were to the Allies during the war?
19. To what extent, in your opinion, were the top army officials involved in setting media policy?

General conclusions
20. What would you say are your major conclusions about your relations with the news media during the Gulf conflict?

CONTENT ANALYSIS OF LINKAGE STORIES

A Nexis search was conducted to locate all articles (including editorials) which appeared in the *New York Times* which dealt with the issue of linkage before the actual war. The search looked for any articles which appeared after August 2, 1990 which contained the key words: "linkage," "Palestinian," and "Iraq." A total of seventy-six articles were analyzed, three of which could not be coded (category 99).

Two independent coders were given the following coding sheet. There was an 86 percent agreement rate when looking at each individual coding value, and a 91 percent agreement rate when looking at the general categories as described in Table 8.1 (e.g., good news for Iraq).

Coding instructions

You will be reading a group of excerpts which were taken from news stories which appeared before and during the Gulf war in the *New York Times*. These articles all deal with questions about whether the conflict with Iraq should be linked to the Israeli–Palestinian conflict. You are to give each one a code according to the following list of categories.

Articles which say someone is in favor of linkage
1. Any article which says that *Iraq* is in favor of linkage.
2. Any article which says that *other countries or leaders* favor or would consider some type of linkage. *Note that this sometimes means that they reject one type of linkage but accept another type.*
3. Any *editorial* which favors/would consider some type of linkage.

Articles which say someone is against linkage
4. Any article which says that the *United States* opposes linkage.
5. Any article which says that *other countries or organizations* oppose linkage.
6. Any *editorial* which opposes some type of linkage.

Articles which have mixed information about linkage
7. The fact that the Bush Administration, the United States, or the United Nations is either having *mixed feelings* or sending *mixed signals* about whether or not there should be *some type* of linkage between the issues.
8. The fact that the *US disagrees with Iraq or other countries* about whether there should or should not be some type of linkage between the two issues.
9. The fact that there is an *internal debate going on within certain countries/organizations* (excluding the US and the UN) over the idea of linkage. This includes articles which suggest that certain countries are *changing their minds* and *giving up* the idea of linkage.
10. Any article which *links the incident of the Temple Mount* (the riot which resulted in many Palestinian casualties) to the Gulf conflict.

Note this includes *any article* which refers to what happened at the Temple Mount (even if it is focused on someone denying there is/ should be a link between the two).

99. Any article or editorial which you find *difficult to code* into one of these categories.

IMPORTANT GUIDELINES FOR CODERS

1. First read the paragraph where the word "linkage" appears. This has been placed in bold. If you can give a code based on this information there is no need to read the rest of the article. If you are not sure read the entire excerpt. If you are still not sure give it a code of 99.

2. When in doubt refer to the *first and major* reference to the concept of linkage. For example, if the first point is that a certain country is in favor of linkage and only later does the article mention that the US disagrees with this position you would code it 2. If it starts with the disagreement between the US and another country you would code it 8. You can also look at the headline in order to help you.

3. There are only two categories which deal with *editorials* (3 and 6). Editorials are listed as such and you should ignore all other categories (except for 99). Do not worry about how the person describes the situation but only whether the writer is in favor or against some type of linkage.

4. If a person (e.g., the Foreign Minister of Iraq, or Arafat) is quoted as describing a situation and not their own opinion code the situation as if it were being described by a journalist. Thus, if Arafat says that Iraq is in favor of linkage you should code it 1. If on the other hand Arafat says that he is in favor of linkage you should code it 2.

References

ABC Television Network (1991a). *Nightline*. February 13

ABC Television Network, (1991). *World news tonight with Peter Jennings*. February 13

Adoni, H. and Mane, S. (1984). Media and the social construction of reality: toward an intergration of theory and research. *Communication Research*, 11, 323–340

Alinsky, S. D. (1971). *Rules for radicals*. New York: Vantage

American Jewish Committee (1982). Report of interviews with foreign correspondents who covered the Lebanese War from Israel in the summer of 1982. New York: American Jewish Committee

Ball-Rokeach, S. and DeFleur, M. (1976). A dependency model of mass media effects. *Communication Research*, 3, 3–21

Bennett, W. L. (1983). *News: the politics of illusion*. Second edition, New York: Longman

(1989). Marginalizing the majority: conditioning public opinion to accept managerial democracy. In M. Margolis and G. Mauser (eds.). *Manipulating public opinion*. New York: Dorsey Press

(1990). Toward a theory of press–state relations in the United States. *Journal of Communication*, 40, 103–125

Bennett W. L. and Paletz, D. L. (eds.) (1994). *Taken by storm: the media, public opinion, and US foreign policy in the Gulf war*. Chicago: University of Chicago Press

Berger, P. and Luckmann T. (1966). *The social construction of reality*. Garden City, NJ: Doubleday

Blau, P. F. (1964). *Exchange and power in social life*. New York: John Wiley & Sons

Blumler, J. G. and Gurevitch, M. (1986). Journalists' orientations to political institutions: the case of parliamentary broadcasting. In P. Golding, G. Murdock, and P. Schesinger (eds.). *Communicating politics: mass communications and the political process*. Leicester, UK: Leicester University Press

Boorstin, D. (1961). *The image: a guide to psuedo-events in America*. New York: Atheneum

Carey, J. W. (1985). Overcoming resistance to cultural studies. In M. Gurevitch and M. Levy (eds.). *Mass communication review yearbook*, V, 17–20

Cohen, A. A., Adoni, H., and Bantz, C. R. (1990). *Social conflict and television news*. Newbury Park, CA: Sage

Cook, T. E., (1987). Show horses in house elections: the advantages and disadvantages of national media visibility. In Jan Pons Vermeer (ed.). *Campaigns in the news: mass media and congressional elections.* Westport, CT: Greenwood Press

Danielian, L. H. (1988). From "bouncing bosoms" to the ERA: LA Times coverage of LA NOW: mass media activities from 1980–1983. Paper presented at the International Communication Association convention, New Orleans

Davis, D. K. (1990). News and politics. In D. L. Swanson and D. Nimmo (eds.). *New directions in political communication.* London: Sage

Dayan, D. and Katz, E. (1992). *Media events: the live broadcasting of history.* Cambridge, MA: Harvard University Press

Deacon, D. and Golding, P. (1994). *Taxation and representation: the media, political communication and the poll tax.* London, UK: John Libbey

DeFleur, M. L. and Ball-Rokeach, S. (1989). *Theories of mass communication.* Fifth edition, White Planes, NY: Longman

Denzin, Norman K. and Lincoln, Yvonna. S. (1994). Introduction: Entering the field of qualitative research. In *Handbook of qualitative research.* London: Sage

Dordick, H. S. and Wang G. (1993). *The information society: a retrospective view.* Newbury Park, CA: Sage

Dorman, W. and Livingston, S. (1994). News and historical content: the establishment phase of the Persian Gulf policy debate. In W. L. Bennett and D. L. Paletz (eds.). *Taken by storm: the media, public opinion, and US foreign policy in the Gulf war.* Chicago: University of Chicago Press

Edelman, M. (1988). *Constructing the political spectacle.* Chicago: University of Chicago Press

Emerson, R. (1972). Power–dependence relations. *American Sociological Review,* 27, 31–41

Entman, R. (1989). *Democracy without citizens.* New York: Oxford University Press
   (1991). Framing US coverage of international news: contrasts in narratives of the KAL and Iran Air incidents. *Journal of Communication,* 4, 6–27

Entman, R. and Page, B. (1994). The news before the storm: the Iraq war debate and the limits to media independence. In W. L. Bennett and D. L. Paletz (eds.). *Taken by storm: the media, public opinion, and US foreign policy in the Gulf war.* Chicago: University of Chicago Press

Fialka, J. J. (1991). *Hotel warriors: covering the Gulf.* Washington, DC: Woodrow Wilson Center Press

Fishman, M. (1980). *Manufacturing the news.* Austin: University of Texas Press

Fiske, S. T., Kinder, D. R., and Larter, W. M. (1983). The novice and the expert: knowledge based strategies in political cognition. *Journal of Experimental Psychology,* 19, 381–400

Galtung, J. and Vincent, R. L. (1992). *Global glasnost: toward a new world information and communication order?.* Cresskill, NJ: Hampton Press

Gamson, W. A. (1988). Political discourse and collective action. In B. Klandermans, H. Kriesi, and S. Tarrow (eds.). *From structure to action: social movement participation across cultures.* Greenwich, CT: JAI Press Inc.

(1989). News as framing. *American Behavioral Scientist*, 33, 157–161

(1990). *The strategy of social protest* second edition, Belmont, CA: Wadsworth Publishing Company

(1992). *Talking politics*. New York: Cambridge University Press

Gamson, W. A., Croteau, D., Hoynes, W., and Sasson, T. (1992). Media images and the social construction of reality, *Annual Review of Sociology*, 18, 373–393

Gamson, W. A., and Lasch, K. E. (1983). The political culture of the social welfare policy. In S. E. Spiro and Y. Yuchtman-Yaar (eds.). *Evaluating the welfare state: social and political perspectives*. New York: Academic Press

Gamson, W. A. and Modigliani A. (1989). Media discourse and public opinion on nuclear power: a constructionist approach. *American Journal of Sociology*, 95, 1–37

Gamson, W. and Stuart D. (1992). Media discourse as a symbolic contest: the bomb in political cartoons. *Sociology Forum*, 7, 55–86

Gamson, W. and Wolfsfeld, G. (1993). Movements and media as interacting systems. *Annals of the American Academy of Political and Social Science*, 528, 114–125

Gandy, O. (1982). *Beyond agenda setting: information subsidies and public policy*. Norwood, NJ: Ablex

Gannett Foundation (1991). The media at war: the press and the Persian Gulf conflict. Columbia University, NY: Gannett Foundation Media Center

Gans, H. J. (1979). *Deciding what's news: a study of CBS Evening News, NBC Nightly News, Newsweek and Time*. New York: Pantheon Books

Garrett, L. (1991). The dead. *Columbia Journalism Review*. May–June, 32

Garrow, D. J. (1978). *Protest at Selma*. New Haven, CT: Yale University Press

Gitlin, T. (1980). *The whole world is watching*. Berkeley, CA: University of California Press

Glasgow University Media Group (1985). *War and peace news*. Philadelphia: Open University Press

Glassner, B. and Morena, J. (1989). *The qualitative–quantitative distinction in the social sciences*. Boston, MA: Klumer Academic Publishers

Goldenberg, E. (1975). *Making the papers: the access of resource-poor groups to the metropolitan press*. Lexington, MA: Lexington Books

Graber, D. (1984). *Processing the news*. New York: Longman

Grossman, M. B. and Rourke, F. E. (1976). The media and the presidency: an exchange analysis. *Political Science Quarterly*, 91, 455–470

Hackett, R. A. (1991). News and dissent: the press and politics of peace in Canada. Norwood, NJ: Ablex.

Hallin, D. (1986). *The uncensored war*. New York: Oxford University Press

(1987). Hegemony: the American news media from Vietnam to El Salvador, a study of idoleological change and its limits. In D. Paletz (ed.). *Political communication research*. Norwood, NJ: Ablex

Hallin, D. C. and Gitlin, T. (1994). War, popular culture and television. In W. L. Bennett and D. L. Paletz (eds.). *Taken by storm: the media, public opinion, and US foreign policy in the Gulf war*. Chicago: University of Chicago Press

Hammond, W. M. (1991). The army and public affairs: a glance back. In L. J.

Mathewes (ed.). *Newsmen and national defence: is conflict inevitable?*. Published under the auspices of the US Army War College Foundation Inc., Washington, DC: Brassey Inc

Harwood, R. (1988). Double standards toward death. *Washington Post*, May 22, 22

Hawk, B. (ed.) (1992). *Africa's media image*. New York: Praeger

Henderson, C. (1992). The filtered war. In H. Smith (ed.). *The media and the Gulf war*. Washington, DC: Seven Locks Press

Hilgartner, S. and Bosk, C. (1988). The rise and fall of social problems: a public arenas model. *American Journal of Sociology*, 94, 53–78

Irvin, C. L. (1992). Terrorists' perspectives: interviews. In D. Paletz and A. P. Schmid (eds.). *Terrorism and the media*. Newbury Park, CA: Sage

Israel Foreign Ministry (1988). Know the answers: disturbances in the territories. Background paper, December 12, Information Department: Jerusalem

Iyenger, S. (1991). *Is anyone responsible? How television frames political issues*. Chicago: University of Chicago Press

Iyenger, S. and Simon, A. (1994). News coverage of the Gulf crisis and public opinion. In W. L. Bennett and D. L. Paletz (eds.). *Taken by storm: the media, public opinion, and US foreign policy in the Gulf war*. Chicago: University of Chicago Press

Jansen, G. H. (1991). A war to defend principles. *Times of India*, January 23, 12

Joan Shorenstein Barone Center on the Press, Politics, and Public Policy (1993). Turmoil at Tiananmen: a study of US press coverage of the Beijing spring of 1989. Cambridge, MA: John F. Kennedy School of Government, Harvard Unversity

Jowett, G. S. (1992). Toward a propaganda analysis of the Gulf war. In B. S. Greenberg and W. Gatz (eds.). *Desert Storm and the mass media*. Cresskill, NJ: Hampton Press

Kallich, M. and MacLeish, A. (1962). *The American revolution through British eyes*. New York: Harper and Row

Katz, E. and Levinsohn, H. (1994). Slight decline in support for autonomy. Press release of the Louis Guttman Institute for Applied Social Research, Jerusalem, June 14

Kellner, D. (1991). *The Persian Gulf TV war*. Boulder, CO: Westview Press

Knightley, P. (1975). *The first casualty*. New York: Harcourt Brace Jovanovitch

Lang, G. E. and Lang, K. (1994). Press coverage as prologue: media coverage of Saddam's Iraq 1979–1990. In W. L. Bennett and D. L. Paletz (eds.). *Taken by storm: the media, public opinion, and US foreign policy in the Gulf war*. Chicago: University of Chicago Press

Lau, R. (1986). Political schemata, candidate evaluations and voting behavior. In R. Lau and D. Sears (eds.). *Political cognition*. Hillsdale, NJ: Lawrence Erlbaum Associates

Lau, R. and Sears, D. O. (1985). Social cognition and political cognition: the past, the present, and the future. In R. Lau and D. Sears (eds.). *Political cognition*. Hillsdale, NJ: Lawrence Erlbaum Associates

Lederman, J. (1992). *Battle lines: the American media and the intifada*. New York: Henry Holt and Company

Levinsohn, H. and Katz E. (1994). Jordan accord strengthens (not weakens) public support for autonomy accord. Press release of the Louis Guttman Institute for Applied Social Research, Jerusalem, August 15

Lichter, R. (1992). The instant replay war. In H. Smith (ed.). *The media and the Gulf war.* Washington, DC: Seven Locks Press

Lichter, R. and Lichter L. (1988). Israel in crisis: coverage of Israel's Palestinian problem. *Media Monitor,* 2, no. 4, 1–3

   (1991). The instant replay war: television news coverage of the Persian Gulf war, *Media Monitor,* 5, no. 4, 1–4

Makovsky, D. (1989). Media impact. *The Jerusalem Post Magazine,* August 25, 4, 5, 10

Manheim, J.B. (1991). *All of the people, all of the time.* Armonk, NY: Sharp Inc

   (1994). Managing Kuwait's image during the Gulf conflict. In W. L. Bennett and D. L. Paletz (eds.). *Taken by storm: the media, public opinion, and US foreign policy in the Gulf war.* Chicago: University of Chicago Press

McDaniel, A. and Fireman, H. (1992). The President's "spin" patrol. In H. Smith (ed.). *The media and the Gulf war.* Washington, DC: Seven Locks Press

Mishal, S. with Aharoni, R. (1989) *Speaking stones: the words behind the Palestinian intifada.* Tel Aviv: Hakibutz Hameuchad [Hebrew]

Molotch, H. and Lester, M. (1974). News as purposive behavior: on the strategic use of routine events, accidents, and scandals. *American Political Science Review,* 39, 101–112

Molotch, H., Protess D. L., and Gordon, M. T. (1987). The media–policy connection: ecologies of news. In D. L. Paletz (ed.). *Political communication research: approaches, studies, assessments.* Norwood, NJ: Ablex

Morrison, D. E. and Tumber, H. (1988). *Journalists at war: the dynamics of news reporting during the Falklands conflict.* London: Sage

Mowlana, H., Gerbner, G., and Schiller, H. I. (1991). *Triumph of the image: the media's war in the Persian Gulf – a global perspective.* Boulder, CO: Westview Press

New York Times (1990a). Bush assails Israeli lack of restraint. October 10, A10

   (1990b). Excerpts from speech by Bush at Marine post. November 23, A16

   (1991a). A final pause. January 13, A19

   (1991b). Text of Hussein's radio speech dealing with war and peace. February 22, A9

Newsweek (1991). April 15

   (1992). The day Bush stopped the war. January 20, 10–19

   (1994). Blood bath. February 14, 10–14

   (1995). When words are the best weapon. February 27, 18–21

Paletz, D. L., and Entman, R. M. (1981). *Media, power, politics.* New York: Free Press

Paletz, D. L. and Shmid, A. P., (eds.). (1992). *Terrorism and the media.* Newbury Park, CA: Sage

Paletz, D. L. and Vinson, C. D. (1992). Two international incidents in the world's press. Paper presented at the American Political Science Association Meeting in Chicago

Patterson, T. (1993). *Out of order.* New York: Alfred A. Knopf

Protess, D. L. and McCombs M. (1991). *Readings on media, public opinion, and policy making*. Hillsdale, NJ: Lawrence Erlbaum Associates

Raboy, M. and Dagenais, B. (1992). *Media, crisis, and democracy*. London: Sage

Reese, S. (1991). Setting the media's agenda: a power balance perspective. In J. Anderson (ed.). *Communication yearbook*, XIV, 309–340

Reese, S., Grant, A., and Danielian, L. (1994). The structure of news sources on television: a network analysis of "CBS News," "Nightline," "MacNeil/Lehrer," and "This Week with David Brinkley." *Journal of Communication*, 44, 84–107

Roach, C. (1990). The movement for a new world information and communication order: a second wave?. *Media Culture and Society*, 12, 283–308

Robinson, M. and Sheehan, M. (1983). *Over the wire and on TV*. New York: Russel Sage Foundation

Roeh, Y. and Nir, R. (1993). Reporting the *intifada* in the Israeli press: how mainstream ideology overrides "quality" and "melodrama." In A. Cohen and G. Wolfsfeld (eds.). *Framing the intifada: people and media*. Norwood, NJ: Ablex

Rokeach, M. (1960). *The open and closed mind*. New York: Basic Books

Ryan, C. (1991). *Prime time activism*. Boston, MA: South End Press

Schattschneider, E. E. (1960). *The semi-sovereign people*. New York: Holt, Rinehart, and Winston

Schiff, Z. and Ya'ari E. (1990). *Intifada: the Palestinian uprising – Israel's third front*. New York: Simon and Schuster

Schoor, D. (1991). Ten days that shook the White House. *Columbia Journalism Review*, July–August, 21–23

Sears, D. (1985). Schematic variant of symbolic politics theory. In R. Lau and D. Sears (eds.). *Political cognition*. Hillsdale, NJ: Lawrence Erlbaum Associates

Sewell, W. H. (1992). A theory of structure: duality, agency, and transformation. *American Journal of Sociology*, 98, 1–29

Sharkey, J. (1991). *Under fire: US military restrictions on the media from Grenada to the Persian Gulf*. Washington, DC: The Center for Public Integrity

Shiffer, S. (1990). Rabin chastises Aloni: you failed in your position. *Yediot Ahronot*, January 14, 1

Shoemaker, P. J. and Reese, S. D. (1991). *Mediating the message: theories of influences on mass media content*. New York: Longman

Smith, H. (ed.) (1992). *The media and the Gulf war: the press and democracy in wartime*. Washington, DC: The Seven Locks Press

Snow, D. A., and Benford, R. D. (1988). Ideology, frame resonance, and participant mobilization. In B. Klandermans, H. Driesi, and S. Tarrow (eds.). *From structure to action: comparing social movement research across cultures*. Greenwich, CT: JAI Press Inc.

Soderlund, W. C. and Schmitt, C. (1986). El Salvador's civil war as seen in North and South American press. *Journalism Quarterly*, 63, 268–274

Sprinzak, E. (1991). *The ascendance of Israel's radical right*. New York: Oxford University Press

Staggenborg, S. (1993). Critical events and the mobilization of the pro-choice movement. *Political Sociology*, 6, 319–345

Stronthoff, G. G., Hawkins, R. P., and Schoenfeld, A. C. (1985). Media roles in a social movement: a model of ideology diffusion. *Journal of Communication*, 35, 135–153

Taylor, P. (1986). The semantics of political violence. In P. Golding, G. Murdock and P. Schesinger (eds.). *Communicating politics: mass communications and the political process*. Leicester, UK: Leicester University Press

Tilly, C. (1978). *From mobilization to revolution*. Reading, MA: Addison-Wesley

Times of India (1991). War and peace, editorial, January 23, 1

Tuchman, G. (1973). *Making news*. New York: Free Press

Turk, J. V. (1986). Information subsidies and media content: a study of public relations influence in the news. *Journalism Monographs*, No. 100

Twain, M. (1970). *The war prayer*. New York: Harper Colophon Books

Waldman, S. R. (1972). *An exchange theory of politics*. Boston, MA: Little, Brown and Company

Walsh, E. J. (1988). *Democracy in the shadows: citizen mobilization in the wake of the accident at Three Mile Island*. Westport, CT: Greenwood Press

Wimmer, R. D. and Dominick, J. R. (1991). *Mass media research*, third edition, Belmont, CA: Wadsworth

Wolfsfeld, G. (1984a). Collective political action and media strategy: the case of Yamit. *Journal of Conflict Resolution*, 28, 1–36

(1984b). The symbiosis of press and protest: an exchange analysis. *Journalism Quarterly*, 61, 550–556

(1991). Media, protest, and political violence: a transactional analysis. *Journalism Monographs*, no. 127

(1993a). The role of the news media in unequal political conflicts: from the *intifada* to the Gulf war and back again. Research paper R-8, Joan Shorenstein Barone Center, John F. Kennedy School of Government, Cambridge, MA: Harvard University

(1993b). Introduction: framing political conflict. In A. Cohen and G. Wolfsfeld (ed.). *Framing the intifada: people and media*. Norwood, NJ: Ablex

Wolfsfeld, G. and Rabihiya, Y. (1988). Communication and control in times of crisis: Israeli censorship in the occupied territories. *Canadian Journal of Communication*, special issue, December, 96–101

Zaller, J. R. (1992). *The nature of mass opinion*. New York: Cambridge University Press

Index